SENSE OF SAFETY
ART IN A TIME OF WAR

Contents

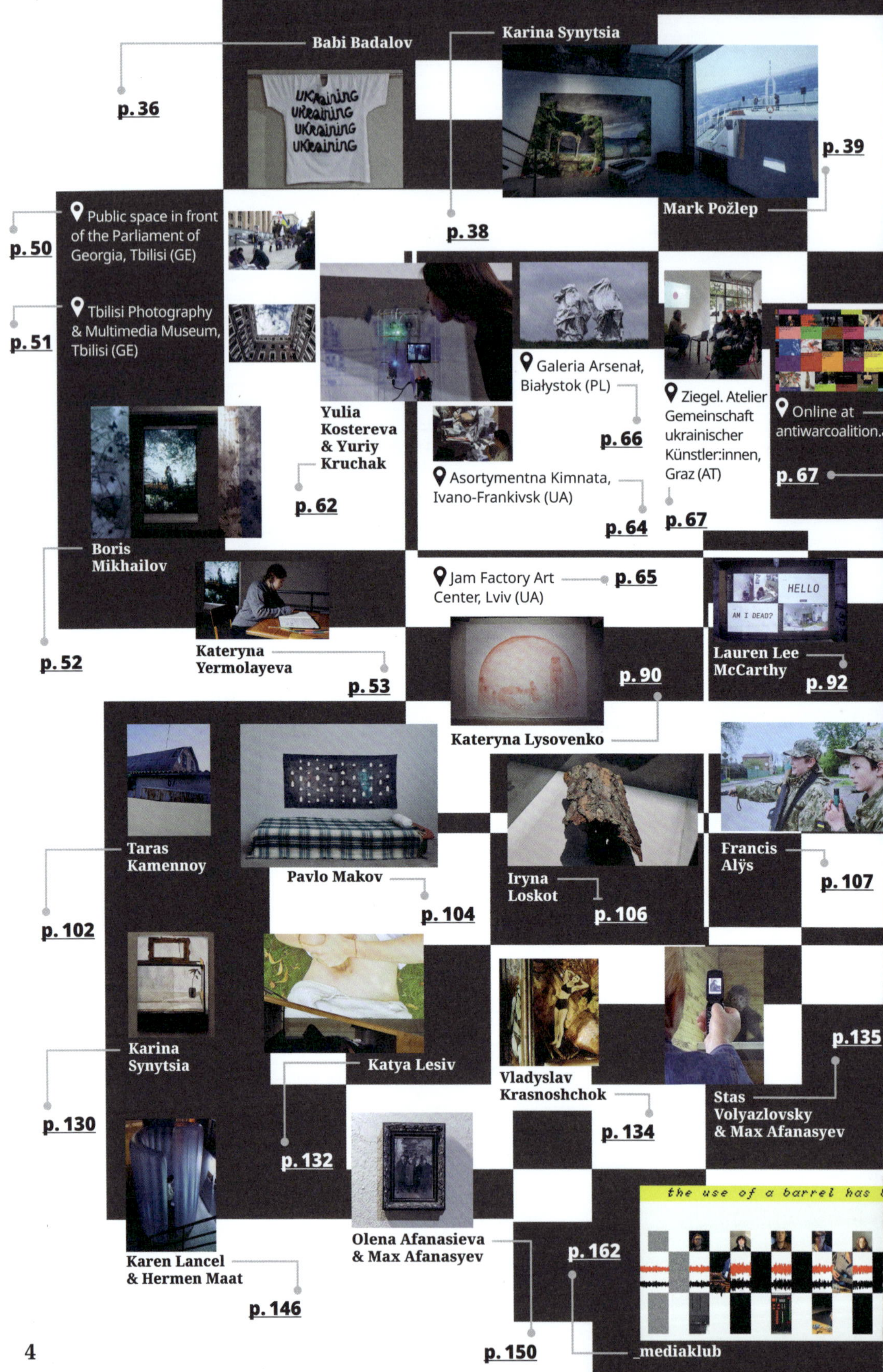
Babi Badalov
p. 36
UKRaining
UKRaining
UKRaining
UKRaining
Karina Synytsia
p. 38
p. 39
Mark Požlep
Public space in front of the Parliament of Georgia, Tbilisi (GE)
p. 50
Tbilisi Photography & Multimedia Museum, Tbilisi (GE)
p. 51
Yulia Kostereva & Yuriy Kruchak
p. 62
Galeria Arsenał, Białystok (PL)
p. 66
Ziegel. Atelier Gemeinschaft ukrainischer Künstler:innen, Graz (AT)
p. 67
Online at antiwarcoalition.a
p. 67
Asortymentna Kimnata, Ivano-Frankivsk (UA)
p. 64
Boris Mikhailov
p. 52
Kateryna Yermolayeva
p. 53
Jam Factory Art Center, Lviv (UA)
p. 65
HELLO
AM I DEAD?
Lauren Lee McCarthy
p. 92
p. 90
Kateryna Lysovenko
Taras Kamennoy
p. 102
Pavlo Makov
p. 104
Iryna Loskot
p. 106
Francis Alÿs
p. 107
Karina Synytsia
p. 130
Katya Lesiv
p. 132
Vladyslav Krasnoshchok
p. 134
p. 135
Stas Volyazlovsky & Max Afanasyev
the use of a barrel has
Karen Lancel & Hermen Maat
p. 146
Olena Afanasieva & Max Afanasyev
p. 150
p. 162
_mediaklub

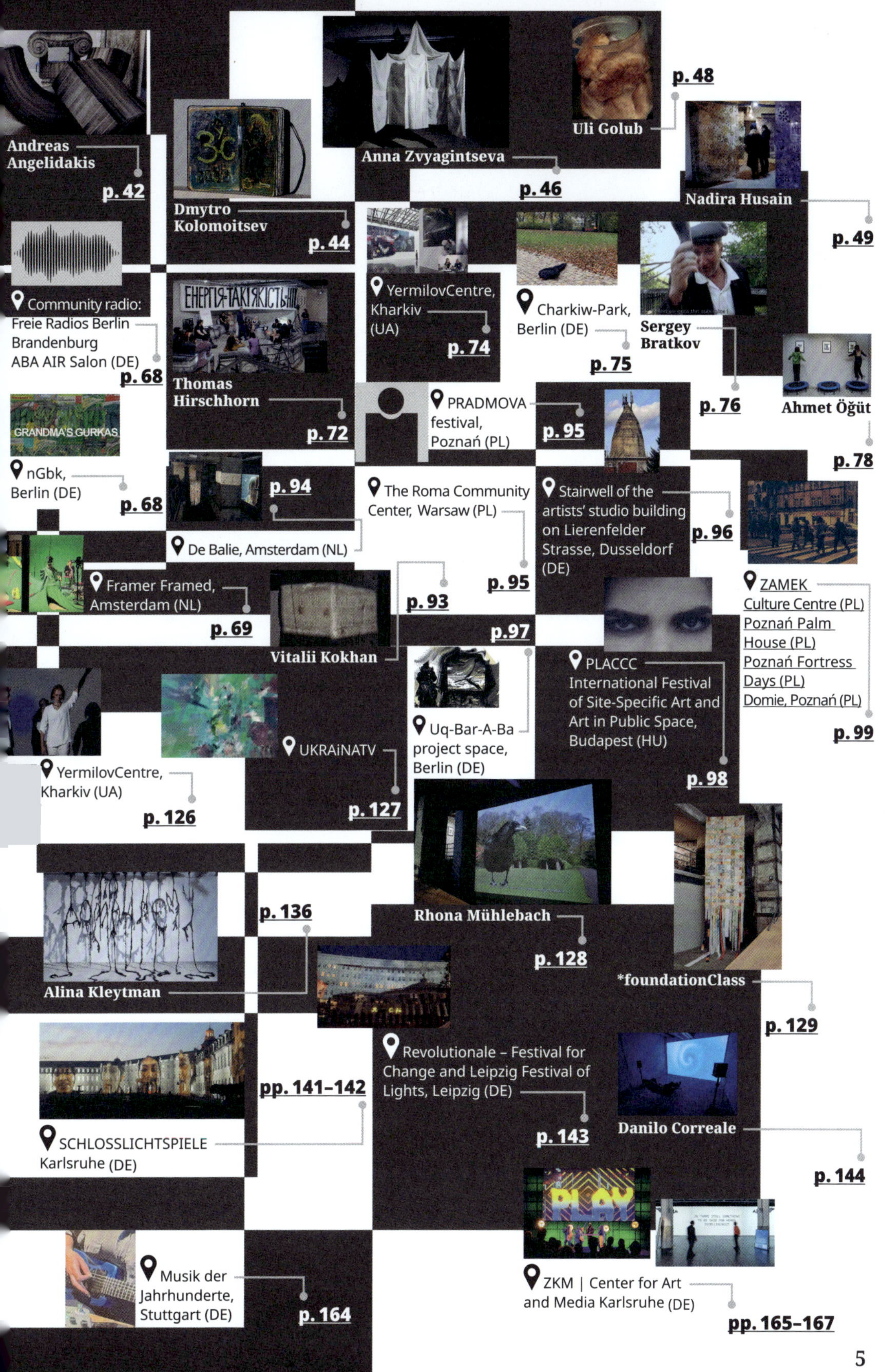
Andreas Angelidakis
p. 42
Dmytro Kolomoitsev
p. 44
Anna Zvyagintseva
p. 46
Uli Golub
p. 48
Nadira Husain
p. 49
Community radio:
Freie Radios Berlin Brandenburg
ABA AIR Salon (DE)
p. 68
Thomas Hirschhorn
p. 72
YermilovCentre, Kharkiv (UA)
p. 74
Charkiw-Park, Berlin (DE)
p. 75
Sergey Bratkov
p. 76
Ahmet Öğüt
p. 78
GRANDMA'S GURKAS
nGbk, Berlin (DE)
p. 68
p. 94
De Balie, Amsterdam (NL)
PRADMOVA festival, Poznań (PL)
p. 95
The Roma Community Center, Warsaw (PL)
p. 95
Stairwell of the artists' studio building on Lierenfelder Strasse, Dusseldorf (DE)
p. 96
ZAMEK Culture Centre (PL)
Poznań Palm House (PL)
Poznań Fortress Days (PL)
Domie, Poznań (PL)
p. 99
Framer Framed, Amsterdam (NL)
p. 69
Vitalii Kokhan
p. 93
p.97
Uq-Bar-A-Ba project space, Berlin (DE)
PLACCC International Festival of Site-Specific Art and Art in Public Space, Budapest (HU)
p. 98
YermilovCentre, Kharkiv (UA)
p. 126
UKRAiNATV
p. 127
Rhona Mühlebach
p. 128
*foundationClass
p. 129
Alina Kleytman
p. 136
Revolutionale – Festival for Change and Leipzig Festival of Lights, Leipzig (DE)
p. 143
SCHLOSSLICHTSPIELE Karlsruhe (DE)
pp. 141–142
Danilo Correale
p. 144
PLAY
Musik der Jahrhunderte, Stuttgart (DE)
p. 164
ZKM | Center for Art and Media Karlsruhe (DE)
pp. 165–167

Introduction by Tatiana Kochubinska

As If This Could Protect Us

This publication is inspired by the exhibition *Sense of Safety*, which took place at the YermilovCentre in Kharkiv in 2024. Kharkiv is a unique center of arts and sciences renowned for its Constructivist heritage, a city that has given the world Nobel laureates in immunology, economics, and physics—Ilya Mechnikov, Simon Kuznets, and Lev Landau. But today, Kharkiv is mostly known to the world for its proximity to the frontline—a city subjected to continual, near-daily shelling and attacks by the Russian army.

It is precisely under these conditions of unceasing terrorist pressure and psychological violence that a new generation of Ukrainians is growing up: the "children of war." As we witness the reemergence of this concept today, we cannot help but remember how deeply it is rooted in our culture and history. First and foremost, it is associated with the children of World War II, that catastrophe that the world vowed never to repeat again. Those who were born or grew up during the Nazi occupation of Soviet Ukraine are now spending their old age under the same shelling and bombings with which their lives began. Though this time around, it is from the descendants of their former allies in the defeat of fascism.[1]

In this cross-cutting context, where the city itself bears witness to history tragically repeating itself, and to the ongoing resistance that stretches across time, the *Sense of Safety* project was born—in a place that is categorically unsafe. Perhaps it answers a human need to create a comforting illusion of safety—even if only temporarily—one that is nonetheless crucial for the survival and the continuity of civilization.

The title and theme of the project were suggested by Maryna Konieva, one of the exhibition's curators and a resident of Kharkiv who chose not to evacuate after Russia's full-scale invasion of Ukraine began. During yet another Shahed attack on the city, on the day before a Zoom meeting with the entire project team, Maryna took cover under a thick blanket from her grandmother. It might have protected her from shrapnel or shattered glass from the large window in her apartment. And so, this need for safety—seemingly delusional under conditions like these—prompted us to develop our curatorial ideas further. What does safety mean—for me personally, for others? What does it mean existentially, socially, and beyond?

At the same time, the YermilovCentre itself, with its dense concrete walls, had effectively served as a bomb shelter since the beginning of the full-scale invasion. This also informed the exhibition's conceptual development, as the space ensured safety simply through its presence. "Space is the medium in which ideas are visually phrased," suggests Robert Storr.[2] In this sense, the YermilovCentre became a medium in its own right, which began to phrase the project's visual language. The exhibition emerged from it, shaped by its materiality, its function, and its embedded condition of safety.

When we began preparing the exhibition, public events were not permitted anywhere else in the city for security reasons. In this regard, the two levels of YermilovCentre's subterranean space were in a privileged position to host many visitors—some coming to experience art, others seeking refuge from air raids.

The *Sense of Safety* project created a situation of safety for visitors, encouraging them to return again and again. Admission is free, as the YermilovCentre is part of Karazin University and operates within a broader educational framework, opening access to art as a space for learning and shared experience.

These reflections—arising from the context, conversations among ourselves, and with the artists—led to various interpretations of safety. Yet, they were all united by one thing: the ambivalence of the concept itself, the tension inherent to it. This tension permeated every work on display. YermilovCentre's director, Nataliia Ivanova, once said that she did not want visitors entering the space to hear the sound of air raids echoing through the artworks again. When selecting the contributions, it was extremely important for us not to re-traumatize viewers, but also not to present life through rose-colored glasses, since our audience is living through a war zone every day. This delicate balance informed the selection of works as well as the development of new commissions.

Fragility, transience, and precarity—whether thematic or technical—were ever-present. We understood that we were making an exhibition in a city that could be shelled at any moment, potentially causing power outages that would plunge all the media works into darkness and make magnificent pieces like the inflatable isolation pillar in Karel Lancel and Herman Maat's *Agora Phobia (Digitalis)* disappear entirely.[3]

In response to these considerations of ambivalence and tension, the exhibition developed a complex, non-linear navigation system: an open framework inviting visitors to chart their own path through a network of thematic blocks that we called "force fields," inspired by the history of scientific research in Kharkiv. In physics, the term describes how non-contact forces can act at a distance, shaping space and time. Within the project's framework, these conceptual fields functioned as lines of tension, solidarity, and interconnectedness.[4]

The non-linear, vertical nature of the exhibition was enhanced by its so-called floating exposition: all the video works on display swapped their locations according to a preprogrammed algorithm. This created shifting relationships between the works themselves and within the viewers' perceptions, offering a fresh experience each time. Through these swaps, the scale of the works also changed. Small projections—for example, the video by Kateryna Yermolayeva housed in a cardboard box—emerged from their confines and appeared on the "big screen" at YermilovCentre, a massive wall connecting the two underground floors. The big screen also served as a central gathering point for the entire exhibition—a kind of agora for public expression, exchange of ideas and practices, and moments of spontaneous togetherness. Over the course of the day, all the video works in the exhibition would eventually be presented there.

Navigating between meanings and works went beyond the confines of YermilovCentre's physical space thanks to *Bridges of Solidarity*—a network of events across various European institutions connecting Kharkiv with other regions and enabling dialogue across communities, geographies, and temporalities. *Bridges of Solidarity* continued throughout the exhibition and after, taking the form of hybrid online and offline events: discussions, screenings, concerts, expanded exhibitions, and public appearances. These included large-scale outdoor video projections in Leipzig and Karlsruhe, performative actions in Tbilisi and Poznań, simultaneous screenings in Kharkiv and Amsterdam, and more. Many of the events took place elsewhere but were always transmitted back to YermilovCentre's agora. *Bridges* embraced established institutions, artists' studios, city streets, and livestreams as spaces of shared presence. Together, these efforts strengthened our network of support and solidarity, while enhancing Kharkiv's visibility on the international art map.

The dispersed exhibition format made it possible to situate *Sense of Safety* within a broader artistic context and reestablish connections between Kharkiv and the rest of Europe through art[5]—defying expectations that a city at war could only broadcast its ruins to the world. On the contrary, it became a place where ideas were brought to life, where creation persisted, and where art continued to flourish. It was art that provided an opportunity to communicate, shape thoughts, and overcome the isolation imposed by the war.

The entire project can also be understood as one big bridge, whose primary purpose was to connect, to heal divisions, and to embody a state of transition. It connected audiences and different realms, the physical and the digital, creating a shared space through their union. First and foremost, it was created in Kharkiv for the local audience. Nevertheless, we also felt that by bringing a large international presence to the city, we could use this gesture to shout to the world: "Look here! People live here! Art is happening here!" The more heavily Kharkiv was bombed that sultry summer, the more resolute we became in our desire to hold the exhibition right here and now. It was as if attention itself could carve out a space of safety and somehow halt the missiles. But it could not. The day after the opening, the young artist Veronika Kozhushko was killed in a Russian strike.[6] Many recalled how, just the day before, she had been jumping—happy, youthful, full of energy—on the trampolines in Ahmet Öğüt's work.

Overnight, the fragility of safety became tangible, and its illusory nature all the more apparent.

The structure of this publication follows the exhibition's multi-layered and multidimensional layout, mirroring its spirit and atmosphere through fluid spaces and media, as well as shifting geographies. It immerses readers in the exhibition environment while also offering retrospective reflections on the project at a moment when the issue of safety is no less globally relevant than it was two years ago.

This book also reaffirms Kharkiv's place on the global art map, demonstrating that despite the war it remains a place of creation rather than a broadcasted ruin. It aims to archive and contextualize the project within the history of exhibitions, situating it in a context of war and highlighting the potential of art to heal, communicate, and overcome. What might initially sound like grandiose claims about the necessity of art during war can become undeniable realities when experienced firsthand.

In addition to documentation, the catalog features thirteen new contributions. It is designed like a transport map, composed of textual-visual lines that guide readers through the voices of artists and contributors, artworks, and bridges of solidarity, conveying the exhibition's feeling as a continuous flow. The publication unfolds like a vortex, an interweaving of events forming an unbroken textual-visual stream. It brings together four types of texts: descriptive texts about the exhibition and artworks presented at YermilovCentre; details of the programming for *Bridges of Solidarity*; retrospective reflections from people who experienced the project on site or from afar; and contextual inserts addressing the context of Kharkiv from personal perspectives.

The publication opens with an essay by Boris Buden, who draws on his experience of the Yugoslav wars and casts Death as a performance artist. He examines how modern warfare—drones, bombs, and technological surveillance—visualizes human vulnerability and turns the pervasive sense of unsafety into a tool of power and manipulation. As a counterpoint, Nataliia Ivanova speaks from an on-the-ground perspective in her extensive interview with Lena Prents. She recounts the earliest days of the full-scale invasion and outlines how YermilovCentre transformed and survived during wartime, illustrating the resilience and continuity of cultural life in Kharkiv.

Oksana Barshynova and Alona Karavai both experienced the exhibition on site and offer complementary perspectives: Barshynova through an art-historical lens tracing vulnerabilities across time, and Karavai through an art-critical lens focused on the immediate, lived vulnerability of war today. Barshynova situates the project within Kharkiv's artistic history, mapping subtle connections between international practices and the city's artistic life through its key loci—from avant-garde movements to underground circles of the 1960s and contemporary practices—highlighting how art and the city have reciprocally shaped each other over time. Karavai focuses on the role of humor as a survival strategy, while weaving in anecdotal and personal experiences. Through memes, jokes, and black humor, she shows how collective laughter enables visitors to process danger, anxiety, and stress, preserving a sense of community while acknowledging chaos and death as part of human experience.

Texts by Asia Tsisar and Bojana Piškur are united by the concept of solidarity. Tsisar, a native of Kharkiv and firsthand witness of the exhibition, writes from a personal perspective that focuses on people, presence, and concrete acts of care, analyzing what an international exhibition can offer a frontline city. Piškur, by contrast, approaches solidarity from a global and historical perspective, tracing its manifestations in artistic and cultural practices, transnational networks, and the Non-Aligned Movement. She shows how solidarity has been enacted across communities and time, linking culture, collective responsibility, and shared experience.

The site—both the city and the YermilovCentre—was decisive in shaping the project. Yet the exhibition was determined not only by place, but also by time. It emerged from a particular historical moment marked by ongoing war, fragility, and uncertainty—from a volatile present in which conditions shift daily and the possibility of showing or experiencing art is never guaranteed. This publication seeks to reflect the importance of site, context, and moment. Its contextual inserts extend the exhibition's navigational system of force fields. At YermilovCentre, these fields acted as spatial guides, connecting the artworks and sparking dialogue between them; in the book, they guide the reader through Kharkiv itself. Here, the force fields become anchors, continually returning us to the site that gave rise to the project. Each contextual insert functions as a case study, reading the city through a particular force field. Taken together, they offer a layered interpretation—informed by a historical perspective yet shaped by the urgency of the present, perceiving not only its light, but also its darkness.[7]

In his essay written through the lens of the force field *Post-Traumatic Ingrowth*, Maxim Rosenfeld speaks about Kharkiv's main symbol, Derzhprom, as a living embodiment of the courage to dream. Serhiy Zhadan emphasizes communication as a lifeline—especially after the full-scale war began—showing how it helps overcome fear and build trust and belonging. Oleksandr Sorokin turns to science in contemporary Kharkiv. He highlights global interdependence and describes how the Institute for Scintillation Materials continues to manufacture crystals for CERN despite the war. Tetyana Pylypchuk, addressing the force field *Asynchrony and the Dream Museum*, shifts the focus from objects to meanings, from preservation to the activation of cultural experience as a source of communal safety. Maryna Konieva examines the infrastructure of care, tracing how the artistic community has turned toward volunteering, personal support, and safeguarding heritage, linking solidarity with the defense of culture. Reflecting on the force field *I'm in My Happy Place*, Borys Filonenko uses the Aza Nizi Maza children's art studio as a case study to show how relocating to the metro provided physical safety, while creative activity and imaginative engagement became a form of psychological and social shelter. Finally, Antonina Stebur gives voice to the public—the exhibition's visitors. Taking Kateryna Yermolayeva's *Collective Diary* as a starting point, she explores how daily routines and shared experiences can be transformed into practices that provide emotional grounding in wartime.

These personal essays, woven throughout the publication, were created in response to each force field and reveal Kharkiv in its manifold richness.

In 1974, Vagrich Bakhchanyan wrote an ironic piece about Kharkiv as the "navel of the earth,"[8] in which he used absurd hyperbole and a jumble of fake "facts" to satirize the language of Soviet propaganda and the very myth of the "great city":

Kharkiv stands on the great river Lopan.

Kharkiv is a very large city.

Judge for yourself.

A plane flight from one side of the city to the other takes 4 hours 42 minutes. Kharkiv is 16 times larger than New York, with 200 million residents (not counting the suburbs).

Every second Kharkiv resident writes poetry, every third paints, every fifth is a physicist, every sixth pens denunciations.

2,174 laureates of the Nobel, Lenin, Stalin, and Shevchenko Prizes live and work in Kharkiv, etc.[9]

But today, this irony has, in some sense, become a form of faith: the hyperbolic myth of Kharkiv has become a means of protecting and sustaining a city under fire.

In developing the exhibition and the book—working on site, designing the exposition, and engaging in the *Bridges of Solidarity* with team members working from different cities and countries—we were constantly asking ourselves how it might be possible to find a way through ruin and trauma, and whether there was any space to imagine the future. The idea of post-traumatic ingrowth, as articulated by Ukrainian social and military psychologist Oleh Pokalchuk, became central to the entire process. He suggests that if you listen carefully enough, the fear of experiencing an explosion can be transformed into a love of life.

So, dear readers, we invite you to leaf through this book—to watch, to read, to engage, to follow its paths and QR codes—with that same love of life.

---

1. The resurgence of authoritarianism, terror, and manipulation in contemporary politics has led some scholars to describe these developments as a new form of fascism. See interview with Timothy Snyder, "Recognizing the signs of fascism today," *CBC News* (30 May 2025), https://www.youtube.com/watch?v=7PcxC1p-Z-g&t=588s [accessed 7 April 2026].
2. Robert Storr, "Show and Tell," in *What Makes a Great Exhibition?*, ed. Paula Marincola (Philadelphia: Philadelphia Exhibitions Initiative, 2006).
3. See description of the artwork on pp. 146–147.
4. These fields are: *Infrastructure of Care, Post-Traumatic Ingrowth, Routine as a Grounding Practice, I'm in My Happy Place, Asynchrony and the Dream Museum, Communication as a Safe Place,* and *Interdependency and Connectivity*.
5. Dispersed exhibition formats became popular in the 1970s and blossomed in the 1980s. According to Bruce Altshuler, they "came with the growth of biennials outside Euro-American centres." The dispersed nature of the *Sense of Safety* exhibition has become a gesture of deep solidarity across geographies, while simultaneously questioning the binary of centers and peripheries. See: Paula Marincola, ed., *Site Read: Seven Curators on Their Landmark Exhibitions* (Milan: Mousse Publishing, 2019).
6. Veronika "Nika" Kozhushko (born 19 May 2006, Kharkiv; died 30 August 2024, Kharkiv) was a Ukrainian artist, poet, and volunteer.
7. According to Giorgio Agamben, "the contemporary is the person who perceives the darkness of his time as something that concerns him, as something that never ceases to engage him. Darkness is something that more than any light turns directly and singularly toward him." See Giorgio Agamben, "What Is the Contemporary?," in *What Is an Apparatus? and Other Essays*, trans. David Kishik & Stefan Pedatella (Stanford: Stanford University Press, 2009), p. 45.
8. Bakhchanyan was a Kharkiv-born underground artist. See detailed biography on p. 61.
9. Translated from Russian by Iaroslava Strikha. Source: Research Platform, PinchukArtCentre.

Sense of Safety, opening of the exhibition at YermilovCentre, 2024.
Photo: Oleksandr Osipov.

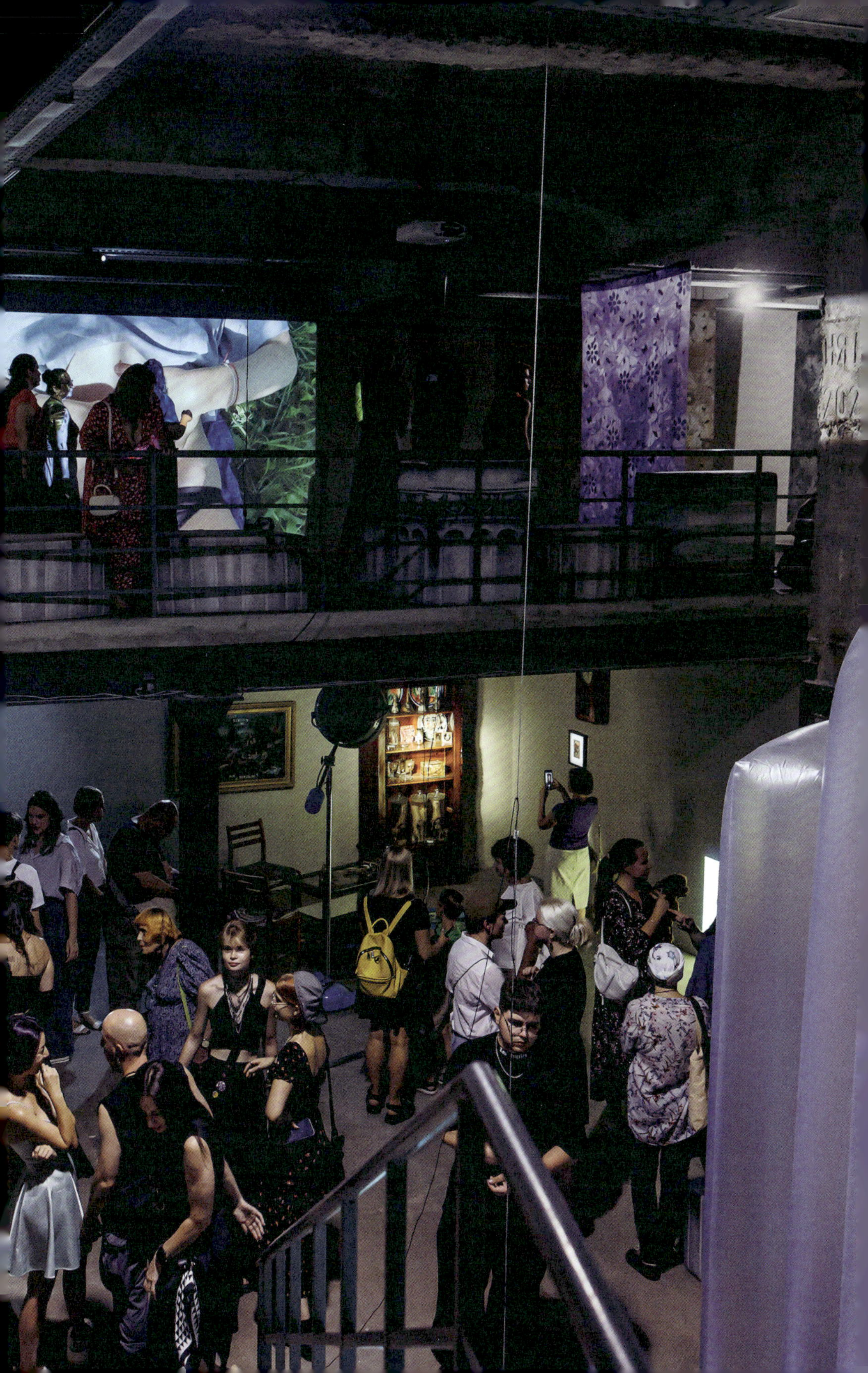

Boris Buden

Do you want the total safety? Yeeeaaah!—Towards the Milky Way Biennial

More than thirty years ago, during the Yugoslav wars, the sense of safety and its gradations were quite simple. It was a matter of physics, or more concretely, of the difference between the speed of light and the speed of sound. The former is, as we know, vastly faster. So if you were able to notice the difference between the flash of a bombardment and its sound, you could consider yourself safe. The longer the interval between the two, the stronger the feeling of safety. To put it simply, the bombs were falling on someone else's head, not on yours. At least for the time being.

This simple law of physics no longer applies in today's Ukraine. Sound has overtaken light. The moment you hear the buzz of a drone marks the existential turn from safety to unsafety. And by the time the light arrives on the scene, it might already be too late. What is left to be seen is Death coming to take you. The feeling of safety or unsafety is no longer based on the laws of physics: it can't be experienced through the differing speeds of light and sound, nor can it be measured by the distance between the two. Oddly enough, it seems that rapid technological advancement has slowed our perception of (un)safety, though only to make Death swifter—and more performative! Like a theater bell ringing to announce the start of the show, the sound of a drone rings up the curtain for Death's own performance, the drone's aerial *danse macabre,* the last show a human target's eyes will ever see. But Death is a serious artist, one who documents its performance most fastidiously—though, of course, not from the perspective of the audience. Death is no bystander, far less a witness. It is a perpetrator, and that is what makes its performance truly performative. What Death films, it kills, giving remote audiences, and posterity in general, the unique chance to identify with its gaze. Those who survive us will have seen us through the eyes of our death—thanks to the tremendous technological development that gave us this little flying device equipped with a camera. The drone has given Death eyes and even made it an artist.

Now, when it comes to art, we know it is ill-advised to put constraints on our imagination. This is especially the case with the technologically driven post-human turn in art and culture. So let's imagine a new pavilion in Venice for the largest and most populous nation the world has (n)ever seen: the nation of dead humans. Whomever we appoint as the curator, the artist will always be the same: Death itself. Picture its vast video archive from Ukraine, the final moments of thousands of soldiers and civilians, shot by Death itself. Here the double meaning of "shooting"—firing a weapon and filming—has collapsed into a single act: shooting means shooting; performance becomes performative.

Let us now go back a hundred years to the Soviet Union of the 1920s. Among the key figures of the Soviet film avant-garde is a young newsreel and documentary film director Dziga Vertov. He developed a film technique called "Kino-Eye" with the goal of liberating film from the fictional world of theater and confronting it with real life. For Vertov, the camera in his hands is a new, technologically generated eye that advances our perception of the world and reveals dimensions of life otherwise inaccessible to "mere" human vision. By expanding and deepening human experience, it activates our latent potential for transforming the world. Vertov's Kino-Eye was more than a new film technique; it was a movement, a group of film makers with a mission bigger than filmmaking itself. Film can change the world ... for the better, of course.

You might think you know how the story unfolded back then: Vertov proved to be just as mistaken as the communists were about the revolutionary transformation of the world—a dream that culminated in the horrors of totalitarianism. Film has no social mission, nor does technological progress have any intrinsic ideological meaning. And the illusion that it might be otherwise has cost us dearly.

But wait. Aren't we talking about the field of art where imagination can freely invent alternative histories in order to speak the truth—not about the past but about our present? So, imagine there was a member of the Kino-Eye movement who Vertov was fully unaware of, the most devoted and attentive admirers of his new film technique, someone who not only fully identified with its mission but, moreover, has never been disappointed by its historical results. Radical change remains possible, though not necessarily for the better.

Perhaps Death was there too, taking a break after the First World War. Leaning back to observe humanity's rapid technological progress was in any case less stressful than toiling on the frontlines. Moreover, these advancements inspired Death's own imagination. By moving around with the camera or attaching it to a mobile device like a motorbike or car, Vertov hoped to expand our gaze on the world and life. Death, however, had different ideas about how to use this technique—to expand its own gaze on us from the great beyond. And now, a century later, it flies around with a camera in its hands. The Kino-Eye is now a "Death-Eye."

It isn't hard to imagine that nuclear warheads will soon be outfitted with cameras too. And by then, we would have to ask ourselves: Who would then be the audience of humanity's last moments? Whose gaze will our species perform its death throes for?

But stop! Our imagination has gone too far. Art is no excuse for cynically abandoning the reality we live—and die—in. Reality still matters: the reality of the war in Ukraine, of Russian aggression, of the global struggle between democracy and authoritarianism, of international justice, economic interests, human rights ... A view of the world in which such real human concerns only appear as trivialities is closer to pathological delusion than serious thinking. And isn't it also morally abject to ignore the real injustice and human suffering we are now witnessing on a near daily basis?

Don't be so sure! A new tendency in contemporary British ethical philosophy called Longtermism might prove us wrong. It is an offshoot of traditional Utilitarianism, whose ideal is summarized in the well-known formula "the greatest happiness for the greatest number of people." Longtermism, however, projects this happiness into a very, very distant future, from the perspective of which our present concerns, including dire threats to humanity like global warming or nuclear war, look like grim but ultimately brief and negligible episodes in a much longer story. According to William MacAskill, one of the movement's leading thinkers, if human history were a novel, we would still be on the very first page.[1] In fact, the happiness this theory projects into the future won't even be realized on Earth but rather in a universe colonized and populated by our descendants. By then, our numbers will have reached 10^{58}. In this future—not hundreds or thousands, but rather of millions or billions of years away—happiness will be the most trivial thing in human life. Each human will enjoy living standards higher than the richest individuals can afford today. This is probably one reason why Longtermist research projects have been heavily funded by Silicon Valley billionaires like PayPal founder, Peter Thiel, and one of the Skype founders, Jaan Tallinn, not to mention Elon Musk.

For the Longtermists, we must learn to look beyond the short-sighted priorities of our contemporaries. Our choices today should be made for the sake of the generations who will inhabit a far distant future. Their safety—the total safety required for their promised happiness—is what matters, not ours. Whether we are currently safe or not, or whether we might perish through nuclear war or climate collapse, is of little interest to the Longtermist. And they care even less about who wages wars against whom, winners and losers, perpetrators and victims. Only a history stretched to the horizon of eternity can set us free from such mundane ethical concerns—and provide us with total safety.

How does Death feel about this future? First, there is hard work ahead, with millions or billions of us to be ushered into the beyond, but then there is also the prospect of retirement in the far, far future. According to the Longtermists, rapid technological advancements should eventually make it possible for humans to overcome death. They have a variety of techniques to these ends in mind: genetic engineering, uploading our consciousness via brain-computer interfaces, and nanorobots that repair damaged cells or reverse aging. It goes without saying that these immortal super-beings of the distant future will be more technological than biological, which is why they will be able to outpace the speed of light and colonize the entire universe. In this multi-galactic paradise—the Longtermists unironically call their project "paradise engineering"—we will enjoy a life of radical abundance, endless happiness, total safety, and infinity. The post-humans will ultimately abolish death and become immortal.

You might think Death would resent the prospect of being abolished in the future—or of dying itself. Quite the contrary! Not only can it not imagine its own death, it doesn't fear unemployment either. What sounds to us like a neoliberal techno-utopian pipe dream appears to Death as a rather plausible communist future—that is, communism for Death, not for us. Given its ceaseless labor during the revolutions of recent history, it would hardly be unfamiliar with Karl Marx's ideal of a communist society freed from toil, where individuals can devote their abundant free time to whatever activities they like. In Marx's famous words, they will be free to "hunt in the morning, fish in the afternoon, rear cattle in the evening, criticise after dinner."[2] But how would Death escape the eternal boredom of a world without classes and class struggles, a world of total harmony where every post-human has become far richer than any capitalist's dreams? There is only one possible answer: make art. What else? This is the work of the Death-Eye today: uploading clips of thousands of final moments in Donbas or Gaza, and perhaps soon from the cameras of nuclear warheads, streaming the agony of our species in near real time. Could there be any better exhibit for Death's show in the pavilion of dead stars—one of the most prestigious at the famous Milky Way Biennial?

Again, you might think I am exaggerating vastly. There aren't any facts in our present reality to support such nonsense. But let me remind you of some facts that you might want to check yourself.

Émile P. Torres, a drop-out from the Longtermist movement, claims that their ideas have become increasingly powerful due to infiltrating foreign policy circles and major governing institutions like the United Nations.[3] In an article at *UN Dispatch*, one reads that "the foreign policy community in general and the United Nations in particular are beginning to embrace longtermism."[4] Supposedly, it has also had a significant impact on the UN's 2024 Summit of the Future. According to Timnit Gebru, one of the leading experts in AI ethics, "Longtermism is everywhere in Silicon Valley."[5] In their race to create advanced AI, companies like OpenAI and DeepMind also draw on the Longtermist ideology. And then there are the rich and powerful people who support it, like the aforementioned Elon Musk, CEO of SpaceX, who considers Longtermism "a close match" for his own philosophy.[6] Unsurprisingly, the movement is also backed by tens of billions of dollars. In short, it has become a global force and, according to Torres, it is currently "building momentum." If you don't believe me, just google it yourself.

Such ideas about rapid technological development sidelining humans in order to follow its own logic are not entirely new. They even relate to our most crucial safety concerns, the question of war and peace.

In his late years, Friedrich Engels expanded his research on the history of capitalism to not only include the development of the means of production but also the means of destruction, meaning the technological and social means of warfare. Although he more or less maintained the materialist view that the industrial strength of a country determines its military strength, he also allowed for the possibility that it might happen the other way around. As German sociologist Wolfgang Streeck shows in his analysis of Engels' late writings, the advancement of military technology can fundamentally drive civilian technology—a dynamic that has been confirmed a hundred years later with the development of the Internet.[7] Observing the endless modernization of armaments in late nineteenth-century Europe, Engels concluded that technological progress generates a dynamic of its own, an *Eigendynamik* intrinsic to the arms race that forces states to constantly catch up with one another, so as not to fall behind. Eventually, the arms race becomes a proximate cause of war in its own right.

As Streeck emphasizes, this renders the classical distinction between aggression and defense meaningless. It is the *Eigendynamik* of arms races—that is, the autonomous escalation of the means of destruction—that dictates the boundaries between war and peace. What Engels described as "the systematic development of mutual one-upmanship in armaments"[8] operates quite independently of human will. In this view, the civilizational collapse of Europe brought about by WWI, which Engels had clearly predicted, was not just the result of an economic crisis. As Streeck argues, it was the consequence of an arms race getting "out of the hands of an incompetent political class."[9]

Is this already the case in today's Ukraine? Is it true that the boundary between safety and unsafety, between war and peace, is slipping out of human control?

Perhaps things haven't gotten that far, or at least not yet. What if Ukraine's fate still lies in human hands and can still be decided by the will—or if you prefer a softer version, the responsibility—of the world's political elites? Then this fate might look like the post-war reality of the former Yugoslavia.

Just a reminder for those who might have forgotten: the so-called wars of Yugoslav succession—there were five of them—took almost ten years in total, from 1991 to 2001. Let us put aside the question of what caused these wars or who actually started them—there will never be agreement on that—to ask who ended them and how? Apart from the total exhaustion of human, economic, and moral resources (even Death got tired), the decisive role in pacifying the region was assumed by the United States. The rest of Europe only vacillated between further fueling the conflicts, moralizing about them from a distance, and providing humanitarian aid—which was the most useful thing it did in the end. In terms of political and military involvement, the rest was done by the Americans. The political representatives of the warring parties—almost all of them war criminals with some even responsible for a genocide—were forced to the negotiating table, where they had no choice other than agreeing to the terms dictated by the US supervisors. The peace treaty for Bosnia and Herzegovina was in fact negotiated and signed in Dayton, Ohio. The logic was simple: accepting the reality established by military force. In short, the territory belongs to whoever has the most boots on the ground. This also included the results of ethnic cleansing and genocide, which were simply accepted as a *fait accompli.* Peace was not achieved by undoing the violent mess of war, but by adapting to the results.

The Western powers did not pacify the former Yugoslavia with clean hands. The USA, the EU, and NATO staged regime changes, launched illegal military interventions, committed war crimes, and broke the bounds of national sovereignty. Moreover, the American negotiators also secured lucrative business contracts with the signatories of the peace treaties. Yet all of this was tolerated simply because there wasn't any other guarantor of peace, and because Western power effectively operated with impunity. That impunity, of course, did not extend to any of the local perpetrators or parties involved. The UN had already established the so-called Hague Tribunal, or more precisely the International Criminal Tribunal for the former Yugoslavia (ICTY), during the war. During the 25 years of its activity, the court indicted more than 150 individuals and gave 91 of them sentences that would add up to over a thousand years. However, the hope that the judicial closure of the war would finally bring about "peace and reconciliation" remains largely disappointed. Almost all of the sentenced criminals are still celebrated as national martyrs at home.

The post-war condition of the territories in the former Yugoslavia has but one name: *pax americana.* It is not an order of peace and security, let alone of democracy and prosperity. Rather it is a sort of post-democratic, post-sovereign regime, a form of governance limited to managing the fallout of permanent social, political, and economic instability. What passes for peace is perhaps better described as a suspended war, where the ubiquitous sense of unsafety becomes the most vital source of political power. It is a condition of constant ideological and political manipulation mobilized through fear and resentment.

Does this look like a realistic prospect for Ukraine today? Or shall Death quicken its grim work, hurrying us along toward a life of total safety—not in eight or ten billion of years, but perhaps just three or four. As the saying goes, hope dies last.

---

1. See William MacAskill's own definition, "Longtermism" (July 2022), https://www.williammacaskill.com/longtermism [accessed 11 February 2026].
2. Karl Marx, "The German Ideology" (1846), in *Marx-Engels Collected Works* vol. 5 (New York: International Publishers, 1976), p. 47.
3. Émile P. Torres, "Longtermism poses a real threat to humanity," *The New Statesman* (3 August 2023), https://www.newstatesman.com/ideas/2023/08/longtermism-threat-humanity [accessed 11 February 2026].
4. Mark Leon Goldberg, "How 'Longtermism' is Shaping Foreign Policy | Will MacAskill," *UN Dispatch* (15 August 2022), https://undispatch.com/how-longtermism-is-shaping-foreign-policy-will-macaskill/ [accessed 11 February 2026].
5. Quoted in Émile P. Torres, "Longtermism poses a real threat to humanity," see note 3.
6. Ibid., see note 3.
7. Wolfgang Streeck, "Notes on the Political Economy of War," *Review of Keynesian Economics,* vol. 12, no. 3 (Autumn 2024), pp. 293–307, https://wolfgangstreeck.com/wp-content/uploads/2024/09/streeck_2024.pdf [accessed 11 February 2026].
8. Friedrich Engels, "Introduction to Sigismund Borkheim's Pamphlet *In Memory of the German Blood-and-Thunder Patriots 1806–1807*" (1887), in *Marx-Engels Collected Works* vol. 26 (New York: International Publishers, 1990), p. 451.
9. Wolfgang Streeck, "Notes on the Political Economy of War," see note 7.

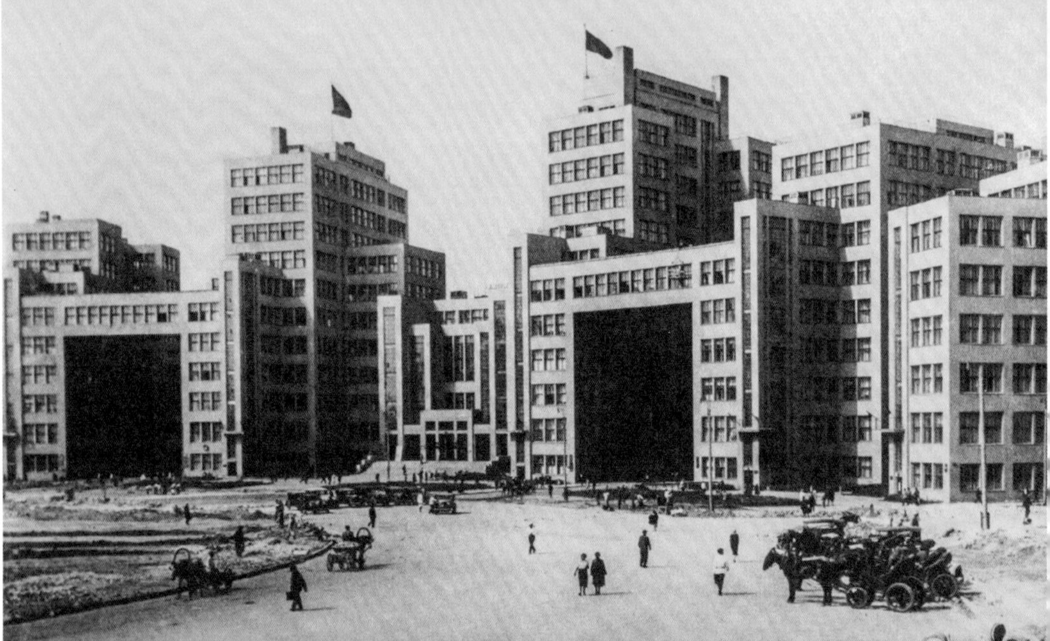

Dreaming Is a Good Thing

Maxim Rosenfeld

POST-TRAUMATIC INGROWTH

The name of this force field is borrowed from psychology, where the term post-traumatic growth describes the personal transformation that happens following a traumatic event which has disrupted one's sense of a safe world. War disrupts every regime of stability and seemingly any vision of the future. Safety, as a civilizational achievement, fades into the background yet becomes all the more urgently desired. This force field encourages us to think about the possibilities for the future. It asks how we can transform traumatic experiences into artistic expressions and find ways to respond to acute moments of crisis marked by fear and pain in order to reshape those experiences into new ones. The practices gathered under the auspices of *Post-Traumatic Ingrowth* do not seek to forget or erase trauma, but rather acknowledge it, foster empathy, and strengthen social ties, thereby forming a safe field of communication.

Some cities have recognizable symbols: the Eiffel Tower in Paris, Big Ben in London, and St. Sophia Cathedral in Kyiv. Kharkiv is no exception, and its main symbol is the monumental Derzhprom building on Freedom Square. Yet, as is often the case, when you start asking yourself what exactly Derzhprom is supposed to symbolize or why it is so iconic, the first answers that come to mind are fairly trite: it is the first reinforced concrete building, the first Soviet skyscraper, an early example of a new style in architecture—constructivism—and other such journalistic tour-guide clichés. Since 2022, the building has acquired another cliché about the heroic pathos of war and the resilience of Kharkiv's people: *Derzhprom is reinforced concrete.* Honestly, the formula that represents Kharkiv and Ukraine so well around the world feels annoying when you're in the city. I mean, *reinforced* concrete is something super static, rooted, lifeless, and I've always thought of Derzhprom as something lively, dynamic, active, and even able to fly. For me, it has never just been a symbol of building material, construction technique, or the philosophy of new architecture, but also a symbol of the ability to dream and the courage to make those dreams come true. I'm lucky to live close to this special building, and, weirdly enough, after so many years of my regular encounters with Derzhprom, it still inspires me and gives me strength. This is what happened to me, and I'm sure it's happened to thousands of other people too.

I remember one such scene well from early March 2022. I stayed in deserted Kharkiv, which was under shelling. On Freedom Square, the recently bombed-out regional administration building still stood there "proudly"; it was freezing, the wind was blowing snow across the completely desolate city, and it was strangely

erzhprom building. Reproduced from V. Bysov and G. Mikhailov, *harkiv: The Capital of Constructivism, 1923–1934* (Kharkiv: Dim Reklamy, 2019). ource: https://constructivism-kharkiv.com

quiet—not a sound could be heard. There was a sense of collective shock over the madness of what was happening, and I could clearly feel the end of history, or at least the end of my own history. Leaving home, I walked along my usual route to the square and cautiously turned my head toward the Derzhprom building. And it didn't let me down. With windows blown out and glass scattered everywhere, it stood there, battered but beautiful and magnificent, and it seemed to smile and say: "Everything will pass. More to come. Get through this day. Look to the future. Keep dreaming." It didn't let me down even in that terrible moment of my life—it saved me once again. And this would happen again and again, and not only to me. After all, this building was not just supposed to be millions of cubic meters of solid reinforced concrete, square kilometers of glazing, or high-tech engineering solutions, but the embodiment of a bold dream. To understand this, we need to look at the history of its creation.

It happened exactly one hundred years ago. In 1925, the situation was critical and, as we would call it today, post-traumatic. Following World War I, the revolution, the civil war, radical changes in life, and devastation, a sort of hangover set in. One had to build a new life, rethink the past, and shape the future. On the one hand, the State Industry Building project was intended to answer the demand for an office center for a large group of state trusts. And on the other hand, it was a kind of experiment in an innovative approach to design, architecture, and construction. From the point of view of philosophy and psychology, this is a very important aspect: crisis fosters abstraction and restores the freedom to dream. It might seem that the crisis is a remarkably inappropriate time for dreaming, but it is during these times that the most daring projects and phenomena are born. So, architect Oleksandr Molokin developed a competition program that clearly defined the expectations for the future building and outlined its innovative approach.[1] The competition was held in one stage, and the winner was the project designed by architects Serhii Serafimov, Samuil Kravets, and Mark Felger with the motto "Uninvited Guest."[2] Its very name clearly defined the character of the winner. When researching the history of the competition and the entire construction, I read many articles by Serafimov, the chief architect of Derzhprom. I realized that, in many ways, that work was a true miracle of divine revelation for the architect, literally a ghost that haunted his imagination like an uninvited guest. The creator understood that he had designed a timeless masterpiece. It is no coincidence that the figure of Derzhprom is engraved on Serhii Savych's gravestone, as it was his lifetime achievement.

But a project on paper is far from being a grand realization. To implement a large-scale project, one needs an engineer and a team of construction workers. Pavlo Rottert performed another miracle.[3] He believed his dream could come true despite the complete lack of materials, technology, and skilled professionals. Dreaming is a good thing, but it takes courage to make dreams come true. What unfolded over two years on an empty lot behind the University Garden was a true miracle. Rottert recruited several thousand construction workers and organized a production school for craftsmen, as such an innovative project required inventing and developing new technologies and solutions, as well as learning how to use them right away. In addition, students from the Polytechnic Institute helped with a number of engineering tasks, and for them, that job was a formative academic experience. Practically speaking, that whole experiment was more like a risky adventure with a pretty low chance of success—there was basically no guarantee of achieving the expected result. In fact, it was constantly a frontier—a dangerous boundary of the unknown—and being in this situation is very unpleasant, uncomfortable, and unsafe. However, this is the only way to move toward something new. The dreamers were rewarded with success. The result exceeded expectations, as it became apparent that the amazing buildings of Derzhprom were inspiring hundreds of other dreamers: artists and writers, physicists and poets, teachers and engineers. The construction of Derzhprom became a hymn to the reality of daring dreams, and it marked the beginning of "our twenties"—a time of revolutionary avant-garde activity across various fields.[4]

Nevertheless, the physical embodiment of Derzhprom should not be perceived as a monument to a dream. A monument is a reminder of the past, and a dream cannot be in the past tense; it is alive and immortal. Another telling story about treating Derzhprom as a living entity is connected to its second father, engineer Pavlo Rottert. According to the recollections of his colleagues, after moving to Moscow for work in the 1930s, Pavlo often visited Kharkiv—the city of his youth, his love, and the place where his children and grandchildren lived. During his last visit in 1954, he took a taxi from the train station to the square, asked the driver to wait a few minutes, walked up to the wall of Derzhprom, hugged it, stood there for a while, returned to the car, and went back home. He died a few weeks later. For him, it was important to say goodbye to Derzhprom before his death, as if it were a close relative, a loved one, a living being.

Derzhprom is an undeniable architectural masterpiece, but not only that. It is a hymn to bold dreams and passionate enthusiasm. That is why it keeps inspiring and saving us in the most challenging times. It is emblematic that the building is located on Freedom Square. In my opinion, there is a special meaning behind this. Once, in 2014, the YermilovCentre, which is situated in the basement of the nearby University building (also designed by Serhii Serafimov, by the way), held an art event titled *Freedom Square.* The project was a response to the Euromaidan events, and its curators invited me to give a lecture about Freedom Square. Back then, I contemplated what true freedom meant to me and concluded that it was the ability to dream. After all, in our bold dreams, we are not limited by reinforced concrete technology and engineering structures, political realities of war, or financial constraints of the project—we are free to dream and fly, which is why I called that lecture "Dreaming does no harm" and dedicated it to Derzhprom. Since then, for me, as well as for many other people, Derzhprom has been a savior, a source of inspiration, and a close relative.

1. Oleksandr Molokin (1880–1951) was an architect, professor, and educator. He defined the competition program for the Derzhprom building and provided the theoretical justification for the project. He was the author of a number of landmark buildings in Kharkiv.
2. Serhii Serafimov (1878–1939) was an architect, educator, professor, and Doctor of Architecture. Samuil Kravets (1891–1966) was an architect and the chief architect of Metroproekt. Mark Felger (1881–1962) was an architect.
3. Pavlo Rottert (1880–1954) was a civil engineer and construction organizer, Doctor of Technical Sciences, professor, corresponding member of the Academy of Architecture of the USSR, and chief project engineer.
4. "Our Twenties" is a term describing a period of rapid cultural, scientific, and technological growth after the end of the World War I, comparable to the Roaring Twenties in the United States and the Goldene Zwanziger (Golden Twenties) in Germany.

Land for Which So Much Blood Has Been Shed Cannot Remain Unsown*

* The title is drawn from a quote attributed to Vasyl Yermilov.

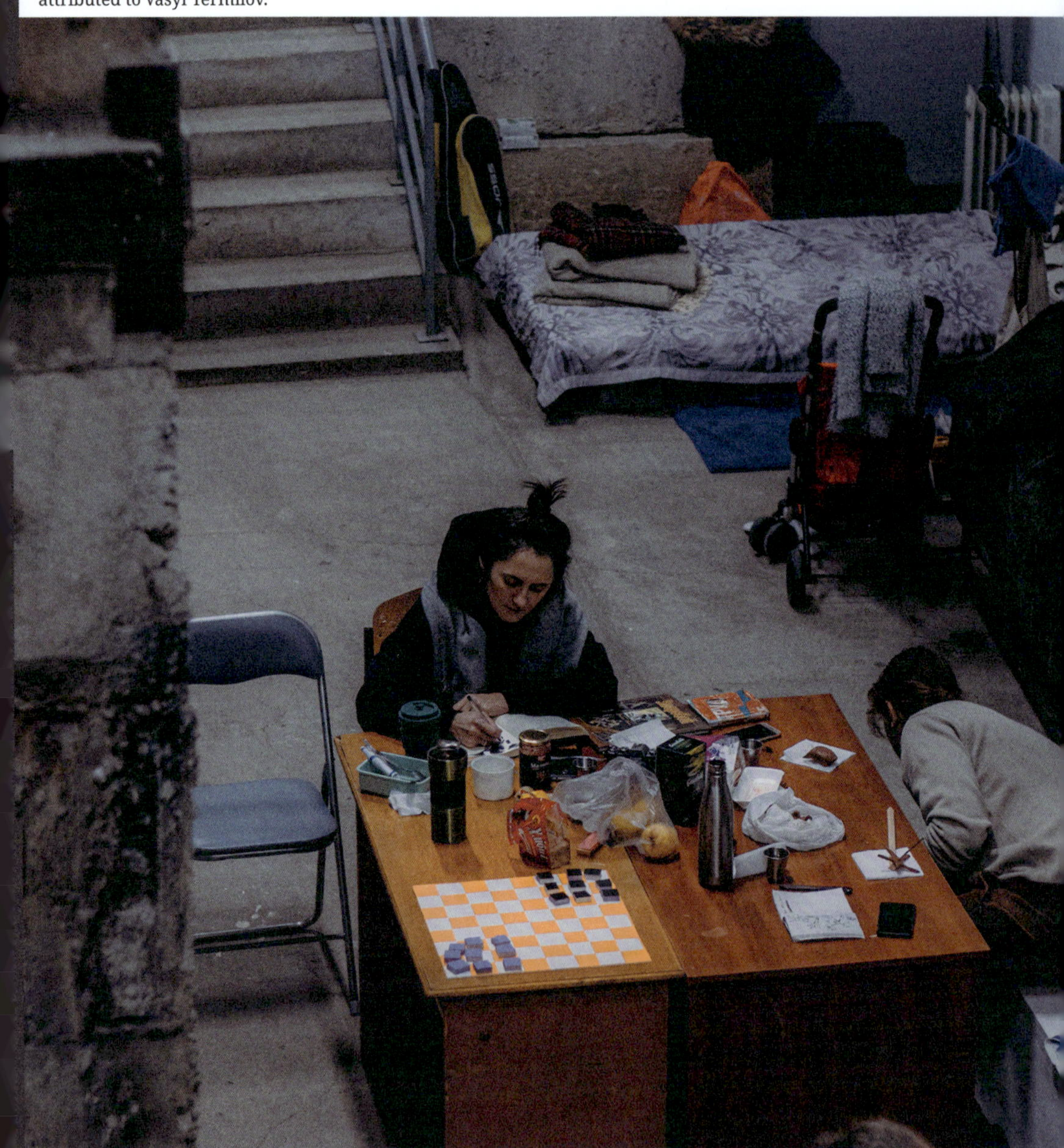

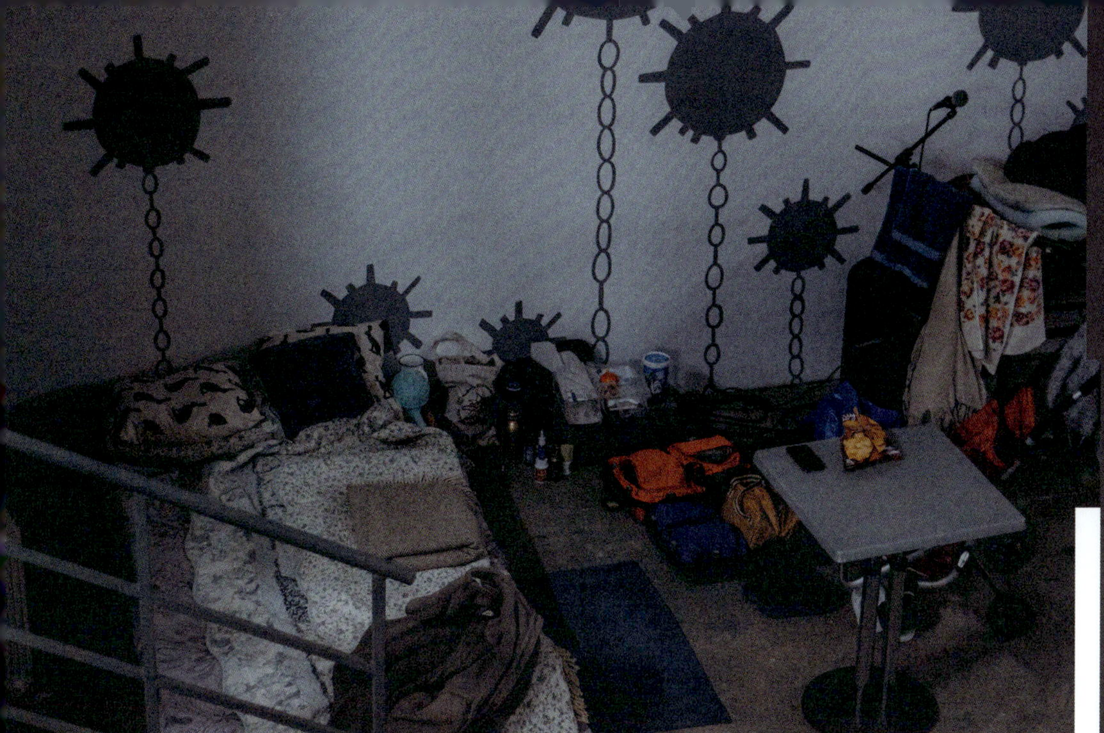

Lena Prents: Nataliia, how did you learn about the beginning of the Russian invasion of Ukraine? Do you remember that moment?

Nataliia Ivanova: Of course I remember it. That morning will stay with me for the rest of my life. I woke up to explosions. We all woke up to explosions in Kharkiv. They were clearly audible, and it was very, very frightening. On 22 February, we had opened an exhibition at the YermilovCentre; I was still feeling the pleasant afterglow of the opening. Then on 24 February, at half past four in the morning, it vanished instantly. When people used to say that life is divided into before and after, it sounded like a cliché. But it is true. I live in the Kholodna Hora district of Kharkiv, near the highway leading to Kyiv. By six in the morning, there were already kilometer-long queues of people trying to leave the city. They stood in those lines around the clock, and it was immediately clear that there was no point in even trying to join them.

LP: Early in the morning of 24 February 2022, I received a message from an acquaintance: “Lena, you’re probably asleep, but when you wake up, you’ll learn that the war has indeed begun.” The laconic nature of that message burned more sharply than the official news. After all, those of us who were socialized in the late Soviet Union were convinced that the Second World War had been the last major war. We grew up with the slogans “No war” and “Peace to the world!” The characters in Svetlana Alexievich’s book *The Unwomanly Face of War* recalled how they fired all the ammunition they had left into the air as fireworks to celebrate victory—because it would never, ever be needed again.

ermilovCentre as a bomb shelter in the beginning of Russia’s full-scale invasion of
kraine, February 2022. Photo: Marharyta Rubanenko. Courtesy of the YermilovCentre.

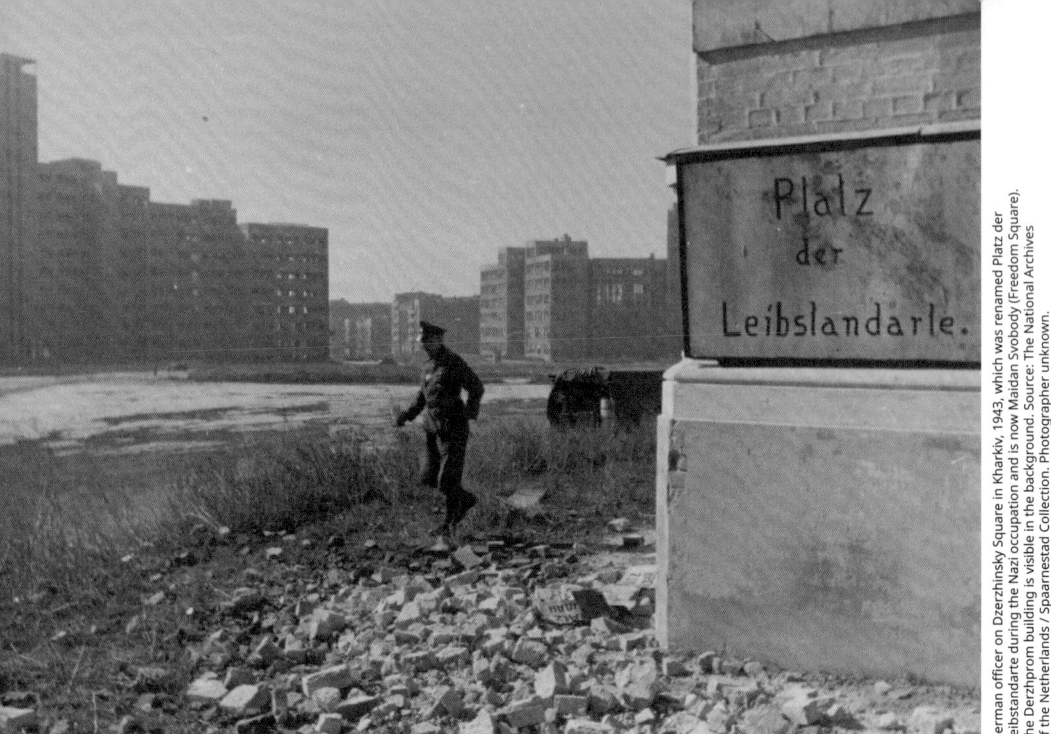

German officer on Dzerzhinsky Square in Kharkiv, 1943, which was renamed Platz der Leibstandarte during the Nazi occupation and is now Maidan Svobody (Freedom Square). The Derzhprom building is visible in the background. Source: The National Archives of the Netherlands / Spaarnestad Collection. Photographer unknown.

NI: Yes, we didn't witness the Second World War, but we grew up knowing about it. And in my imagination, war meant total collapse. Food disappears; people and enterprises are evacuated; entire cities are emptied. It means you must either leave immediately or stay behind, knowing that the territory may be occupied. We remember the historical footage of the German occupation of Kharkiv.[1] But today, this is a different war. On 24 February, we just didn't know that yet. I thought tanks would arrive any moment. And tanks did enter the streets; there were sabotage groups; there were street battles. All of that happened, but episodically. Gradually, we began to understand that it is still possible to live, to work, to love, even to have children under such conditions. And that one must live today, rather than postpone life until after victory.

LP: On 24 February 2022, the YermilovCentre published a post: "The YermilovCentre is closed until Monday! Stay strong. Take care of yourselves and your loved ones. Keep calm." Did you really reopen on Monday, four days later? How did you find your bearings? How did you figure out what should come first—personal safety, responsibility for the team, for the place? The YermilovCentre is located in a university building; it is a two-level basement space that can function as a bomb shelter. It can—but at that moment it wasn't one yet.

NI: At first there was only fear and no understanding whatsoever of what needed to be done. I can't say that I was brave or decisive, or that I quickly came up with a plan for how to shelter everyone in the YermilovCentre—how to give people a place to gather, to sleep, to feel safe. But at some point, you simply have to make a decision, and you make it. In the university chat, a message appeared saying there would be no work that day; everyone stayed home and waited for further instructions or made decisions on their own. In our YermilovCentre chat, we contacted the staff members who work with us, and they said: "Nataliia Valentynivna, we've already come to the YermilovCentre because there is shelling where we live." They lived in Oleksiivka, which the Russians had started shelling along with Saltivka;[2] tanks were entering through Oleksiivka, and it was terrifying there. If my colleagues were already at the YermilovCentre, then of course I went there as well. We began calling friends, colleagues, artists, telling them they could come and stay here in the bomb shelter. And people came—with sleeping bags, backpacks, children, dogs, and cats—and somehow settled in. There were about fifty of us. Later, we created a chat and called it "Hotel YermilovCentre."

Over the years, we had accumulated a great deal of material in the basement—panels, boards, podiums, stands—from which artists quickly improvised sofas, beds, and chairs. Everyone had their own place to sleep. The space is large, so no one disturbed anyone else. We set up a food area with shelving. There was even a special room for cats.

On the fourth or fifth day, we started going out to pharmacies, shops, and the supermarket outside. Standing in kilometer-long queues at the supermarket was very frightening, because planes were flying over the city. When a plane flies overhead and you hear the roar of this enormous machine, fear takes over completely—it doesn't even need to drop anything; your heart simply stops.

LP: And did Oleh Kalashnik's exhibition *Enfant terrible*, which you opened on 22 February, remain open? You were living among and with art.

NI: Strangely enough, amid this endless tracking of news, messages, conversations about what was happening, and what would happen to us and to the country, a desire emerged to talk about something else as well.

The artist Pavlo Makov was with us, along with his wife.[3] That year, he was representing Ukraine at the Venice Biennale. I called him and suggested that they move to the YermilovCentre. At first he refused, but literally half an hour later he called me back and said that a missile had become lodged in the asphalt near their building. It hadn't exploded—it was as if it had simply gotten stuck there. This was how territory was being marked for shelling. His work for the Biennale was in Kyiv, ready to be shipped. But no one knew what would happen next, or whether Makov would go to Venice at all. Makov speaks both Italian and English and was giving countless interviews to international media. And then I said to him: well, instead of telling everyone separately, why don't we do an artist talk here, where you can speak about your project? And that's what we did.

LP: They say that during catastrophes and wars, the perception of time becomes heavily distorted—it can slow down or speed up. Listening to you, it feels as if you are describing months or even years. Yet in reality, we are talking about days and weeks—time became so compressed by the succession of events and reactions.

NI: Yes. Around 6 March, our electricity was cut off—and everything depended on electricity. Without power, there is no life in the YermilovCentre. We did have various camping and emergency supplies, but all of that is very temporary; it is impossible to live like that for long. By that point, most people had already left the YermilovCentre. For those who remained, I suggested going to my village in the Sumy region, where I run artist residencies. I usually travel there via Okhtyrka, which was being mercilessly shelled, with Russian troops stationed 10 kilometers away. So we took a detour through the Poltava region. There was slush; the snow froze and then melted. Once we arrived in the village, we immediately asked everyone who had stayed at the YermilovCentre to send photos and videos to a chat. Using this material, we created an online project, *How Are You?*—a response to the first hours and days of the war: how it felt, where we lived, what forms of support existed.

LP: Nataliia, theoretically you could have just closed the institution and not worried about it at all, right?

NI: Of course, it would have been possible to close the institution. Theoretically, I could have left the country or switched to an entirely online mode of work. But there are arguments on the other side as well: there is a safe, comfortable space in the city center where events of various formats can be held for large numbers of people. And you know that you are able to ensure full operation, and that the work of many people depends on you. At that point, you don't want to leave—it becomes an obvious decision. You stay and do what is important for your institution right now.

I created this center and developed it over ten years. Many other people also worked to make the YermilovCentre what it is today: curators, artists, managers, not only from Kharkiv but from all over Ukraine. How could I just close it and leave? And there was also the understanding that we could still do a great deal—for the city, for the country, for the university. I think about it this way: if you can do something, then do it.

We hosted many events, including those not strictly related to contemporary art, sometimes two or three a day: a press conference in the morning, a charity concert in the evening, sometimes meetings and briefings in between. The Kharkiv Media Hub operated here. After the Ukrainian counterattack in 2022, part of the Kharkiv region was liberated, and bodies were later exhumed in the Izium forest. We all learned about this horrific tragedy. Many journalists, including international ones, were working in the city, and they needed a place to work. Their insurance policies required them to remain in a bomb shelter during air raid alerts. But how can you work if air raid sirens sound 24/7? We had the best possible space for this.

At the same time, it was important for me to preserve the YermilovCentre specifically as a cultural institution. I wanted to keep doing cultural projects, to continuously fill the space with exhibitions, events, educational programs. We saw that these formats were needed. Perhaps even more than before the war.

LP: You say these events were needed. But needed by whom? Your audience must have changed significantly. I looked it up: before the war, Kharkiv had around 400,000 students. Many must have left, along with your regular visitors. And although new people arrive during any war, that doesn't automatically make them an audience for cultural events.

NI: To be honest, I don't even know how many people were in Kharkiv in 2022. At that time, if even 10–20 percent of the residents were still living in an apartment building, one person per stairwell, that was already considered good. But it felt to me as though everyone who was in Kharkiv was with us. The university has 20,000 students. If even 10 percent of them physically remained in the city, that is already 2,000 people.

There were many volunteers cooking and delivering food, distributing medicine; there were many journalists. Everything had changed, but people still came to us.

You are right: there used to be 400,000 students, and then there were 300,000 internally displaced people. Some of them will move on, but many will stay. The YermilovCentre has four staff members: myself and three managers who were students just yesterday. They still have much to learn and much experience to gain, even though they are highly motivated. And working with deeply traumatized people, such as displaced persons from the Luhansk and Donetsk regions, requires specialized knowledge and experience. Imagine losing everything in the middle or toward the end of your life. Entire families with children are now living in dormitories in Kharkiv. It may sound strange to speak of "dreams" in this context, but I dream of working with them and for them.

My second dream is for Kharkiv to regain its status as a unique city of extraordinary architecture, science, and culture, and for the world to recognize it as such. It must not remain a place known only for Northern Saltivka, the largest residential district of Kharkiv, which has been completely devastated—there is not a single place left intact. This is a tragedy for the city, but it must not become its defining feature.

As much as time, energy, and the number of people allow, we dream of Kharkiv entering the global cultural community with narratives beyond war and destruction.

LP: I know that this was precisely the main motivation for Tatiana Kochubinska when she contacted you on behalf of antiwarcoalition.art with a proposal to create a large international collaborative project. This was not about Western aid to a bombed-out Kharkiv, nor about the self-realization of young curators. It was about something else: putting Kharkiv, with its unique architectural ensemble, historical cultural heritage, and artistic scene, back on the map of Europe.

NI: Yes, and it was extremely important. In general, the question of preserving cultural institutions in a city is a city-forming issue, at least that's how I see it. If, hypothetically speaking, all that remained in the city were industrial enterprises, restaurants, cafés, and the Barabashovo market, then this would no longer be Kharkiv as we know it, love it, and value it. You know, the war also became a catalyst for creating new art and culture spaces. When we opened the YermilovCentre as a contemporary art center, I thought that similar spaces and galleries would start popping up like mushrooms after the rain. The miracle did not happen then, but it is happening now. In 2023, the initiative Some People opened the Center for New Culture. DRUK popped up in the building of a former book factory,[4] which was beautifully restored in accordance with the principles of architectural heritage conservation. There are theaters there, as well as artists' studios. That is why it was important that the YermilovCentre also continued to function in accordance with its mission.

LP: *Sense of Safety* was the first international project at the YermilovCentre after the beginning of the full-scale invasion. Could you speak about the cultural, and perhaps also the political, dimension of this project?

NI: For me, it was essential; there was no other way. Of course, we could simmer in our own problems for as long as we like, hold events just for ourselves, and only exhibit Kharkiv artists. That would be justified—they deserve it, and they must be shown. But if we want Europe and the wider world to learn about Kharkiv in precisely the context we are discussing now, then we have to create international projects. I am deeply grateful to Thomas Hirschhorn for coming. I very much want artists to find the courage to come here. I cannot insist on this today, nor can I guarantee their safety. But I am profoundly thankful to everyone who does come. They can spread information about what they have seen: how we work, how the city lives, and what is happening here. They witness this war with their own eyes.

LP: The curators of *Sense of Safety* have said that today the YermilovCentre is one of the safest places in Kharkiv—an ideal place to think about both feelings and safety. You have said before that for you there is no question at all about whether it makes sense to produce art projects during the war. It is simply not up for debate.

NI: It is not up for debate.

You see, people don't just want to go to work, hide during air raid alerts, step out into a corridor during the workday, return home exhausted, eat, then go to sleep—often on the floor in a hallway away from the windows, just in case there is an air raid at night. People want something more, because they are human. They want to go to an exhibition, a lecture, or the cinema. At the exhibition *Pairs Skating* by Wolfgang Tillmans and Boris Mikhailov,[5] an elderly man came to us several times. He would take a chair and sit in front of the monitor to watch the recorded conversation between the two artists from beginning to end.

In 2022–2023, we sometimes cleared our space for theater productions, because theaters didn't have anywhere to perform except bomb shelters. I watched the play based on Serhiy Zhadan's *A Harvest Truce*, staged by our Shevchenko Drama Theatre, about ten times. And many spectators did as well. The plot is very heavy: at the beginning of the fighting in the Donbas in 2014, two brothers attempt to bury their deceased mother with dignity during a ceasefire. We had a full house every time.

It is extremely important for people to have a place where they can meet and talk, discuss what they have seen in an exhibition, a theater performance, or a film, or simply exchange a few words. It seems to me that today art not only fulfills a communicative function between artist and viewer, but also between visitors themselves. Because it is precisely in moments of communication that you realize life is going on. Here it is. The one and only. And the task of an institution is to sense which questions need to be addressed today.

LP: Sometimes in Berlin I attend public meetings and workshops with curators, or receive invitations to participate in them. Their aim is to exchange experiences and thoughts on strategies and curatorial practice under changing political and social conditions: the rise of right-wing tendencies in society, cuts in cultural funding, the growing precarity of artistic labor. I often experience a sense of déjà vu: I have heard all this before, and we have discussed it already. We curators work with words, and words make it easy to exaggerate things: to turn a small gesture of help into political solidarity against a certain catastrophe, or a few successful events into the creation of a community. In other words, to present something small, exceptional, or local as universal. I do not exclude myself, or our municipal gallery of contemporary art, from this widespread institutional practice of triumphant self-presentation. But I think we should all make more of an effort to measure our curatorial experience of relative well-being and stable structures against the experience of colleagues living in conditions of fragility. Now, at the end of 2025, we see that the war in Ukraine remains open-ended and uncertain, with no clear prospects for resolution, while the international community oscillates between long-term support for Kyiv and attempts at mediation. Has your curatorial practice changed during the war? Has your understanding of curatorial tasks changed?

NI: You see, I live in Ukrainian realities, so I am a curator, a manager, and a director all at once. We choose which projects to work on next and plan one or two years ahead. Because to realize a project in our space, money is needed. Of course, we know how to make exhibitions without it, but if you want to do a large, high-quality project, you have to look for funding. In that sense, my algorithms and methods have not changed. And it is simply wonderful that I can continue doing the work I was doing before the war. I did not have to change anything; I did not have to move to another country; I live in my beloved city, and I can work offline. Thank God, everything is fine with my residency. Yes, there are Shahed drones flying past the window ... that is our reality now. But overall, we are in a relatively safe place. So what is there to change? Do your work, and that's it.

We already have ongoing projects that I believe we are obliged to continue. Supporting young curators and artists is extremely important. Right now, we are hosting the exhibition *Show Your Documents* curated by Yurii Rassokha and Petro Chekal.[6] The curators are young; one of them is my student. Last year, we submitted a grant application that was successful, and now we have realized this project. That, in turn, led me to the idea of launching a competition—an open call for young curators. The winners will have the opportunity to realize their ideas at the YermilovCentre.

LP: Behind you, I see a round object that looks like a portrait of Vasyl Yermilov (1894–1968). In art history, his name is most often associated with the revolutionary Soviet avant-garde of the 1920s—the utopian project of creating a new human being and new society through total experimentation. The Kharkiv Art and Industrial Institute, in whose founding Yermilov participated in 1922, is often compared to the Bauhaus. Yet, unlike the cosmopolitan trajectories of that time, Yermilov remained in Kharkiv throughout his life, with only brief interruptions, shaping the city's visual, cultural, and artistic identity. In Yermilov's expression and understanding, experimental innovation was particular—local, rooted, gentle, and poetic. He regarded teaching as a practice of freedom. Even under conditions of repression and persecution, his visual language carried an impulse of renewal and a belief in the possibility of a different future. So is Yermilov's figure your source of strength and inspiration—the cultural foundation that gives stability and meaning to the entire institution?

NI: Yes, what you see here is a work by Inna Pedan, an artist and designer. She was among the architects and designers who worked on the YermilovCentre space together with Ihor Ostapenko (1951–2023) and Andrii Khvorostianov. They were also the ones to propose the name YermilovCentre. In 2015, Inna created this collage and placed within it a quotation by Yermilov: "Land for which so much blood has been shed cannot remain unsown." This speaks directly to us today. We must already be thinking about what we will sow our land with, and what we will do. I want to develop cooperative projects, expand the residency, and deepen international collaboration. We have something to show. And of course, there is no time to postpone anything. Everything must be done now. That's how it is.

The conversation between Nataliia Ivanova and Lena Prents took place on 30 October 2025 via Zoom.

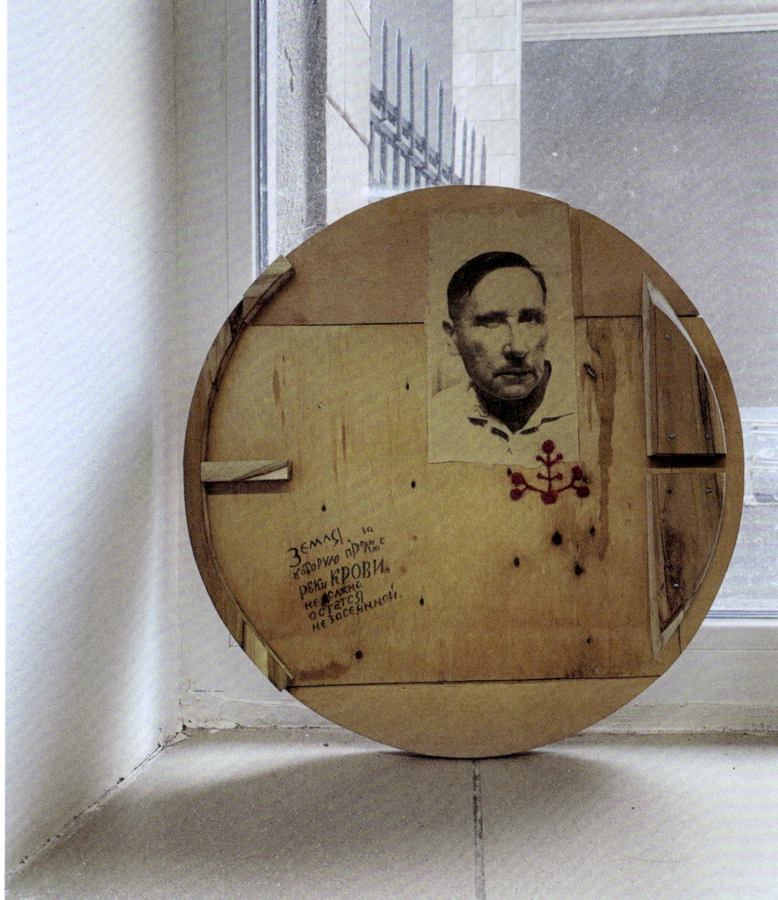

Office at YermilovCentre, featuring a collage by Inna Pedan depicting Vasyl Yermilov, 2026. Photo: Vlad Nikorchuk.

---

1. The occupation of Kharkiv by Wehrmacht troops began on 24 October 1941 and continued, with interruptions, until the liberation of the city on 23 August 1943.
2. Oleksiivka and Saltivka are large residential districts of Kharkiv that came under intense shelling during the first days of the full-scale invasion and were among the most severely affected areas of the city.
3. In 2022, Pavlo Makov represented Ukraine at the 59th Venice Biennale with the project *The Fountain of Exhaustion* (curated by Lizaveta German, Maria Lanko, and Borys Filonenko). In 2024, the project was presented at the YermilovCentre.
4. DRUK is a cultural and community center that opened after the start of Russia's full-scale invasion of Ukraine, housed in a historic nineteenth-century printing house.
5. The exhibition *Pairs Skating: Boris Mikhailov and Wolfgang Tillmans* took place at the YermilovCentre from 25 April to 28 September 2025. It was curated by Maria Isserlis and Tatiana Kochubinska.
6. The exhibition *Show Your Documents* took place at the YermilovCentre from 17 October to 7 December 2025. It was curated by Yurii Rassokha and Petro Chekal.

Listening Without Fear

Serhiy Zhadan

COMMUNICATION AS A SAFE PLACE

**Communication is a two-way process involving sending a message as well as receiving it.
The safety of communication thus depends on two fundamental principles: the ability to speak and the possibility of being heard.
In other words, *Communication as a Safe Place* not only returns to the question of "Can the subaltern speak?" but also asks "How do we speak in order to be heard and understood?"
Communication as a Safe Place assembles artistic practices that engage with the idea of language as the glue of social interaction. It focuses on the possibility and impossibility of speaking in the face of the Other or in contexts where one is numbed by pain. This force field brings together performative and interactive artistic practices that work around spontaneous or organized collectivity and forge bridges of solidarity between different communities, geographies, and temporalities.**

I remember the opening of Pavlo Makov's exhibition at the YermilovCentre,[1] when war had already broken out in Kharkiv. I remember that sharp, deeply important feeling of being among one's own people, when it seems like you know everyone in the crowded basement. Of course, not everyone actually knew one another, but there was this shared space of belonging. You did not so much recognize the person next to you as feel them. And to feel meant to trust. This is not about a bubble or a closed environment. It is about the markers we use to recognize our own, and about the weight of communication, a weight that has changed fundamentally since the beginning of the full-scale war.

So what lies behind this need to speak and to listen? A rejection of loneliness, isolation, abandonment. A need for another's presence, for external warmth, for being understood from the outside. War can make people distrustful but it also sharpens this need. It deepens our dependence on good news and familiar voices. It pushes us into this circle of our own—a circle where one feels safer, more grounded in meaning.

And what stands in the way? Individual solitude, disconnection from the shared soundscape, from channels of exchange, meaning, and warmth. Fear takes root in silence, in the anticipation that there may be an explosion, a flash, a rupture at any moment. Behind the inability to speak lies the inability to understand one another, the inability to explain oneself, to define oneself. In the absence of normal communication, a vast void opens up—a space for fear and darkness, for manipulation and despair. We feel this especially now, whenever we speak or listen, whether to strangers or friends.

Perhaps this is precisely the time to learn to articulate things that once felt impossible, things we had no habit of voicing, no need to voice. Now more than ever, we can sense how vital these forms of communication are: ways of informing, of exchanging voices, of exchanging love. When you speak, and you feel needed. When you listen, and you are not afraid.

1. The solo exhibition *The Fountain of Exhaustion 1994–2024* by Pavlo Makov took place at the YermilovCentre from 29 March to 29 June 2024.

WHEN SO MUCH IS TAKEN AWAY

When so much is taken away
something is always given in return.
Something useful, like the experience of sudden parting.
Where else could you learn about
how suddenly the thread can break,
how suddenly the confused heart can stop?
Pain.
Pain and hope can return your lost sense of this world.
Give life to your essential being, give it meaning.
Pain and hope, which you never expected,
never talked about at family dinners.
Where else can you hear this voice from the forest
frightened by fire, who else can
focus your sight, tune it
like a grand piano, so that your eye won't go flat,
so you recognize the shadowy beast
in the middle of the field?
You survived
the insane balancing act this winter,
collecting fears like old books
from your parents' library,
so now, how can you complain about the weight
of events that have pushed you
into the cold air of history?
Don't you dare,
don't you dare complain
when those burned by rage don't cry.
The mutilated landscape clenches its teeth,
framed by light,
slashed by moonlight.
Pain and hope unite us
in the openings of the dark sky.
Pain and hope, the lungs of a drowning girl,
as the green pond water is forced out,
return her to life.
Pain and hope,
a house rebuilt after a fire.
But in this rift the past retreats,
a shoreline into the darkness,
only in this expanse of patience
can a hint of appreciation appear for what
made you relevant
this spring, so clear, so precise,
set against the sun,
backlit in the wind.
I saw how sleepy women on trains
grab on to invisible voices,
like on to a thread leading them down the corridor.
I saw how fires of inspiration go out over the heads of men.
How children embrace the shade like a mother.
How dogs fall silent, seeing the sun
move over the city.
But summer will come,
with a great scorched river,
and boys on asphalt soccer fields,
like the letters of the constitution,
will testify to the quality of those born on the border,
the quality and honor of people who since childhood
got used to having their skin ripped off by the harsh asphalt;
got used to the pain and the hope,
and stitched up the torn flesh in the thick
light of July.
And summer will come
with trains that return to the city
like fishermen,
let them return with their catch,
let them carry into the cities our hope,
bitter as smoke,
bitter as
writing . . .

6 July 2022

Babi Badalov

born 1959 in Lerik, Azerbaijan; based in Paris, France

All Wars Made by Men

2024
T-SHIRTS, ACRYLIC
PRODUCED ESPECIALLY FOR THE EXHIBITION *SENSE OF SAFETY*
DONATED TO THE YERMILOVCENTRE COLLECTION

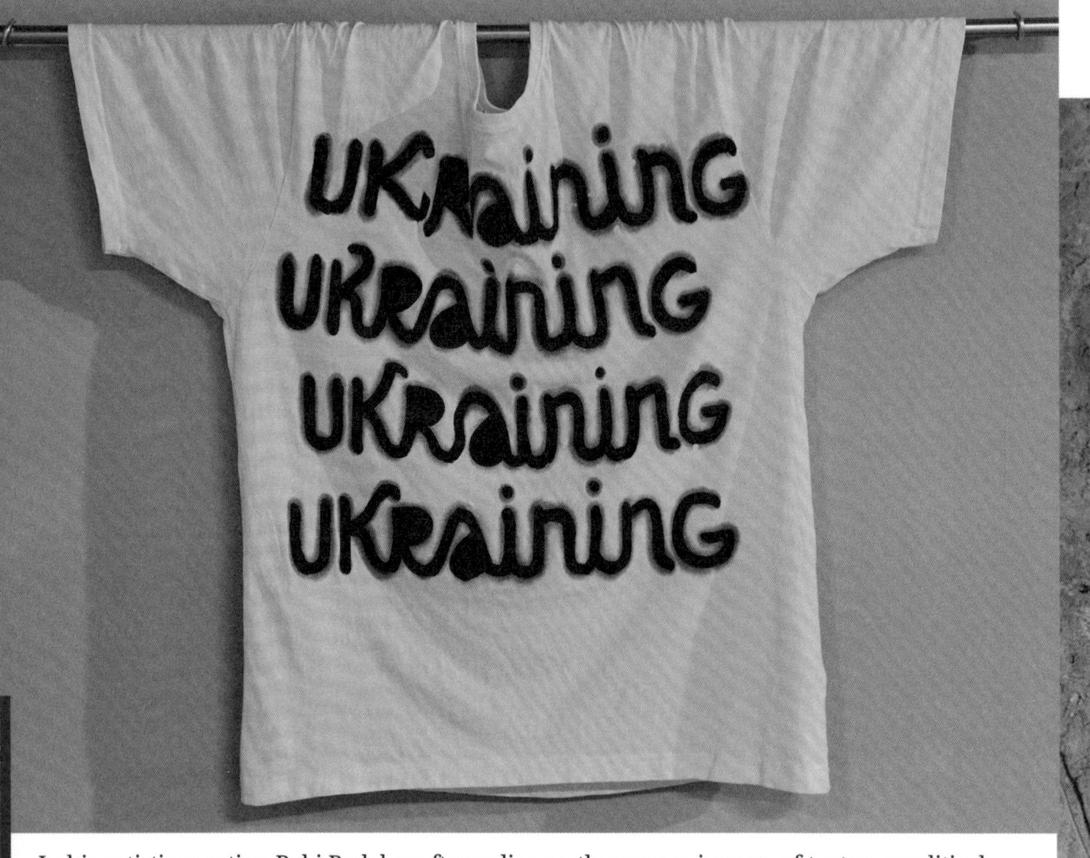

In his artistic practice, Babi Badalov often relies on the expressiveness of text as a political tool. Following the traditions of visual poetry, the artist treats the method, composition, and form of his texts with the same importance as the statements they contain. The artist experiments with a combination of Latin, Cyrillic, and Arabic calligraphic scripts. He unites existing words to create his own language that establishes new meanings. The mixture of languages reflects his own experience as a migrant, as he was forced to change countries before finding refuge in France due to threats of murder in Azerbaijan for his homosexuality. Using both his translinguistic and trans-local experiences, the artist mixes different geopolitical contexts to emphasize the interdependence and interconnectedness of our existence. In addition, his practice is profoundly queer. As a gay man and a political activist, the artist seeks to overcome the binary oppositions deeply rooted in our languages and Western European rationality.

By deconstructing language, he infuses it with sensuality and frankness, avoiding psychologism while amplifying the political sound of specific problems. Badalov's sense of the value of human freedom, the need to express his solidarity with the Ukrainian community, and his desire to support Ukrainian culture prompted him to participate in the *Sense of Safety* project. For the exhibition in Kharkiv, the artist created nine T-shirts with his own inscriptions reflecting his anti-war stance.

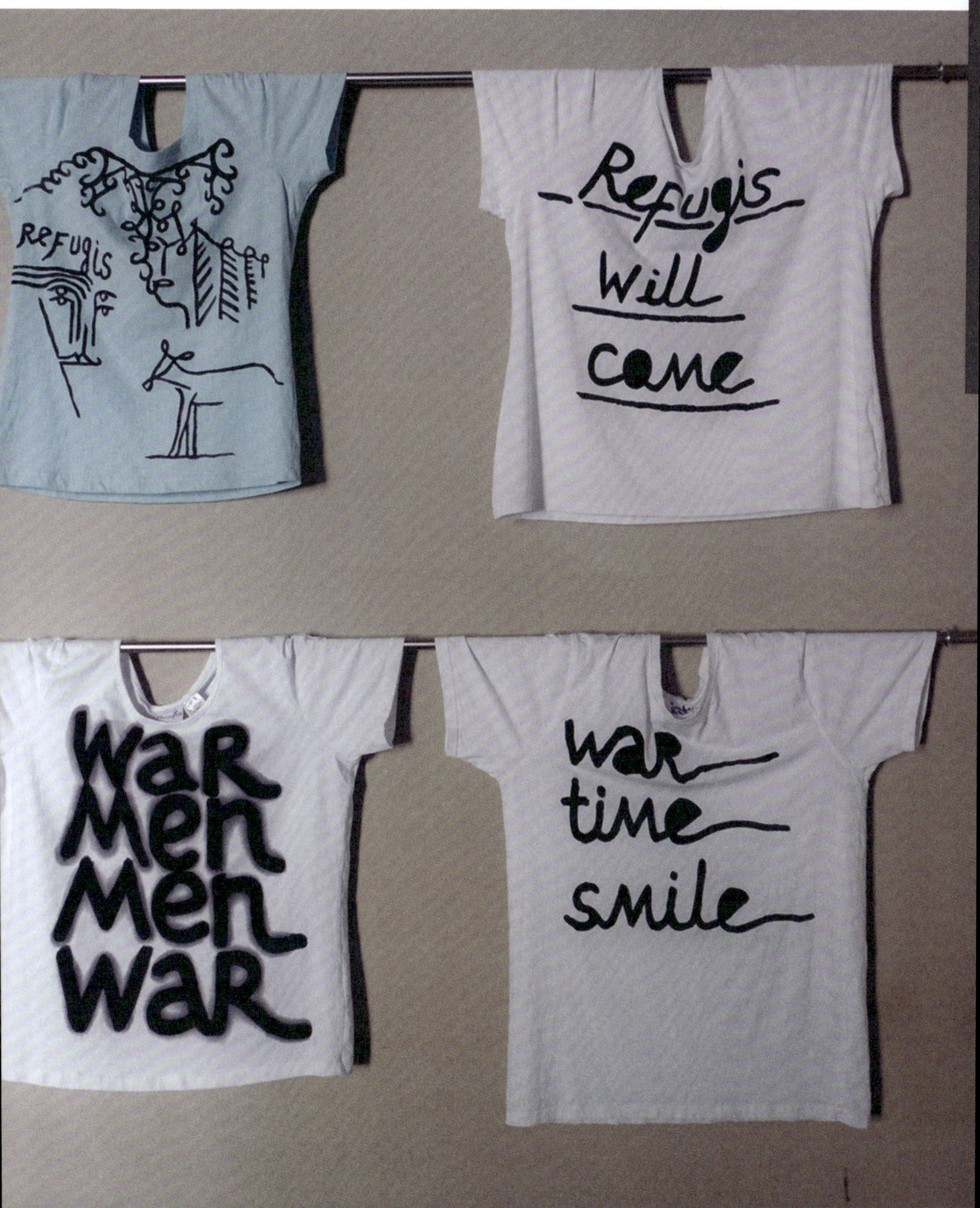

Karina Synytsia

Welcome to Paradise

born 1999 in Sievierodonetsk (now Siverskodonetsk), Ukraine;
based in Kyiv

2023
ACRYLIC ON PHOTO WALLPAPER
COURTESY OF THE ARTIST

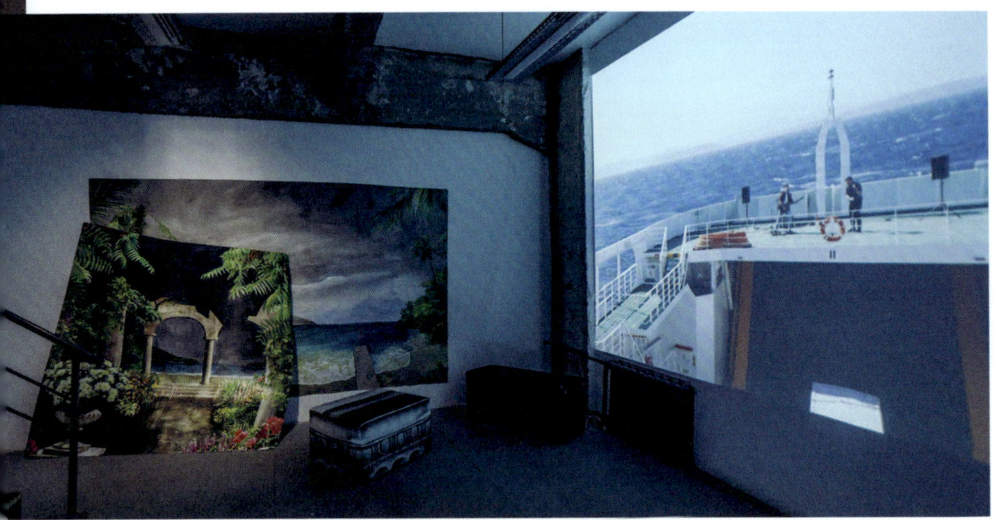

Karina Synytsia explores how external circumstances transform the perception of space and time, using architectural ruins as symbols of forgotten or destroyed emotional states. In her work, the artist transfers memories and emotions into different contexts, creating new forms of existence for familiar things. Her pieces often include elements that remind us of the past but simultaneously reflect contemporary realities, building a bridge between different stages of life. In the project *Welcome to Paradise*, Synytsia draws on the practice of using photographic wallpapers in interiors, which was popular in the 2000s.

Such wallpapers usually depict idyllic landscapes designed to promote relaxation and tranquility. This imaginary comfort zone, which promises "paradise pleasure" through advertising (in this case, Bounty ads from the 1990s), has become firmly entrenched in mass culture. Such landscapes often feature ruins as aestheticized tourist attractions. The artist uses this romanticized form to present the landscapes of occupied Crimea, where scorched earth and recent ruins serve as poignant reminders of the tragedy Ukrainians are currently experiencing.

The ambivalence inherent in the idea of Synytsia's works resonates with the concept of the *Sense of Safety* project, which focuses on the fragile state of safety, for both individuals and the world order as a whole. Synytsia skillfully combines the beauty of nature and architecture with challenging historical, political, and social contexts, forcing viewers to reflect on their emotional state and sensory experience.

Mark Požlep

Permanent Vacation

born 1981 in Celje, Slovenia; based in Ghent, Belgium

2023
VIDEO, 32'
COURTESY OF THE ARTIST
PRODUCED BY CUKRARNA, 2023
WITH SUPPORT FROM THE SLOVENIAN MINISTRY OF CULTURE AND THE URBAN MUNICIPALITY OF CELJE

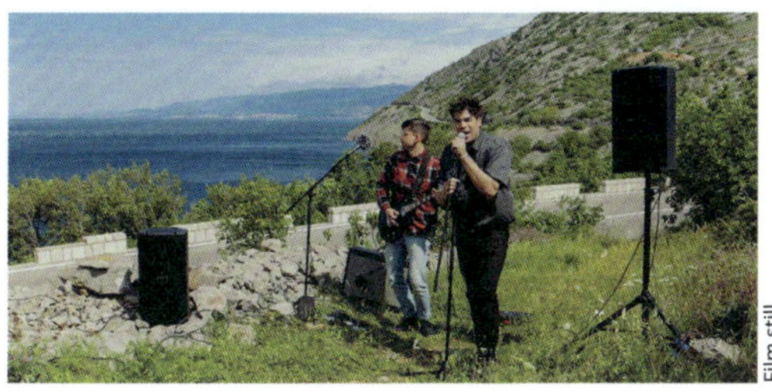

Film still

LYRICS: MUANIS SINANOVIĆ
MUSIC: GAŠPER PIANO
VOICE WORKSHOP: LEJA JURIŠIĆ
CAMERA AND EDITING: YOYPRODUCTION
SOUND MASTERING: JULIJ ZORNIK

Like many of Mark Požlep's projects, *Permanent Vacation* is distinguished by three important components—a journey, the involvement of experts from different disciplines, and a desire to narrate the complicated history of post-traumatic ingrowth while avoiding unambiguous binaries. Together with the economist Igor Feketija, Požlep sets off across the Adriatic Highway—a monumental road spanning 1,006 km from Trieste to the Montenegro-Albania border built from 1945 to 1966. The artist explores how the construction of this road changed the economic, socio-political, and cultural landscape of the region, and how the road affects it today. Like many modernist projects, the Adriatic Highway was built to link civilian and military infrastructures. The road was constructed with the aid of the Yugoslav Army and required 2,000 tons of dynamite. It is a complex interweaving of an almost cinematic reality and was in fact designed to be a scenic journey, like a film seen through the windscreen. Meanwhile, the traces of historical exploitation, violence, and tumult remain hidden in the background.

During the Yugoslav Wars, many hotels along the highway, like the iconic Haludovo Hotel, became shelters for refugees. After the war, these facilities often fell into neglect and ruin. The Haludovo Hotel, for instance, housed refugees before succumbing to privatization and corruption, officially closing in 1995, and it now lies in ruins. The concert/song format that Mark Požlep chooses to convey the research's results is not random. The history of bands that once played cheesy music on the terraces of tourist hotels resonates with the current desolation of the tourist infrastructure and allows the musicians to freely convey complex emotions and absurdities with humor.

Collaborating with poet Muanis Sinanović and musician Gašper Piano, Požlep transforms the narrative into seven songs that were performed in ad hoc concerts at significant sites along the highway. The performances were recorded and edited into a video, allowing visitors to experience the concerts as if they were there.

Karina Synytsia, *Welcome to Paradise*, 2023 (detail). ⟶

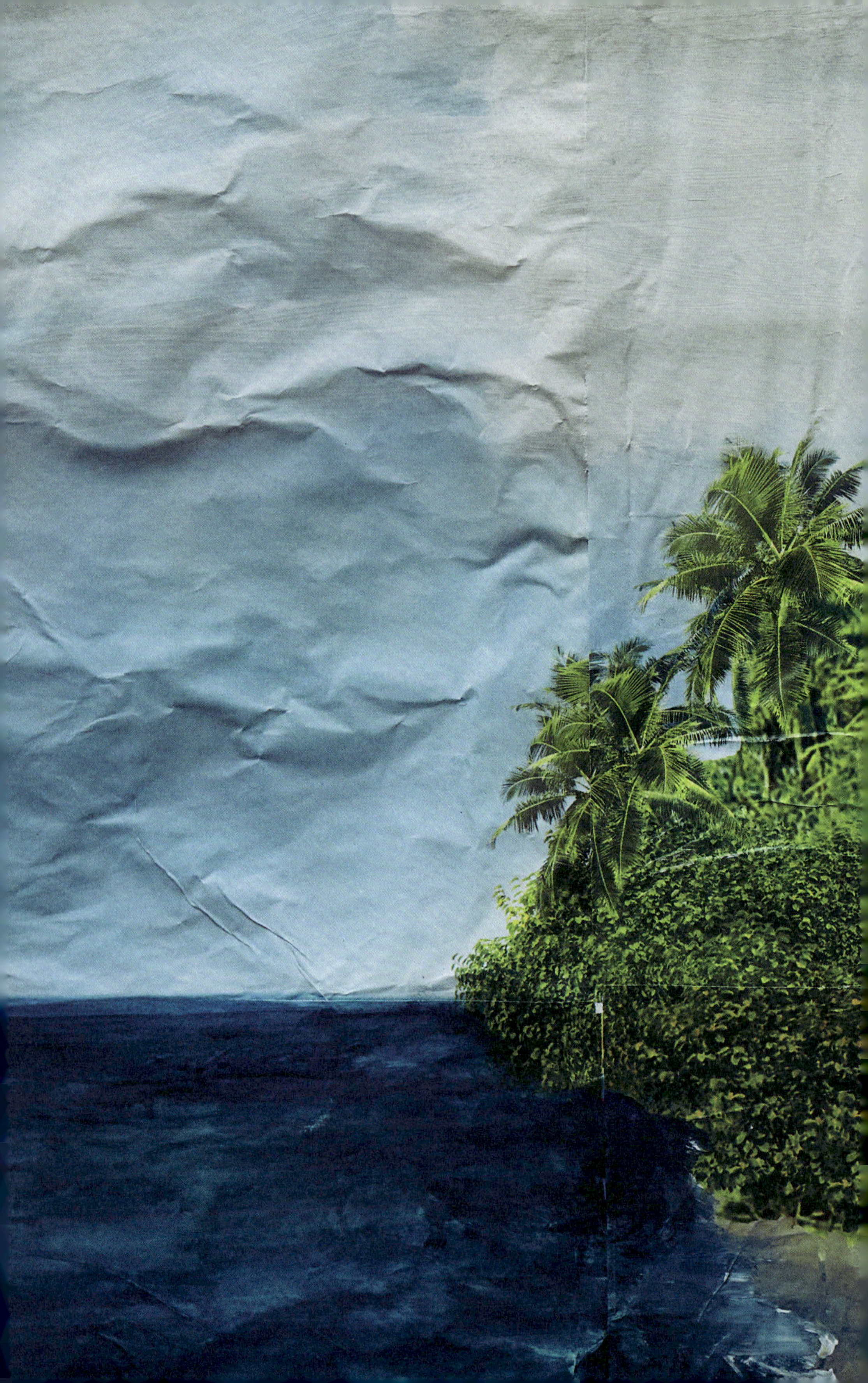

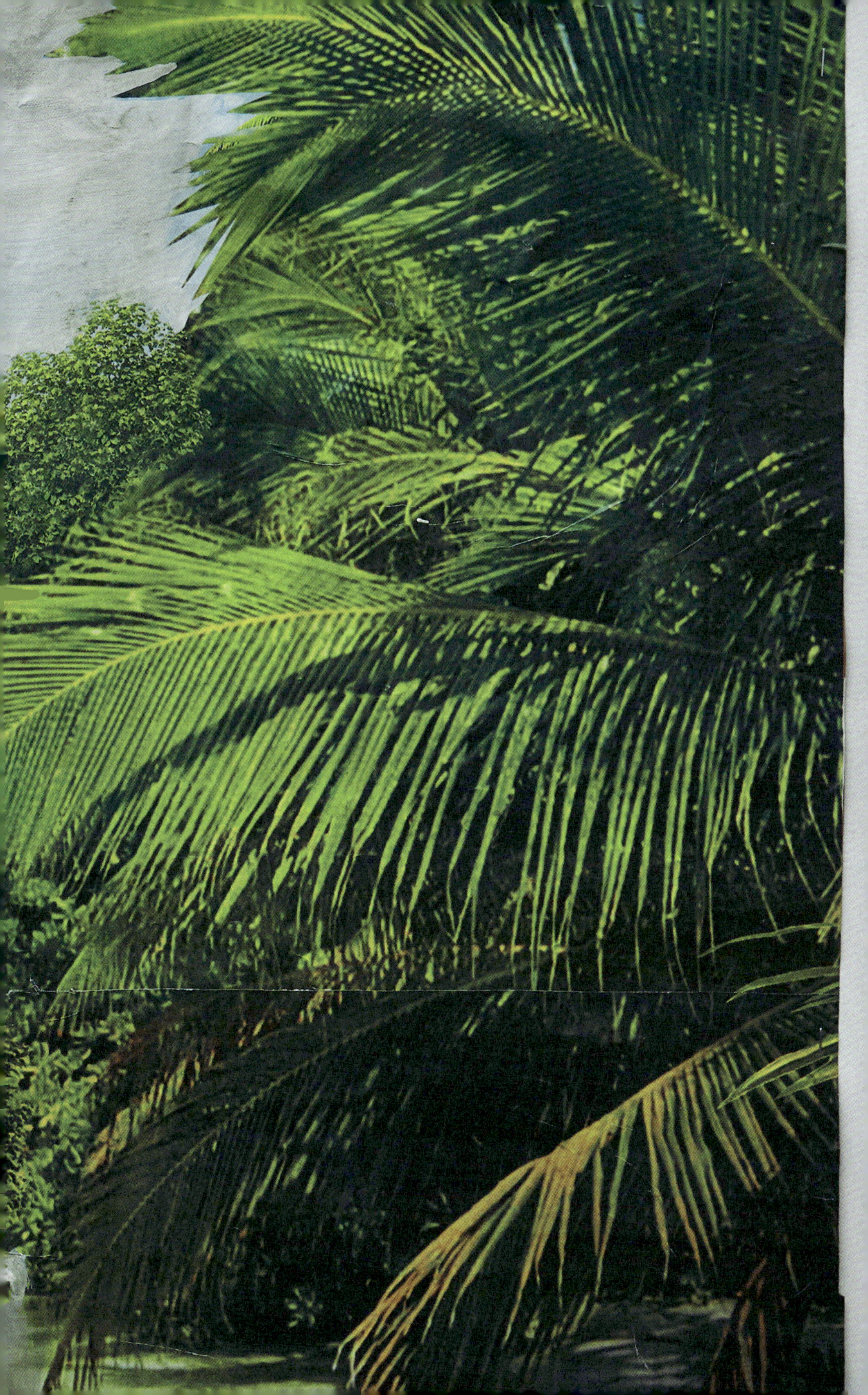

Andreas Angelidakis

born 1968 in Athens, Greece; based in Athens

2022
FOAM AND CANVAS BLOCKS, DIMENSIONS VARIABLE
PRODUCED BY AUDEMARS PIGUET CONTEMPORARY
DONATED TO THE YERMILOVCENTRE COLLECTION

Center for the Critical Appreciation of Antiquity

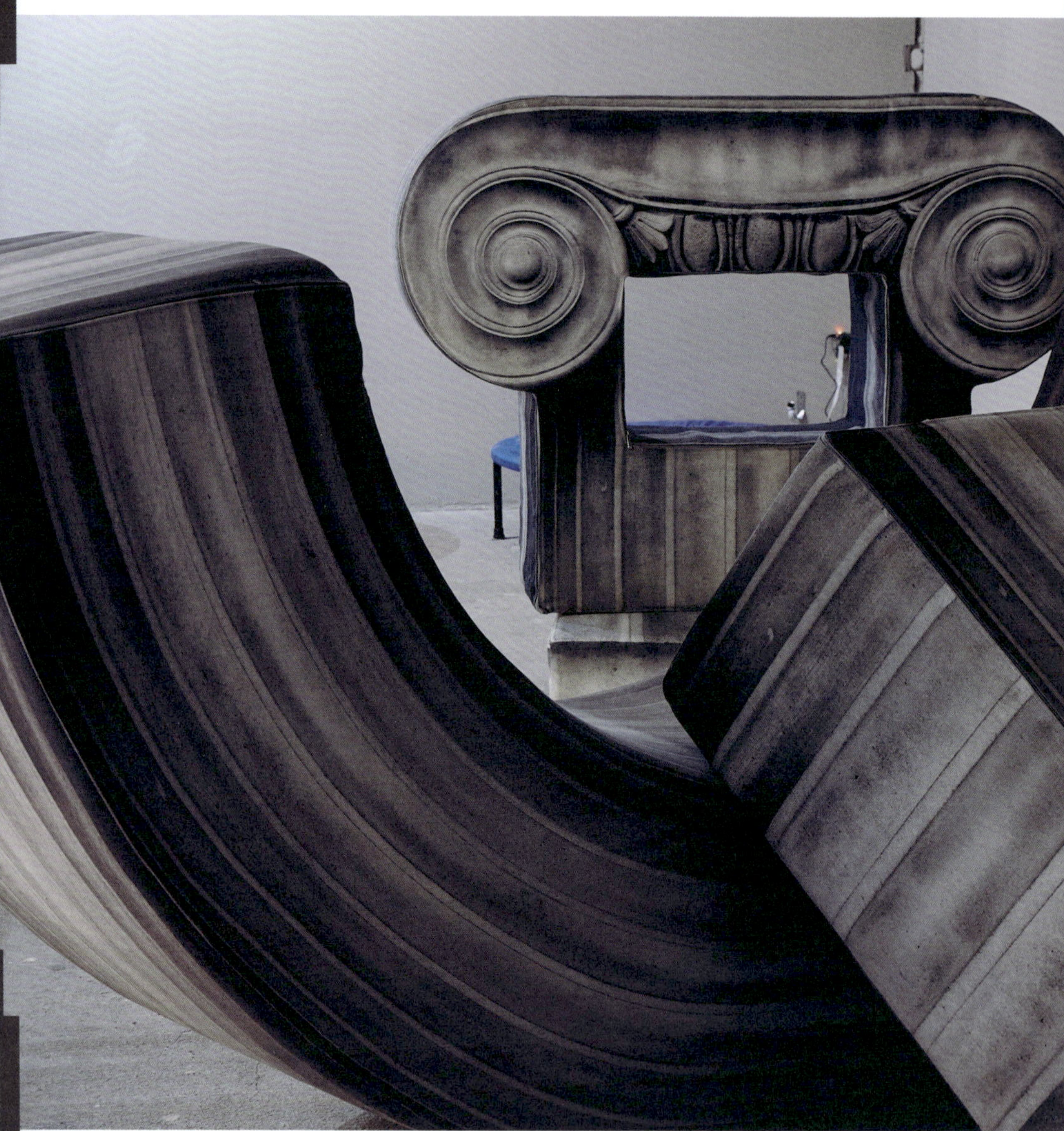

Andreas Angelidakis lives in Athens, a place literally filled with ancient Greek ruins. These ruins are involved in the political economy of nostalgia. At the same time, they can be understood in terms of post-traumatic ingrowth. How can we re-think ruins by suspending processes of alienation and tourist commodification?

In his installation *Center for the Critical Appreciation of Antiquity*, the artist proposes a queer approach to architecture. By reconstructing the existing ruins of the Temple of Olympian Zeus in Athens, he reflects on architecture as a place of social interaction, turning the marble ruins into pieces of soft furniture that visitors can interact with and rearrange. Andreas Angelidakis thus undoes the hierarchy between the people who build a space and those who inhabit it.

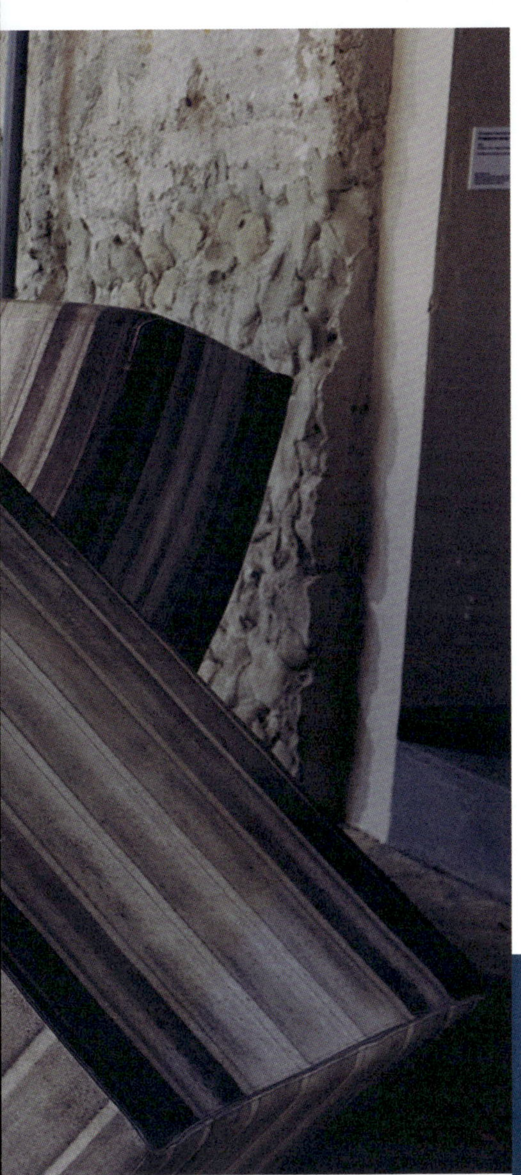

In addition, the installation is a ruin of columns. During emergencies like earthquakes or bomb raids, it is often advised to stay near columns. This practice dates back to the Middle Ages when columns were believed to have apotropaic powers to ward off evil. Historically, towns were constructed around ancient columns to benefit from their protective qualities.

On the one hand, this work shows the fragile nature of safety. The transformation of hard marble into soft furniture refers to the famous phrase "all that is solid melts into air." On the other hand, the artist's gesture of placing and presenting this artwork at YermilovCentre means creating an infrastructure of care. After all, if the space has to become a shelter again, these soft ruins can be used by those seeking refuge from shelling and bombing.

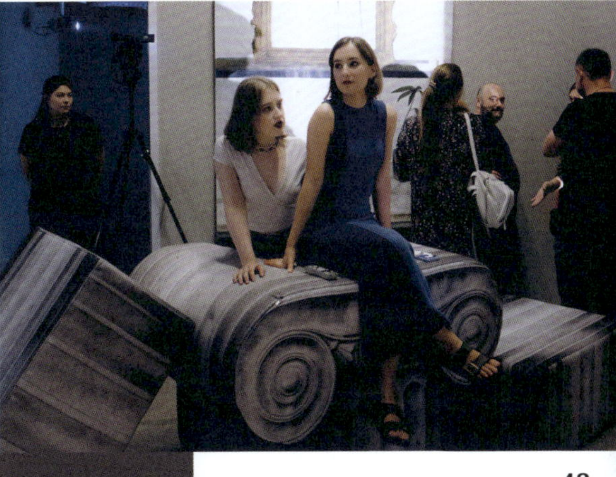

Dmytro Kolomoitsev **Moleskines**

born 1976 in Donetsk, Ukraine; currently in the Armed Forces of Ukraine

2022
ARTBOOKS
COURTESY OF THE GRYNYOV ART COLLECTION

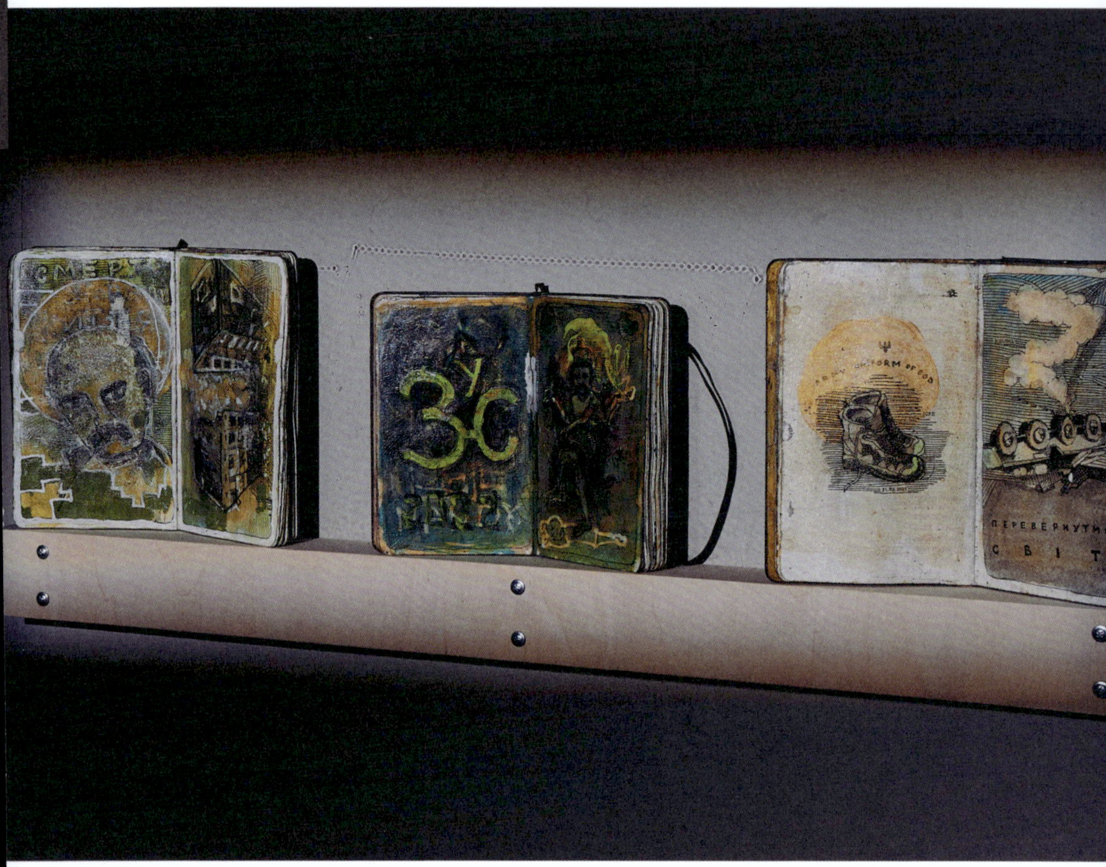

In 2015, Dmytro Kolomoitsev served in the ATO zone (Anti-Terrorist Operation Zone in Ukraine since 2014) and volunteered to join the Armed Forces of Ukraine when Russia's full-scale invasion began. Despite the circumstances, the artist did not stop working during his service. Kolomoitsev reinterprets the soldier's routine into an artistic statement: he makes art installations in his dugout, creating visual diaries of the war that are often filled with Vedic perception.

The project includes artbook diaries in which the artist records significant military events, scenes of soldiers' everyday lives, and his own reflections. The compact form of a notebook is the most convenient for a soldier who has to stay mobile and does not have access to a large arsenal of art supplies. Kolomoitsev's works are humorous and offer a sense of psychological relief by adding a light touch to the most challenging moments.

The image of Taras Shevchenko is a counterpoint in all the Moleskines. Kolomoitsev portrays it as a symbol, an iconic shrine that he deconstructs and brings closer to mass culture. The artist's myth-making in relation to Ukrainian history is also noteworthy here. The final artbook of the four presented is dedicated to exploring the phenomenon of victory. The author traces victory in historical events, small everyday achievements, and fictional stories. By visualizing the desired event, the artist turns a daily ritual into a means of overcoming the traumatic experience of war.

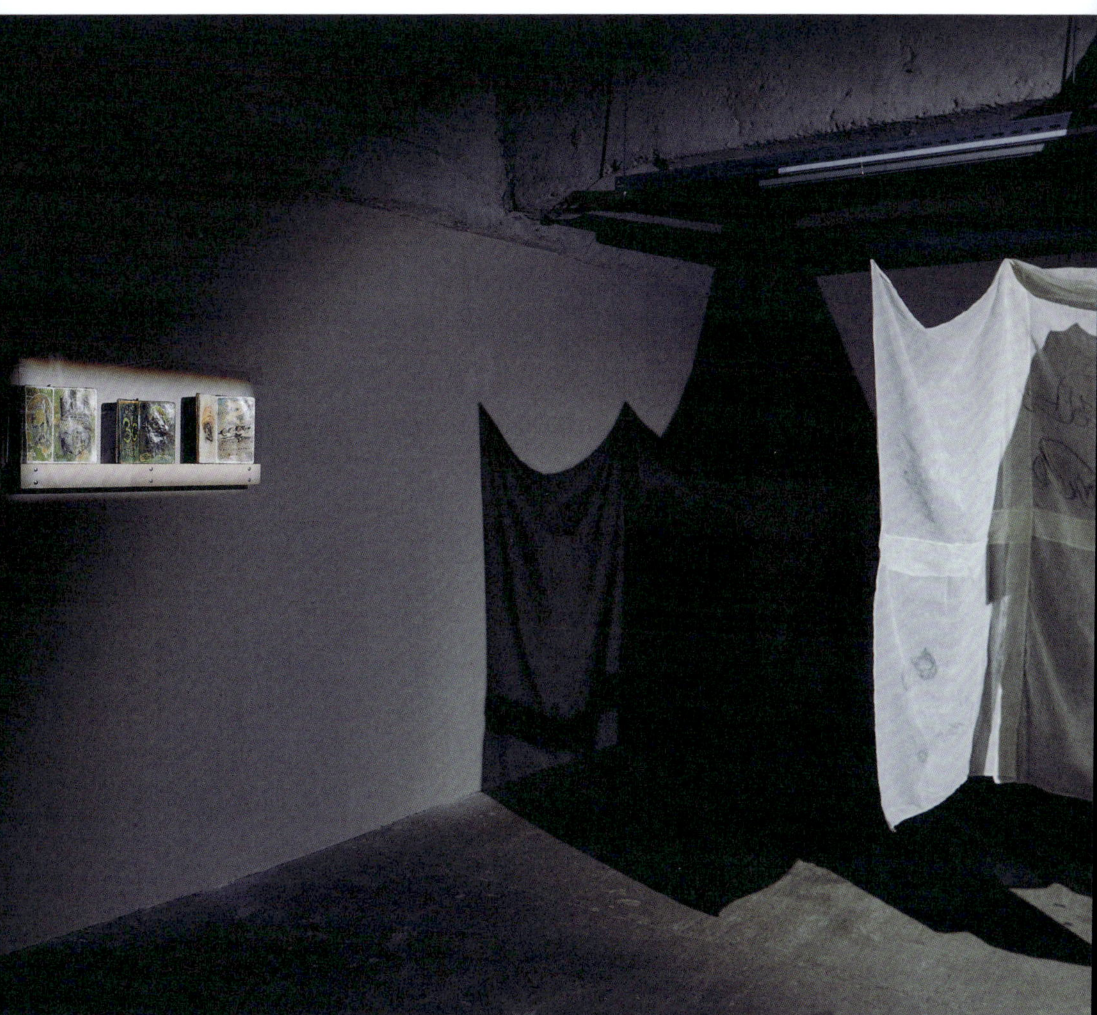

Anna Zvyagintseva

The Nook

born 1986 in Dnipro, Ukraine; based in Kyiv

2023
FABRIC, PENCIL
COURTESY OF THE ARTIST

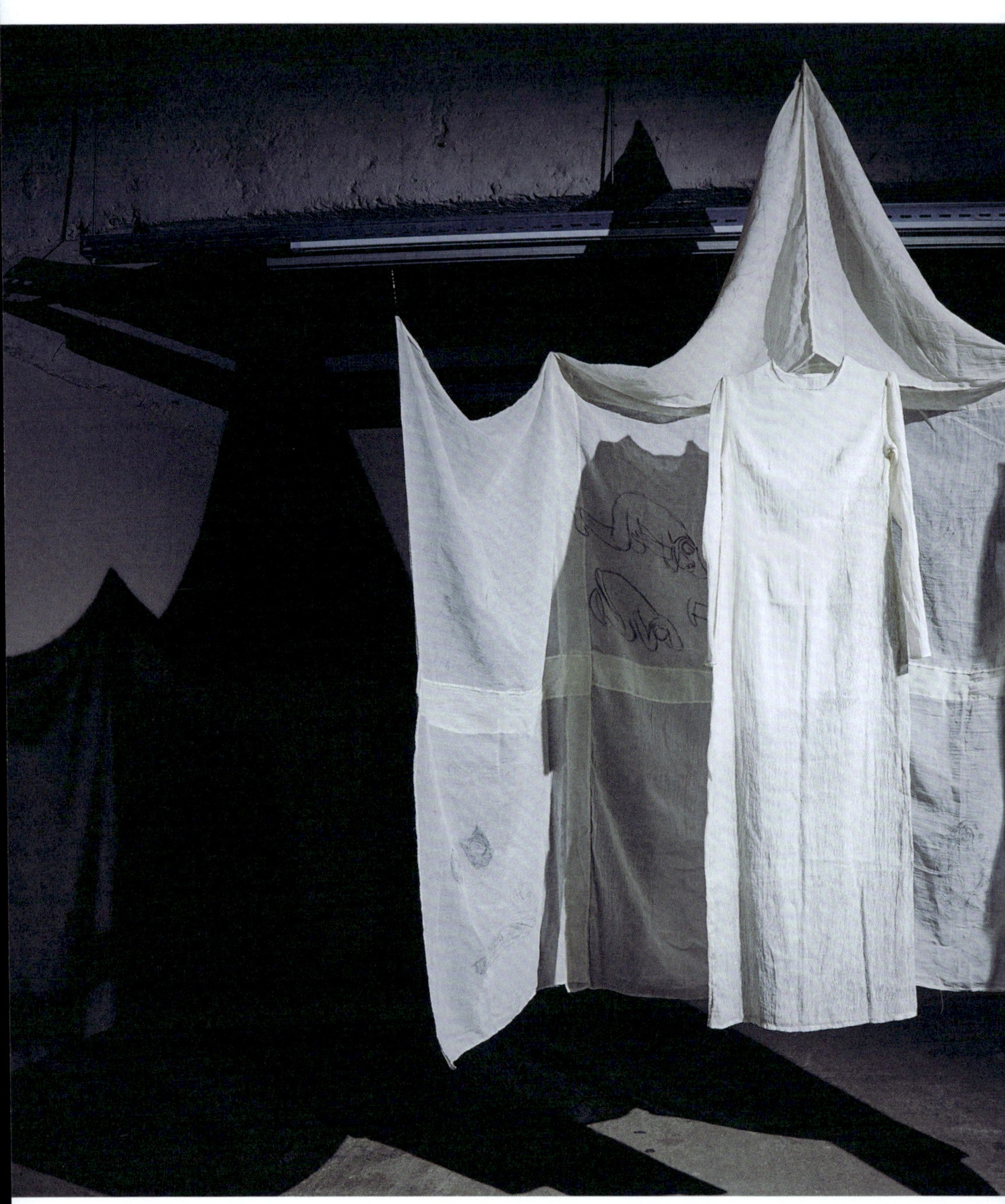

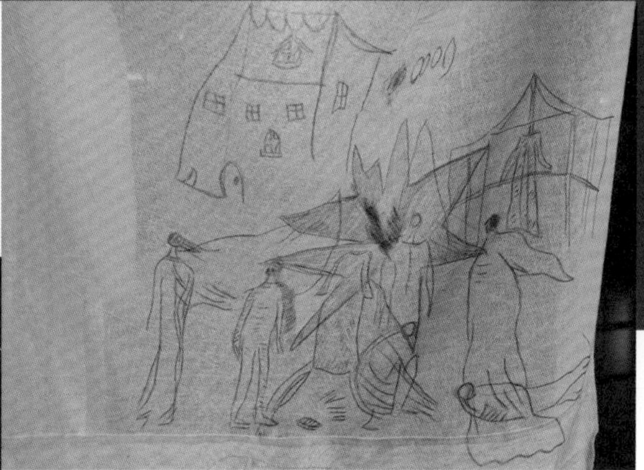

In her artistic practice, Anna Zvyagintseva often references the barely noticeable, intangible aspects of our lives—fleeting moments, insignificant actions, and small gestures. Drawing on personal stories rooted in the country's political realities, the artist offers sensual experiences, reveals human vulnerability, and captures the elusive.

In The Nook, Zvyagintseva creates an object based on schematic children's drawings of houses with windows as eyes and doors as mouths, recreating a familiar and reliable image of a home. The two-dimensional plane of the fabric is transformed into a three-dimensional object that serves as a shelter for the dress inside. The dress in this work functions as a kind of amulet—you can hide in it, wrap yourself in it, and be buried in it, like a cerecloth or shroud. On the dress one can see a drawing of grass, and on the house there are drawings from the artist's visual diary, which she has been compiling since the outbreak of the full-scale invasion.

The work conveys an inner desire and urgent need for safety, even if it is illusory. The cloak house represents comfort and protection, reminding us of the tragic reality of war. However, the grass pattern on the dress also suggests a window onto the future, radiating hope rather than sadness.

Uli Golub

born 1990 in Kharkiv, Ukraine; based in Oakland, California, USA

Notes from Underground

2016
VIDEO, 13'22"
COURTESY OF THE ARTIST

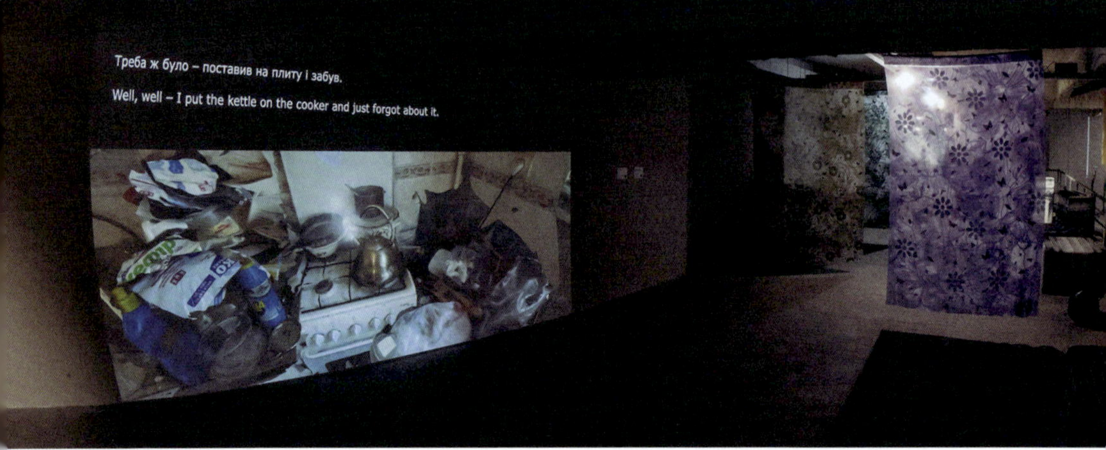

In her artistic practice, Uli Golub often draws on her personal experiences as well as the stories and memories of her acquaintances. The artist primarily works with video, 3D animation, and motion pictures, creating narratives that invite viewers to dream up new realities. Her method is based on storytelling. The artist composes multi-stage plots with a strong emotional component. Though shaped by her own contexts, the scenarios in her work balance fiction and social reality in order to address daily problems and experiences familiar to all humans. As a result, her works often resonate with viewers across a surprising variety of geographical contexts.

Notes from Underground is a story about an enigmatic character living in a cluttered apartment; the prototype is an actual apartment in Kharkiv, which the artist composited into a 3D model. The video seemingly refers to the events around the Revolution of Dignity in 2013–2014, but Golub focuses on the emotional dimensions—the feelings, experiences, and fears of a particular person who suffers from pathological hoarding, which arises from the need to maintain an illusion of safety in conditions of instability. There are so many wartime fears and suspicions shaping the character's actions and thoughts: the fear of hunger, power outages, etc.—all of which have become our reality today, but also share historical echoes with the Holodomor (the Ukrainian Famine) of 1932–1933 and the economic devastation of the 1990s.

Routine daily activities like gathering supplies is necessary to avoid starvation and ensure survival during cataclysms. Despite the near impossible living conditions in this cluttered home, it is the safest space imaginable for the protagonist and he fears losing it. After all, home is the core space that allows him to continue existing.

Nadira Husain

born 1980 in Paris, France; based in Berlin, Paris, and Hyderabad, India

Smoking Ornaments (Lila, Night Blue, Green, Yellow, Brique)

2024
INKJET PRINT ON MUSLIN FABRIC
PRODUCED ESPECIALLY FOR THE EXHIBITION *SENSE OF SAFETY*
DONATED TO THE YERMILOVCENTRE COLLECTION

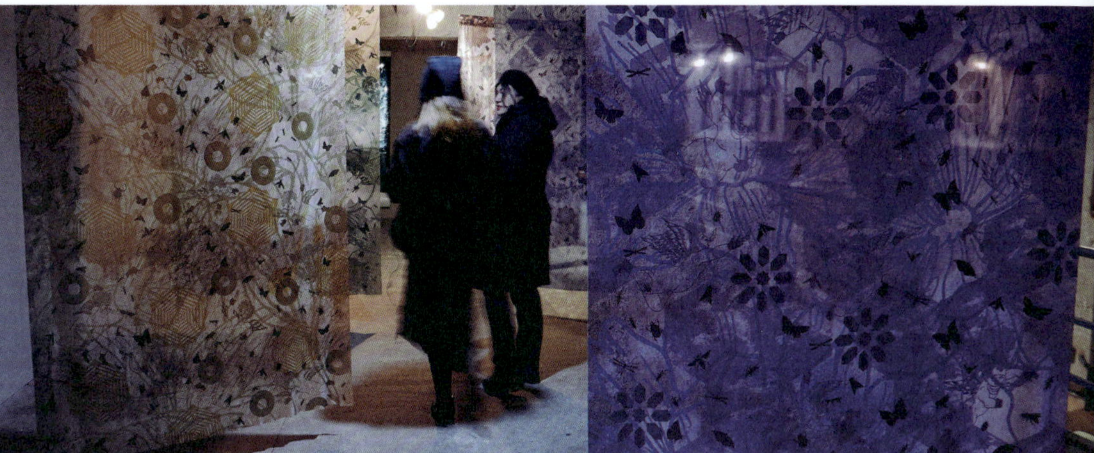

Smoking Ornaments consists of five semi-transparent muslin panels, each printed with ornamental motifs. The background is a reproduction of the solid concrete walls of the YermilovCentre, creating a striking contrast between the concrete's solidity and the fabric's lightness. Concrete is an extremely strong material, used in the construction of bomb shelters and bunkers because it can withstand the impact of shelling. Transposing the concrete walls of the YermilovCentre onto transparent fabric emphasizes ambivalence, fragility, and constant anxiety about safety. In this way, Nadira Husain highlights a feminist understanding of safety as something that requires continuous collective effort.

As in her other pieces, the artist combines figures, symbols, and ornaments from different cultures to create complex images that reflect her own multicultural experience, thus disrupting the Western European hierarchy of classical painting. In European art, ornament has traditionally been seen as something subsidiary to the central image or text. Nadira Husain disrupts this conventional hierarchy as her work is filled almost exclusively with such "secondary" characters and subjects. This move not only forces a rejection of pictorial hierarchies but also refuses a Eurocentric understanding of images. As an artist emerging from the intersection of Indo-Islamic and French cultures, Nadira incorporates a non-European view of ornament as something self-sufficient rather than merely supplementary. The compositions combine traditional motifs found in Islamic art and Mughal art with smoking putti, who disrupt the idea of a central narrative.

The exhibition took place in the public space in front of the Parliament of Georgia and was initiated by Bouillon Group's mobile gallery project *Let Me Show You Something Beautiful*. Instead of a permanent venue, the gallery pops up in various public locations. The presentation included works by photographers from Kharkiv, as well as students and graduates of MYPH (the Mykolaiv School of Conceptual and Art Photography). This gesture was an attempt to reflect on the concept of beauty under conditions of war.

The public format of the exhibition invited passersby to an open conversation—about the war in Ukraine, experiences of resistance, and the cost of freedom. Bouillon Group's mobile gallery allowed art to move beyond institutional spaces and directly engage audiences who are not typically part of the art world, opening up a space of observation, empathy, and reflection.

Visitors at the YermilovCentre, Kharkiv, watch a transmission of a pop-up exhibition in public space by Bouillon Group in Tbilisi, 2026. Photo: Yelyzaveta Koval.

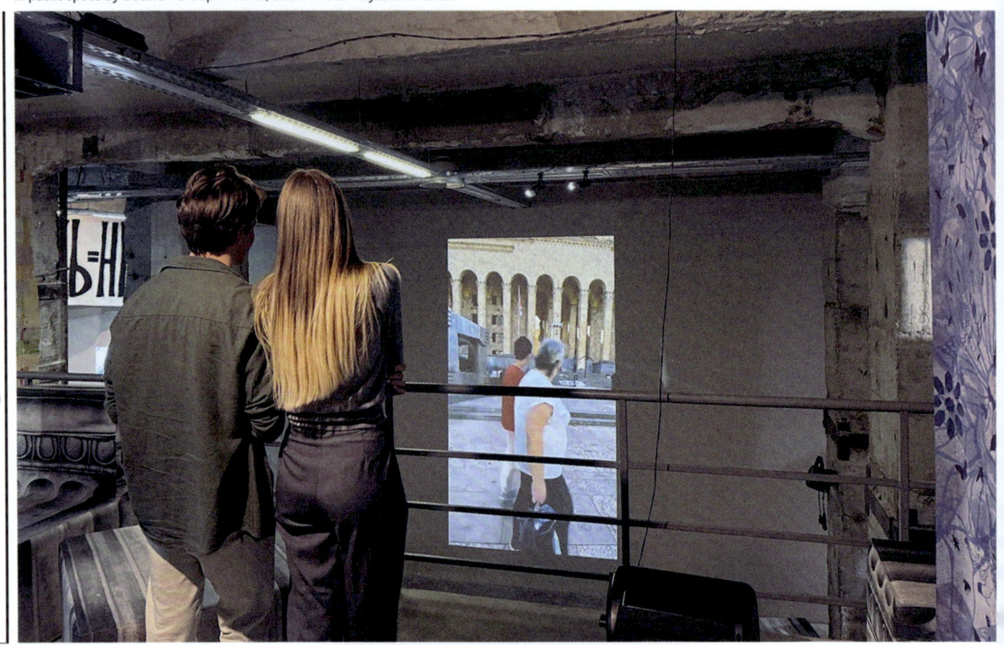

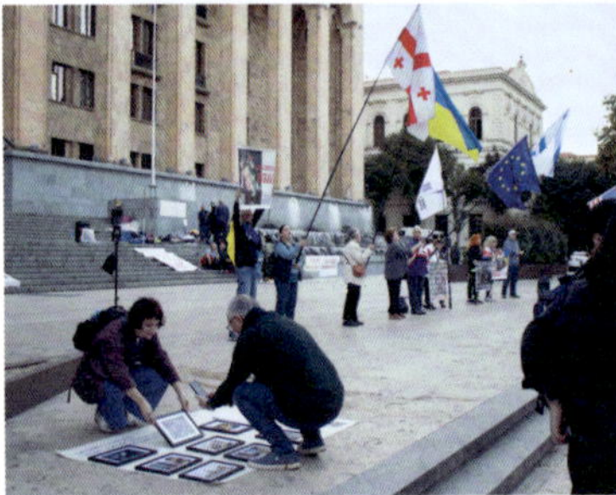

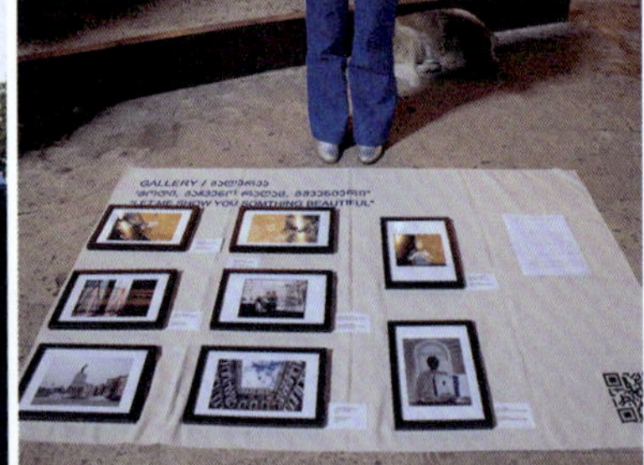

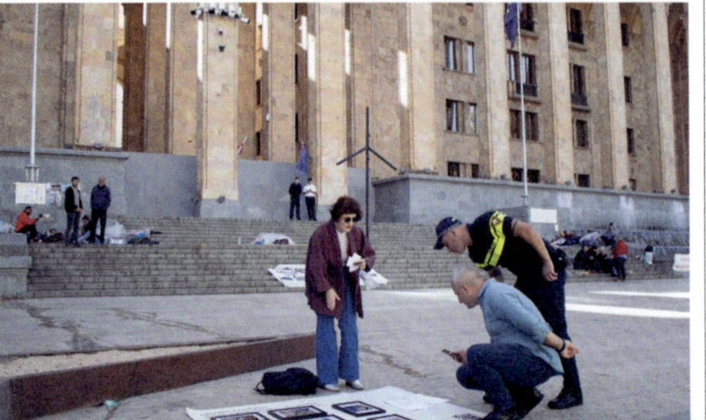

A pop-up exhibition in public space in Tbilisi, featuring Natalia Vatsadze, co-founder of the Bouillon Group, 2026. Photo: Levan Adikashvili.

Let Me Show You Something Beautiful

Pop-up exhibition of Ukrainian photographers

Public space in front of the Parliament of Georgia, Tbilisi (GE)

Date
29.09.2024

Participants
Bouillon Group (GE)
Maria Gorshkova (UA)
Oksana Kami (UA)
Olena Lemberska (UA)
Serhiy Melnychenko (UA)
Oleksandr Osipov (UA)
Stanislav Ostrous (UA)
Ainur Sakisheva (UA)

The discussion took place within the framework of the exhibition *Let Me Show You Something Beautiful* and focused on the complex issues of ethics and aesthetics in photography under conditions of war. Participants discussed how to avoid the romanticization or aestheticization of destruction and suffering, which often appear in images of war. Special attention was given to the work of Ukrainian photographers who depicted events that they themselves have experienced. The photographic medium, which only allows a limited distance between the author and the event, requires particular caution and reflection from the artist. Participants shared practices that help protect themselves from retraumatization, integrating their own experiences into artistic practice while simultaneously creating a space for public reflection on the war. The discussion emphasized the importance of a conscious and ethical approach to depicting war in photography, as well as the role of art as a tool for critical thinking, empathy, and the documentation of reality.

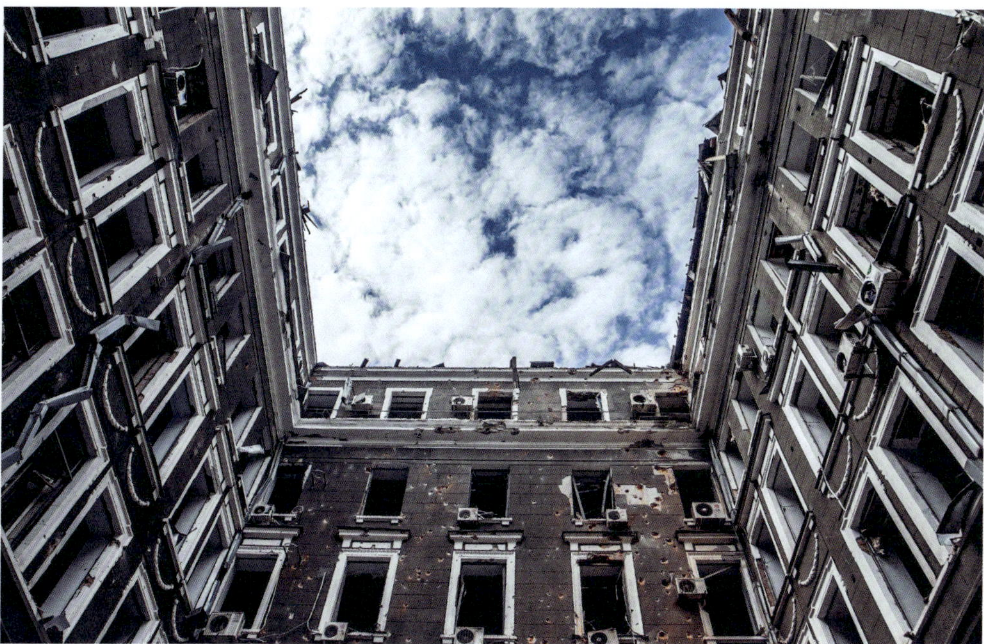

Oleksandr Osipov, *Sky Above the Palace of Labor*, 2022, from the project *In the Streets of Kharkiv* (with Denys Karachevtsev). Courtesy of the artist.

The realization of this exhibition in a public space was extremely important to me. In a country where freedom is restricted and voices are silenced, a conversation about Ukraine, the war, and the people fighting for freedom felt both necessary and personal. There was something powerful in knowing that part of the exhibition was taking place live, in front of people who were not directly involved, yet were watching, experiencing it, and reflecting on the war in Ukraine—here, in Georgia, where state propaganda has paradoxically declared Tbilisi a city of peace. The mobile gallery by Bouillon Group gave us the opportunity to see the dangers behind this so-called peace being offered and to consider its real impact. The public and mobile format allowed the exhibition to reach people directly, creating a space for reflection, doubt, and a sense of the weight of these realities.

Natalia Vatsadze, Bouillon Group.

Exhibition *Let Me Show You Something Beautiful* and a public discussion "Let Me Show You Something Beautiful: Ethics and aesthetics in 'war photography' in Ukraine and Georgia"

Tbilisi Photography & Multimedia Museum, Tbilisi (GE)
Online

Date
10.10.2024

Curated by
Natalia Vatsadze (GE)

Speakers
Khatuna Khabuliani (GE)
Sophia Lapiashvili (GE)
Oleksandr Osipov (UA)
Stanislav Ostrous (UA)

Moderated by
Alona Karavai (UA)

Supported by
The Danish Cultural Institute (LV)
The International Coalition of Cultural Workers in Solidarity with Ukraine (DE/NL/PL/UA)
YermilovCentre (UA)
Ambasada Kultury (DE/LT)
Tbilisi Photography & Multimedia Museum (GE)

Boris Mikhailov

born 1938 in Kharkiv, Ukraine; based in Berlin, Germany

LATE 1960S
C-PRINT
COURTESY OF THE ARTIST AND GALERIE BARBARA WEISS (NOW TRAUTWEIN HERLETH)
THE WORK WAS COMMISSIONED BY THE STATE ART COLLECTIONS OF DRESDEN FOR THE EXHIBITION *KALEIDOSCOPE OF (HI)STORIES. UKRAINIAN ART 1912–2023*

Untitled. From the series Yesterday's Sandwich (Overlays)

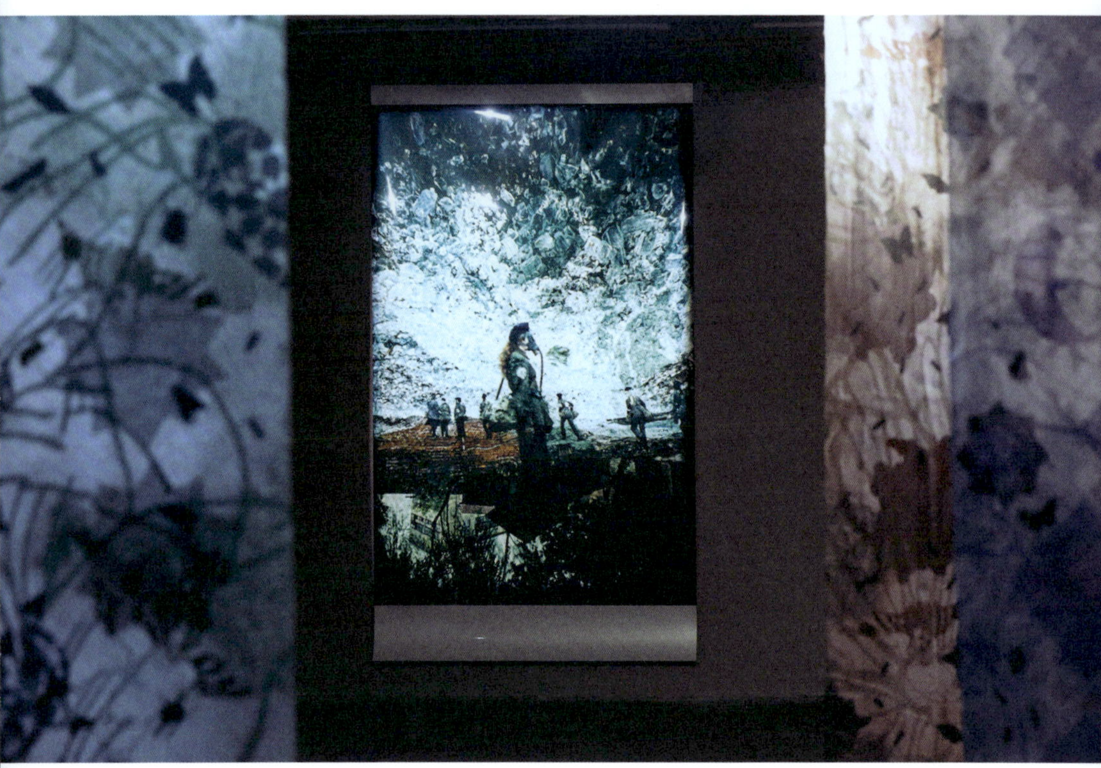

This photograph belongs to Boris Mikhailov's famous series of experimental works known as *Overlays*, which the artist began working on in the mid-1960s. The original print of this particular photograph is signed in pencil: Kharkiv, 1968. The principle of his experiment was to superimpose two frames of film with different images, resulting in a new artistic motif. Combining the ideological language of one frame with the subjective message of the second frame created a third, partly unpredictable image that opened up the possibility of making an artistic and social statement. Initially, Mikhailov demonstrated this series in the form of slides with musical accompaniment, Pink Floyd in particular.

Later, he began to extract specific fragments of the series to make independent monumental works, in which surreal images from the past appear as ominous prophecies of the future, witnessing the tragedies of the present.

Kateryna Yermolayeva

I Just Want Silence

born 1985 in Donetsk, Ukraine; based in Kyiv

2024
INSTALLATION OF 5 GESTURES: SOUND, VIDEO, PERSONAL BELONGINGS, GRAPHIC WORKS (PENCIL, LINER, ACRYLIC ON PAPER), INTERACTIVE ALBUM
PRODUCED ESPECIALLY FOR THE EXHIBITION *SENSE OF SAFETY*

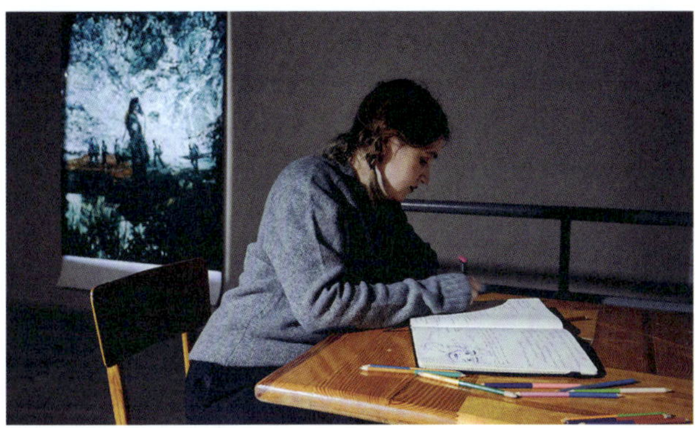

The core of Kateryna Yermolayeva's work lies in combining her deeply personal experiences with observations of others that viewers often perceive as directly addressed to them. She began her career as a graffiti artist under the pseudonym Mikhalych. The anonymity of this play of alter egos allowed the artist to create a space of psychological safety. This play continues in a series of five subtle gestures scattered around the YermilovCentre, in which the artist combines childhood memories, superstitions, and rituals with a contemporary sense of unsafety, which was certainly informed by the feeling of losing her own home in 2014. The artist recreates a temporary sense of home by by including her mother's clothing in the display or evoking childhood rituals, like knocking on the door with grandma using a confidential code only known to loved ones or hiding under a blanket in a cardboard box while watching videos. Darkness is associated with the possibility of rescue and the desire to be unnoticed in difficult situations, both in childhood and now during curfews. She also invites the audience to create a *Collective Diary* where they can share their thoughts and record their own experiences through stories of any tone.

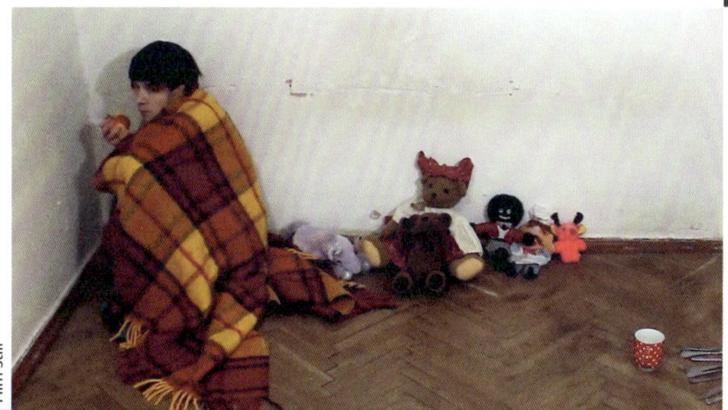

Film still

Oksana Barshynova

Loci of Vulnerability: From the Underground to the Shelter

Nonconformism in Kharkiv's art scene was "quiet" and episodic, like a gunshot in a deaf alley.[1]

During wartime, our relationship with cities undergoes radical change. What only recently seemed stable and reliable becomes fragile and uncertain, incapable not only of protecting its inhabitants but even of preserving itself. Everywhere one senses not protection but threat—in streets, buildings, parks, and squares. Only the underground seems capable of offering sanctuary.

This is why the metro and basement spaces of frontline Kharkiv not only became shelters but also distinctive hubs of artistic life. Aza Nizi Maza in the metro, the YermilovCentre, the basement of the Literary Museum, and artists' underground studios quite literally turned into rare zones of safety—places where people could gather, remember, and dream. They also allowed for the resumption of rituals that reconnected life to peacetime practices: creative work, communication, exhibitions, readings, and performances.

This transformed understanding of the "normality" of everyday and artistic life in Kharkiv—along with its relocation underground during the first months of the full-scale invasion—has reactivated discussions about the memory of place and the need to preserve the city in recollection and imagination. For Kharkiv, this is not the first experience of "reassembling" itself and recovering after a blow. Its landscapes have served as sites for the realization of grand utopian ideas, but also as spaces of control, repression, erasure, and loss.

The underground of the YermilovCentre forms part of Kharkiv's history and mythology, as it belongs to the ensemble of government buildings that includes the iconic Constructivist symbol of Ukraine's capital during the 1920s—the Derzhprom complex. In the spring of 2022, the YermilovCentre became an actual shelter for Kharkiv's residents, a role that is semantically linked to another kind of underground[2]—the artistic one that existed in Kharkiv from the 1960s to the 1980s. Then as now, these undergrounds are united by a shared experience of unspoken danger, the threat of bodily harm, and uncertainty about the future. In the Soviet period, this danger was political and social; during the full-scale war, it is physical and existential.

The key focus of the exhibition *Sense of Safety* at the YermilovCentre is Kharkiv itself—a vulnerable borderland, traumatized yet alive and open. Founded in the mid-seventeenth century as a frontier of the Tsardom of Muscovy, the city transformed during the eighteenth and nineteenth centuries into the capital of Sloboda Ukraine (Slobozhanshchyna), as well as an educational and commercial center. From 1919 to 1934, Kharkiv served as the capital of the Ukrainian SSR. Although this period ended tragically (with the Holodomor, political repressions, and the destruction of the cultural and political elite), it laid the foundations for Kharkiv's distinctive worldview. After enduring the loss of its capital status, the tragic purges of the 1930s, and occupation during the Second World War, Kharkiv experienced a cultural revival in the 1960s. Literature, art, and photography circles emerged within workers' clubs, while the surviving modernists came into contact with a new generation. Within a single decade, Kharkiv became a center of the underground movement, and its landscape evolved into a real and symbolic space for remembering, recovering, and rethinking the city's mythology.

In this article, we will discuss specific loci of the city associated with safety and vulnerability.[3] The focus is on phenomena of the underground, escape, the search for safe spaces, the avoidance of control, and the pursuit of freedom. These goals were achieved in different ways: through the formation of communities, the search for one's place among the courtyards and city streets, the desire to overcome isolation from the outside world, and the marking of the city as one's own, as a familiar domestic space. The primary loci include the room, the courtyard, walls, and streets within a city that is itself understood as a locus[4]—that is, as something personally experienced by the artists featured in this article.

The Room (31 Poltavskyi Shliakh Street)

How private can personal space like an apartment or room be, and where does the boundary lie between control and the provision of safety? These questions are raised by Lauren Lee McCarthy's work *Someone* (2019), which addresses the contemporary dangers posed by technologies that blur the line between the personal and the social. The work turns the viewer into an observer of someone else's private life through surveillance cameras, reminding us of the possibility of total control.

In the second half of the twentieth century in the Ukrainian SSR, rooms, studios, and kitchens became loci of relative safety, where circles of close friends and like-minded individuals could form.

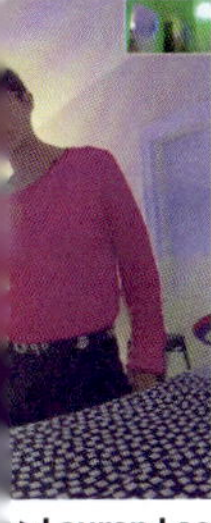

-> Lauren Lee McCarthy p. 92

One such place in late 1950s and early 1960s Kharkiv was the room of the well-known Constructivist artist Vasyl Yermilov,[5] who at the time had been almost completely forgotten. His reputation, however, would be restored during his lifetime: his first solo exhibition opened in Kharkiv in 1962,[6] and an article on his artistic practice was published on the occasion of his seventieth birthday in 1964.[7] From 1963 to 1967, Yermilov taught at the Kharkiv Art and Industrial Institute,[8] where his friend and like-minded colleague Borys Kosarev (1897–1994) also worked—one of the leading Ukrainian stage designers of the avant-garde circle, as well as the author of several photographic series, most notably those documenting the filming of Oleksandr Dovzhenko's *Earth* (1929–1930).

Yermilov's room, which served as both his living quarters and studio, became a shelter for young artists as well as a site for the transmission and transformation of avant-garde ideas. The artist lived in a cramped attic that he loved so deeply that he refused to move elsewhere. Almost everything in it was made by his own hands—from the mailbox and furniture to the window frames. Wall paintings were a distinctive feature of the interior. A sketch of the wall painting around the window shows that the artist added elements marking the space as his own—intimate and homely. In this room, Yermilov received a small circle of visitors, among them Vagrich Bakhchanyan.[9] At the time, the young artist was working as a designer at the Porshen factory and was hardly satisfied with producing posters, notice boards, and wall newspapers. Influenced by his exchanges with studio leader Oleksii Shchehlov, as well as with Yermilov and Kosarev, he began creating abstract works in 1961 that already bore a recognizable absurdist inflection.

A room that offers protection and a sense of intimacy can also generate feelings of enclosure, suffocation, and isolation from like-minded peers. It is but one element within a network that must be built and sustained. For Yermilov, such a network took the form of an ephemeral space of memory, in which he "met" the like-minded figures of his youth—Velimir Khlebnikov, the Syniakova sisters, and others.[10] For Bakhchanyan and his generation, the things they heard and experienced in Yermilov's room became an impetus to seek out kindred spirits in Kharkiv and beyond.

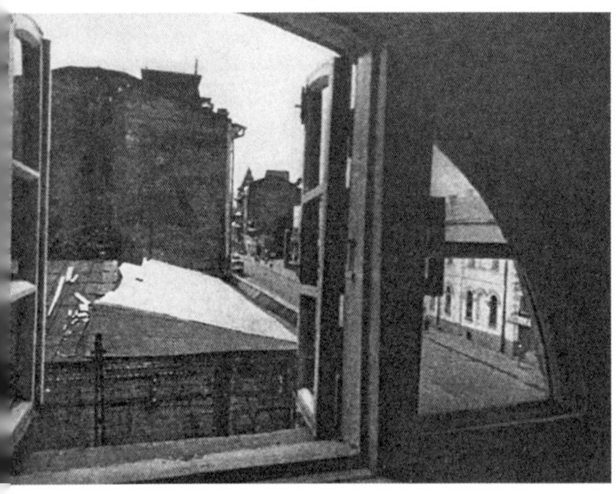

View from the window of Vasyl Yermilov's self-designed living and workspace, Kharkiv, 1970s. Source: Zinoviy Fogel, Vasily Ermilov, Sovetskii Khudozhnik, Moscow.

Between 1961 and 1963, Vagrich Bakhchanyan attempted to present his abstractions abroad, fully aware that such opportunities did not exist in Kharkiv. At that time, Western publications were already available in the USSR, including the newspaper *Les Lettres françaises*, which published the addresses of Parisian art galleries. Bakhchanyan sent letters to them and began receiving catalogues; soon after, one

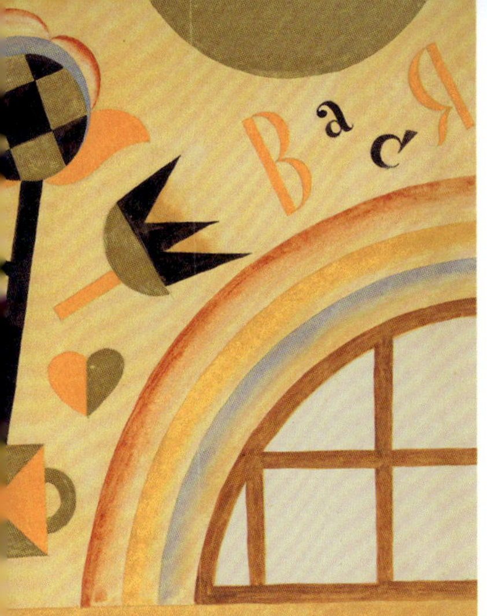

Vasyl Yermilov, *project sketch for painting the wall of Vasyl Yermilov's studio in Kharkiv*, 1921. Watercolor, ink, and bronze on paper on cardboard, 31.7 × 29.2 cm. Courtesy of NAMU (National Art Museum of Ukraine).

gallery invited him to submit his works. Having assembled ten to twelve pieces, he sent them to Paris. The gallery then proposed he participate in an exhibition of young artists and requested works for a solo show. Subsequent attempts to send artworks ended unsuccessfully. The city newspaper *Krasnoie Znamia* published an exposé article denouncing the artist, and a comrades' court was convened at his workplace, where his colleagues condemned him for producing "incomprehensible" works. Labelled "politically unreliable," the artist lost his job and was forced to leave his native city a few years later.

The Courtyard (Sumska Street, opposite the House with Salamanders)

The collective efforts of Kharkiv's underground community were directed towards entering public space, reaching viewers, and engaging with society. Their incompatibility with official artistic doctrine meant that they were barred from publicly presenting their works, deprived of an audience and critical discourse, and excluded from the Soviet art system—often because they lacked formal education or membership in the Union of Artists of the USSR. Instead, the underground artists had to seek out encounters with viewers in more informal spaces beyond the union exhibition halls and museums.

This goal led to the organization of the first street exhibition of non-official Kharkiv artists in the USSR, *Under the Arches*, in one of the courtyards in central Kharkiv in 1965. It lasted only a few hours. Works by Vagrich Bakhchanyan, Anatolii Krynskyi, Mykhailo Basov, Yurii Kuchukov, Anatolii Shulika, Iryna Savinova, and others were shown. The presentation included around forty artworks—paintings, graphic works, photographs, and collages characterized by formal experimentation, with Surrealism and abstraction appearing the most radical. The writers Eduard Limonov, Yurii Miloslavskyi, and Volodymyr Motrych came to support their friends and read poetry instead of giving speeches. At the time, an unsanctioned exhibition was perceived as an act of defiance. Although the artists dismantled it rather quickly, it still had an explosive effect. Persecution followed. Bakhchanyan and his wife, Iryna Savinova, had to move to Moscow in 1967, then later to New York in 1974.[11]

Self-organization as a survival strategy proved illusory. In the second half of the 1960s, the circle of Kharkiv's nonconformist artists dispersed across the world due to official persecution.

This loss of protection—triggered by the attempt to step outside in search of "one's own" space and find like-minded individuals in the wider world—reveals the fragility of ties between individuals, institutions, and places. Today, the need for networks is acutely

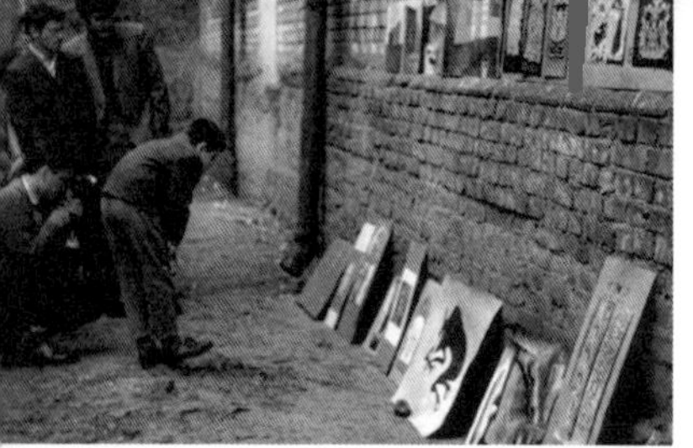

Unauthorized exhibition *Under the Arches*, Kharkiv, 1965.
Photographer unknown.
From the archive of Irina Bakhchanyan.

felt; yet these networks often remain precarious and ephemeral. The installation *All That's Solid Melts into Air (2024)* by Yulia Kostereva and Yuriy Kruchak demonstrates that interconnection is possible, while simultaneously exposing the instability of ties between communities and collective efforts. The work seems to return to the city some of the energy that Kharkiv has given to the world through its talented natives.

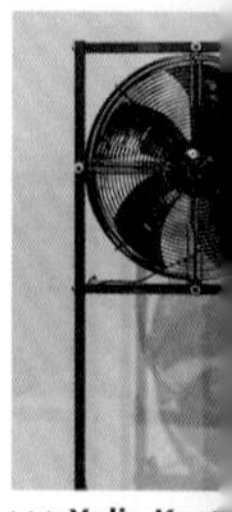

>>> Yulia Kost
&
Yuriy Kru
p. 62

The Wall (18 Kaplunivskyi Lane)

Vagrich Bakhchanyan became a distinctive link between Kharkiv's avant-garde and later artistic practices—conceptualism and text-based art. He is known to have referred to himself as a "word artist," while his authorial strategies explored performativity, corporeality, and imagery in relation to language.

Text is a recurring and structuring theme in Kharkiv. One need only recall that the building constructed in the late 1920s to house the capital's cultural elite was named Slovo, Ukrainian for word. The journal *Nova Generatsiia* (1927–1930), edited by Mykhail Semenko,[12] became a platform for the avant-garde; it was there that the final articles by Kazimir Malevich were published. In the 1920s, many artists worked extensively with language and text, often treating them as propagandistic slogans and narratives. Text is present in Vadym Meller's stage designs for productions by Les Kurbas, in the agitational architectures of Vasyl Yermilov, and elsewhere.

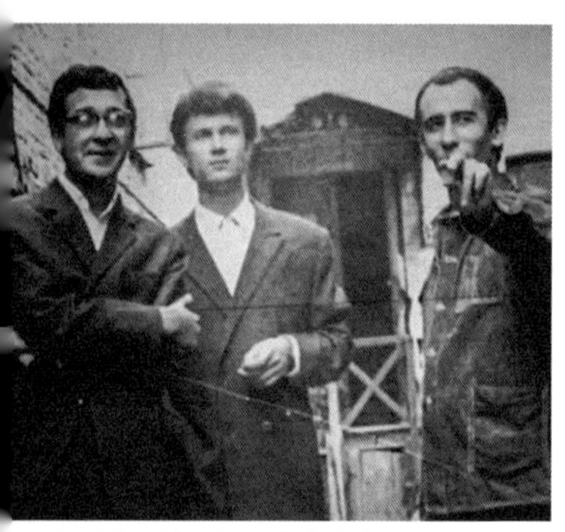

From left to right: writer Yurii Miloslavskyi, writer and political figure Eduard Savenko (Limonov), conceptual artist Vagrich Bakhchanyan, Kharkiv, 1966.
Photographer unknown.
From the archive of Irina Bakhchanyan.

Over time, the word became organically woven into the fabric of the city, resurfacing generations later in the spontaneous writings of Oleh Mitasov (1953–1999), a legendary Kharkiv figure of the 1980s and 90s—the city's "mad genius," who covered buildings with continuous inscriptions. Living in a communal apartment in central Kharkiv, Mitasov wrote enigmatic texts all over the walls and fences of the areas around Pushkinska Street (now Skovoroda Street), Sumska Street, Lenin Avenue (now Nauka Avenue), and his native Chervonopraporny Lane (now Kaplunivskyi Lane). The most common explanation for the deterioration of his mental health is a dramatic story: Mitasov, then a doctoral candidate in economic sciences, is said to have forgotten his dissertation on a tram and consequently failed to obtain his degree. It is believed that this is why he frequently wrote "VEK.VAK," which may be deciphered as Vyshcha Atestatsiina Komisiia (Higher Attestation Commission).

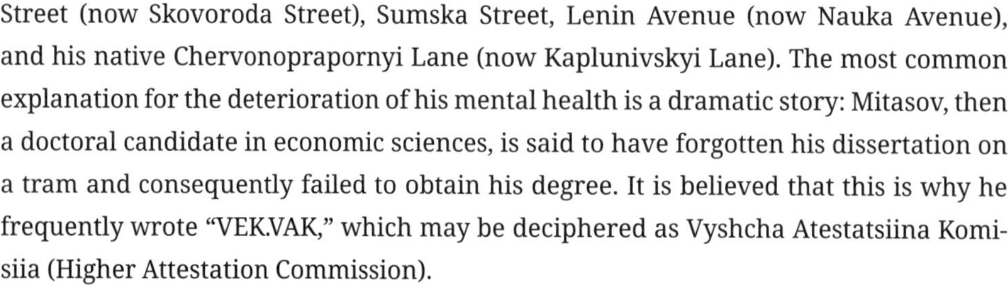

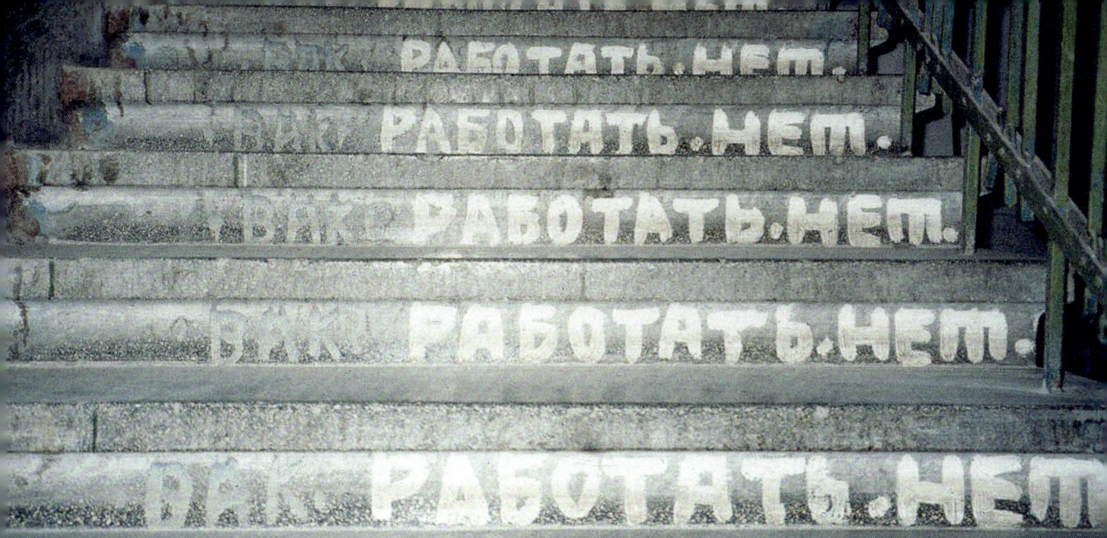

Murals by Oleh Mitasov in the entrance to his own apartment, Kharkiv, 1998–99. Photo: Pavlo Makov.

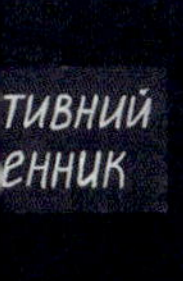

Kateryna Yermolayeva p. 53

Today, this relentless need to paint text on the city's walls can be read as an extraordinary effort to "hide" within writing—to construct an additional layer of protection in a world where the city's walls appear, and indeed are, insufficiently secure. Text preserves memory, offers hope, and prevents us from forgetting what matters; at the same time, it carries an individual intonation, much like the *Collective Diary* (2024) by Kateryna Yermolayeva. It is a comparable attempt to find support in the familiar process of writing and recording thoughts. This intimate act allows one's voice to be separated from the noise of official statements and generalizations produced by wartime reality.

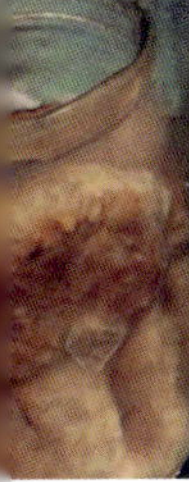

>>> Uli Golub p. 48

Like Mitasov—whose obsessive words filled the space around him, including his own apartment—the character in Uli Golub's video *Notes from Underground* (2016) compulsively accumulates objects and food, seeking protection and stability in them. Apolitical and disoriented like his literary prototype, he attempts to hide in the "underground" of his own imagined sense of safety. Within the literal underground space of the YermilovCentre, the paradox of this shelter becomes especially tangible: a refuge that both protects and imprisons.

The Building (4 Freedom Square)

Even the strongest walls of a building do not guarantee protection; safety requires additional efforts—physical, material, and mental. A building, like a body, is also vulnerable, as shown in *The Nook* (2023) by Anna Zvyagintseva, where the fragile, illusory nature of walls is likened to semi-transparent clothing that neither protects nor conceals.

Anna Zvyagintseva p. 46

As a basic unit of the city and a site of everyday life—routines, meetings, and work—the building is also bound to memories and new experiences. Preserving and re-enacting daily habits and rituals as a way of resisting the entropy of war becomes a

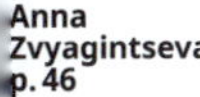

reason to seek out safe spaces for existence. Pavlo Makov's work *Bed, Carpet, Brooch* (2024), directly inspired by the artist's experience of staying together with other Kharkiv residents in the basement of the YermilovCentre during the first months of the full-scale invasion, is an attempt to convey the image of home—a space of "one's own," with walls symbolic or imagined.

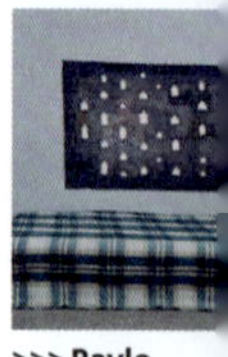

>>> Pavlo Makov p. 104

Within Makov's artistic practice, this work marks a further development of his reflections on the phenomenon of place, where stability is not achieved through tradition or intergenerational transmission, but solely through individual efforts to sustain memories, everyday habits, and rituals. His monumental project *Utopia* (1992–2005) represents a search for reconciliation with the place where one lives, a place where, in his words, "there is nothing to look at."[13] How does one live in a city that has suffered—and continues to suffer—such losses, pain, trauma, and erasure of memory? Makov assumed the role of a documentarian of Kharkiv, drawing on the ways graphic techniques were used before the invention of photography. In his prints, he recorded individual details and fragments of found books, texts, and sketches. Concrete visual elements—Mitasov's inscriptions, training targets in school courtyards, plants from the Botanical Garden, and others—were assembled into his own image of the city, interpreted through corporeality and trace.

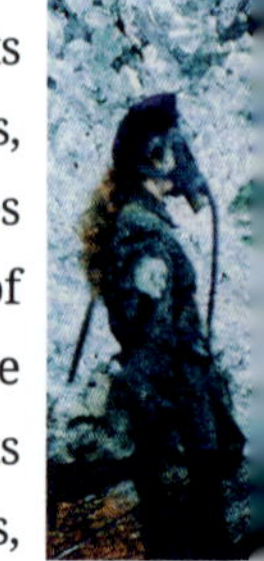

>>> Boris Mikhailov p. 52

The City

The grand attempt undertaken by Pavlo Makov in *Utopia* to rethink Kharkiv through the prism of "one's own" loci—which bear the imprint of history and the presence of loved ones—is one of the efforts to transform the city into a safe space.

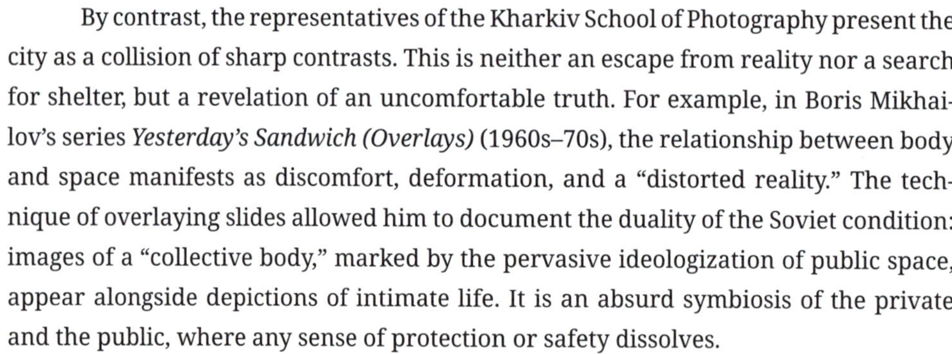

By contrast, the representatives of the Kharkiv School of Photography present the city as a collision of sharp contrasts. This is neither an escape from reality nor a search for shelter, but a revelation of an uncomfortable truth. For example, in Boris Mikhailov's series *Yesterday's Sandwich (Overlays)* (1960s–70s), the relationship between body and space manifests as discomfort, deformation, and a "distorted reality." The technique of overlaying slides allowed him to document the duality of the Soviet condition: images of a "collective body," marked by the pervasive ideologization of public space, appear alongside depictions of intimate life. It is an absurd symbiosis of the private and the public, where any sense of protection or safety dissolves.

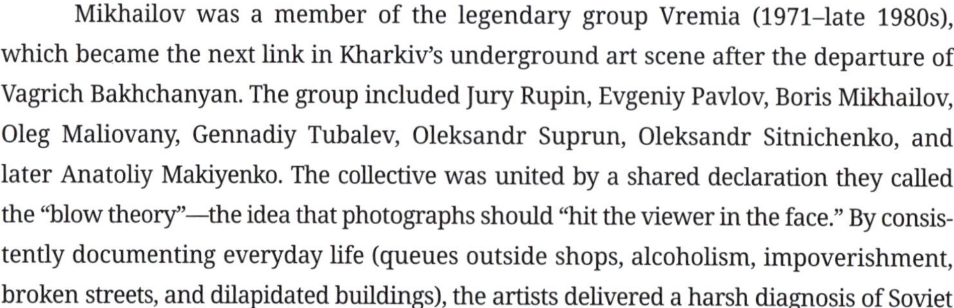

Mikhailov was a member of the legendary group Vremia (1971–late 1980s), which became the next link in Kharkiv's underground art scene after the departure of Vagrich Bakhchanyan. The group included Jury Rupin, Evgeniy Pavlov, Boris Mikhailov, Oleg Maliovany, Gennadiy Tubalev, Oleksandr Suprun, Oleksandr Sitnichenko, and later Anatoliy Makiyenko. The collective was united by a shared declaration they called the "blow theory"—the idea that photographs should "hit the viewer in the face." By consistently documenting everyday life (queues outside shops, alcoholism, impoverishment, broken streets, and dilapidated buildings), the artists delivered a harsh diagnosis of Soviet reality. At the same time, the members of the group critically rethought regional stereotypes of Kharkiv: urbanism, progress, and utopian pathos that had degenerated into standardization, grayness, provincialism, and neglect. In their photographs, Kharkiv's recognizable loci—central squares, Derzhprom, monuments, and official institutions, as well as parks and outskirts—appeared as shadows or threatening reminders from the past.

Sense of Safety unpacks issues of protection and invisibility, which become especially palpable in YermilovCentre's basement space, a place of care and survival. Unlike the avant-garde, Kharkiv's underground art scarcely transformed the urban space; instead, it carefully examined and restored what had been destroyed, erased, or rejected. It reestablished the right to truth, vulnerability, and personal experience in art. Then, artists sought to emerge from the underground; now, we return to it in search of safety. If the avant-garde became "its own antiquity" for the previous generation,[14] the underground is now becoming our topography of survival. In conditions of danger, the city changes, and with it, our ways of seeing and remembering.

---

1. Larysa Savytska, *Art of Kharkiv in the Perspective of the 20th Century* (Kharkiv: Art Map of Ukraine. Kyiv, 2012), p. 8.
2. Terms such as "unofficial art," "nonconformism," and "underground" have regularly been used to describe artistic phenomena that operated outside the paradigm of Socialist Realism and lacked state support.
3. The term "locus" spans a variety of fields, from genetics to psychology. Originally denoting the location of something, it has come to be used in literary studies to describe segments of the existential universe of lyrical subjects within an urban environment, reflecting events and phenomena connected to the trajectory of these subjects. A locus not only "anchors" events to a specific place, but also articulates the interrelation of time and history within a single site, which often has visible or conventionally defined territorial boundaries (a street, a building, a theatre, a room, a porch, a park, etc.).
4. Dmytro Yuriiovych Boklakh, "Definitions and Interrelations of the Categories of Topos, Loci, and the Urban Chronotope and Their Realisation in the Urban Text of a Literary Work," *Bulletin of V. N. Karazin Kharkiv National University*, philology series, no. 74 (2016), pp. 249–257.
5. Vasyl Yermilov (1894–1968) was a prominent Ukrainian artist and a representative of the avant-garde. His entire life was closely connected with Kharkiv. In the 1920s, he worked in industrial graphic design, created agitational tribunes and other mobile architectural forms, designed book and magazine covers, typefaces, and interior decorations that are considered among the finest examples of Constructivism.
6. Vasyl Yermilov, *Exhibition of Works on the Occasion of the 50th Anniversary of Artistic Activity*, exh. cat. Museum of Fine Arts and Kharkiv Regional Union of Artists (Kharkiv, 1962), p. 24.
7. Borys Lobanovskyi, *Decorative Art of the USSR*, no. 12 (1964), pp. 14–17.
8. Present-day Kharkiv State Academy of Design and Arts.
9. Vagrich Bakhchanyan (1938–2009) was a well-known conceptual artist and a representative of the Kharkiv underground. He had no formal art education; his artistic skills were developed at the art studio of the Palace of Culture of the Metalist factory. After the action *Under the Arches* (1965), he was first forced to move to Moscow, then to New York in 1974, where he spent the rest of his life. He experimented with various techniques, working with books, magazine cover design, performance, and texts at the intersection of conceptualism and Sots Art.
10. The Syniakova sisters (in particular Maria Syniakova-Urechyna, 1890–1984) are associated with the early development of the Kharkiv avant-garde. At the Syniakova family estate of Krasna Poliana near Kharkiv, avant-garde artists, writers, and other representatives of new artistic movements from across the Russian Empire gathered.
11. T. Bakhmet, "'The Cherry Pipe' of the Sixties. Kharkiv," in *The Art of Ukrainian Sixties*, ed. Olga Balashova and Lizaveta German (Kyiv: Osnovy, 2015), p. 83. The street exhibition has also been described by Eduard Limonov in *Le Petit Salaud* (Paris: Albin Michel, 1985), p. 25.
12. Mykhail Semenko (1892–1937) was the founder and leading theorist of Ukrainian Futurism (then known as Panfuturism), a poet, and the initiator of numerous publications and actions aimed at promoting avant-garde ideas.
13. Pavlo Makov, *UTOPIA. Chronicles. 1992–2005* (Kharkiv: Dukh i Litera, 2005), p. 41.
14. Larysa Savytska, *Art of Kharkiv in the Perspective of the 20th Century*, see note 1, p. 7.

Yulia Kostereva

born 1973 in Kharkiv, Ukraine; based in Kyiv and in Białystok, Poland

All That's Solid Melts into Air

Yuriy Kruchak

born 1973 in Poltava, Ukraine; based in Kyiv

2024
INTERACTIVE INSTALLATION (MICROPROCESSOR, VENTILATOR, ROTOR, VIDEO CAMERA, LIVESTREAM)
PRODUCED ESPECIALLY FOR THE EXHIBITION *SENSE OF SAFETY*

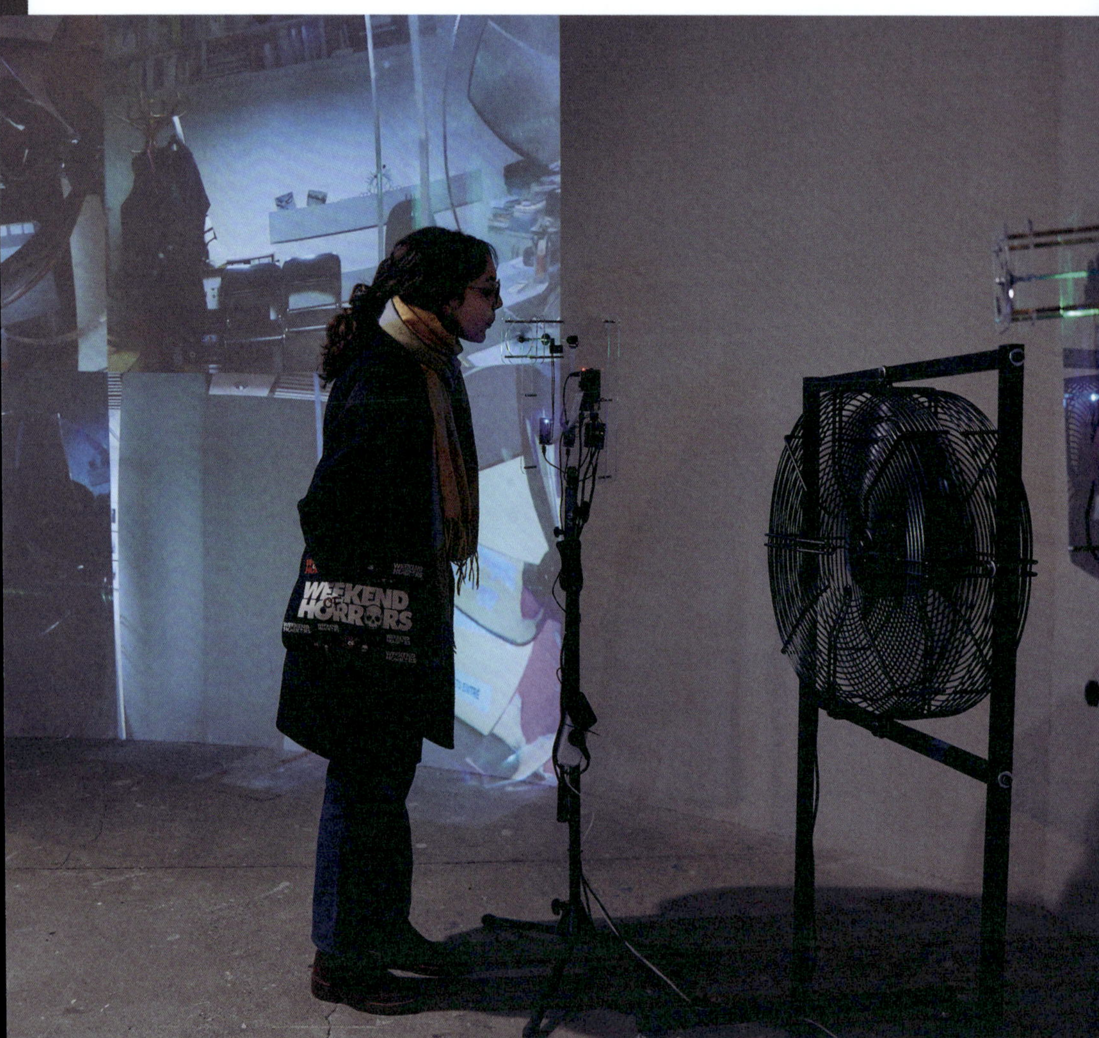

Yulia Kostereva and Yuriy Kruchak's artistic practice is distinguished by its participatory character. The artists do not focus on creating objects for "white cubes" and instead consider art as a space and set of instruments for social interaction and supporting communities. Their work also goes beyond individual practices. In 1999,

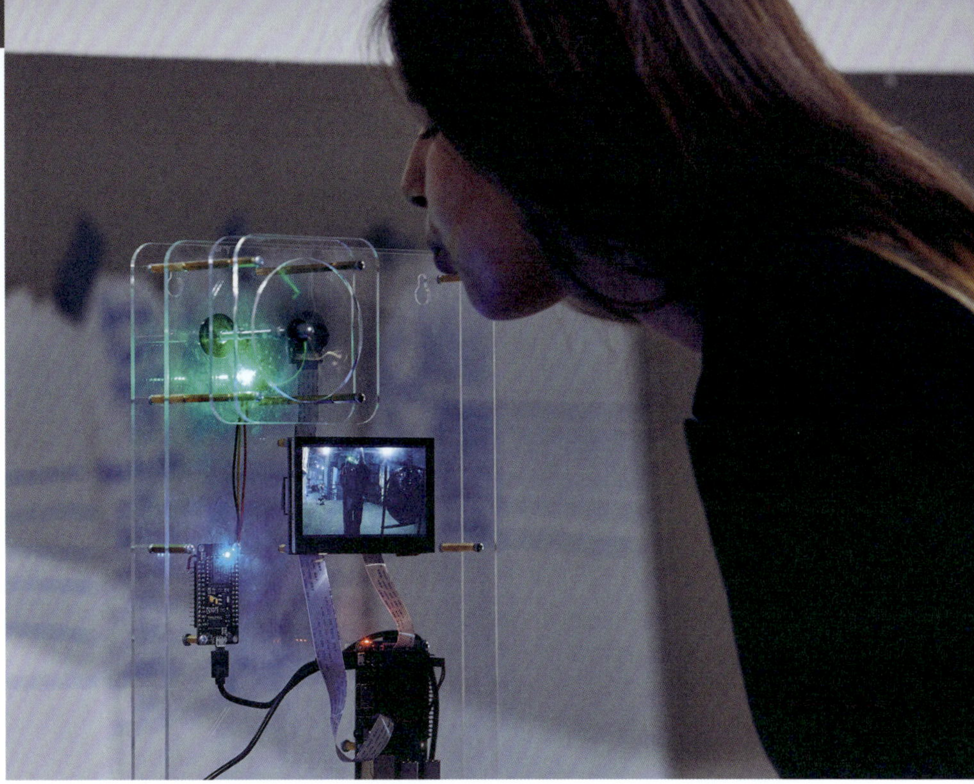

they created the art platform *Open Place*, aimed at building links between different social and professional groups through various practices of knowledge.

The artists are driven by an understanding of interdependence and use cultural and activist practices to connect and mediate social processes. This forms the background of their interactive installation, specifically created for the *Sense of Safety* project. *All That's Solid Melts into Air* highlights the interconnectedness of various geographical contexts, expanding Kharkiv's outreach globally and integrating other geographies. The artwork comprises small rotors installed in various cultural institutions throughout Europe. Each rotor is connected to a central large fan at the YemilovCentre in Kharkiv. When someone breathes on a small fan in any partner location, the large Kharkiv ventilator starts spinning. The more small fans are activated globally, the faster the central ventilator spins. This interactive artwork symbolizes the collective effort and solidarity among different communities, showing how individual actions contribute to a larger movement.

The air here provides a metaphor for the invisible connections between different communities and contexts, which are unseen but essential for the creation and maintenance of safety as a collective infrastructure.

Anchored in the activation of *All That's Solid Melts into Air* by Yulia Kostereva and Yuriy Kruchak, this bridge demonstrated how two Ukrainian cities, located in distant parts of the country, experienced the war with differing intensities. The connection highlighted the uneven geographies of conflict while enabling communication and shared presence through a playful, participatory situation. Building on this gesture, the screening program brought together multiple geographies and explored the collapse of dualities—between game and reality, good and evil, past and future. While children's games recreate the world with sincerity and a sense of truth, adult life is structured by rituals, masking, and role-playing. Using play as both a metaphor and method, the program explored how fear, guilt, and uncertainty are negotiated in contexts where war permeates everyday life, framing play as a fragile yet persistent mode of connection and solidarity.

Discussion at Asortymentna Kimnata, Ivano-Frankivsk. Photo: Taras Telishchak.

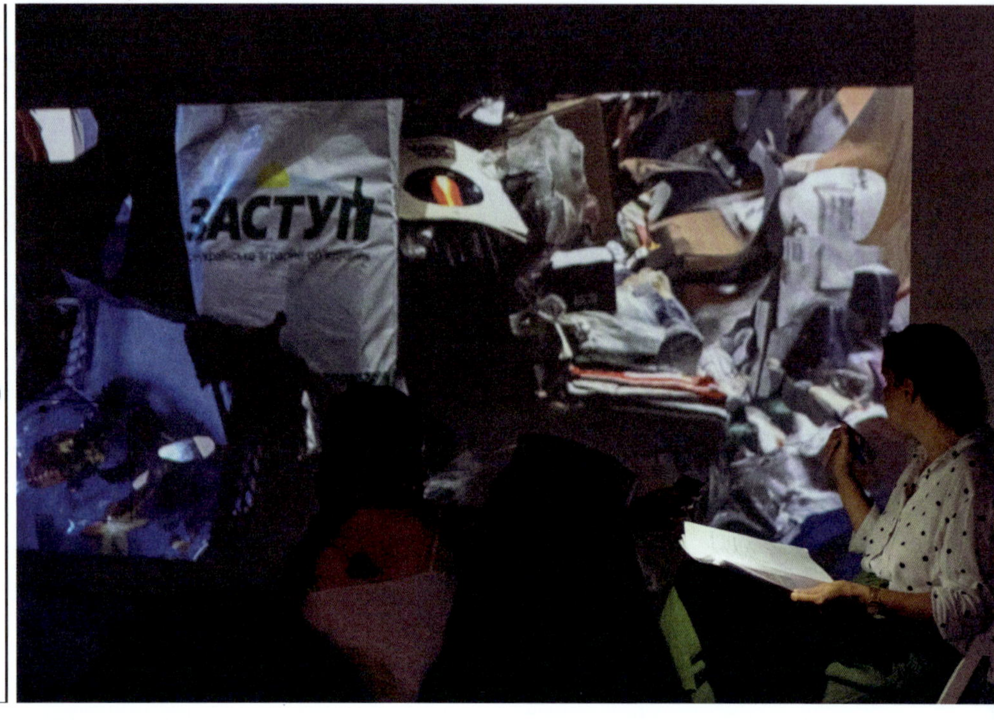

Playing with Safety: No duality, only duality

Video screening, discussion, interactive installation

Asortymentna Kimnata, Ivano-Frankivsk (UA)

Date
06.09.2024

Participants
Alona Karavai (UA)
Olya Polyak (UA)

Artists
Lala Aliyeva (AZ)
Francis Alÿs (MX)
eeefff (BY/DE)
Uli Golub (UA/USA)
Ihar Hancharuk (BY)
Yulia Kostereva & Yuriy Kruchak (UA)
Vitaliy Yankovy (UA/RO)

For me and the entire team of Asortymentna Kimnata, Bridges of Solidarity became a practice of staying focused on what truly matters. Not every format worked perfectly, but the bridges were altogether successful—probably due to the fundamental horizontality of our cooperation, and not least due to the fact that we were talking about Kharkiv.

Alona Karavai

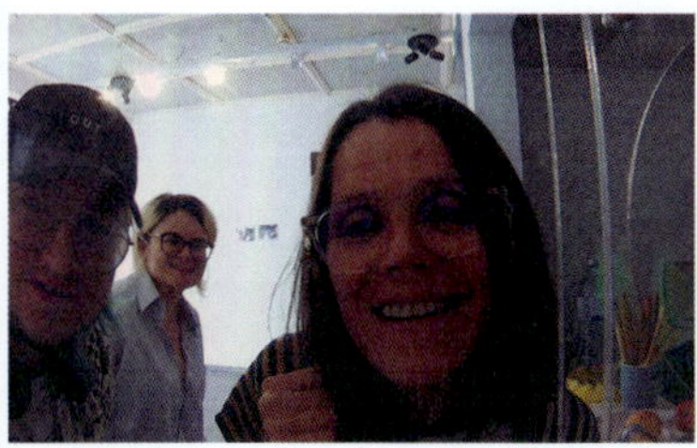

Artist Olia Fedorova and other visitors at Ziegel. Atelier Gemeinschaft ukrainischer Künstler:innen, Graz. Livestream screenshot.

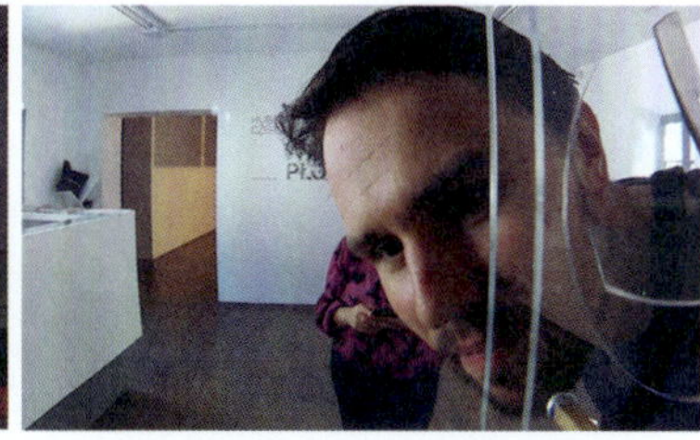

Galeria Arsenał, Białystok. Livestream screenshot.

Artist Luchezar Boyadjiev at ICA – Institute of Contemporary Art, Sofia. Photo: ICA–Sofia.

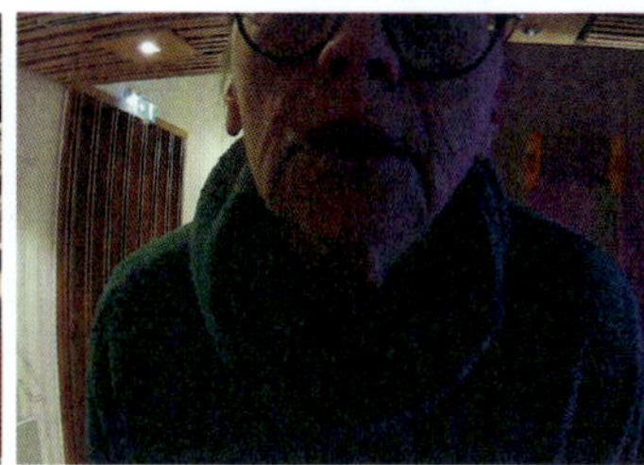

Skövde Kulturhus (SE). Livestream screenshot.

During the project, the installation *All That's Solid Melts into Air* by Yulia Kostereva and Yuriy Kruchak was first activated at YermilovCentre, then traveled to eight art institutions across different cities: Siemiradzki Gallery (Kharkiv, UA), Asortymentna Kimnata (Ivano-Frankivsk, UA), Jam Factory Art Center (Lviv, UA), Voloshyn Gallery (Kyiv, UA), Galeria Arsenał (Białystok, PL), Ziegel. Atelier Gemeinschaft ukrainischer Künstler:innen (Graz, AT), ICA – Institute of Contemporary Art (Sofia, BG), and Skövde Kulturhus (SE).

Photographs document visitors interacting with the work at these locations.

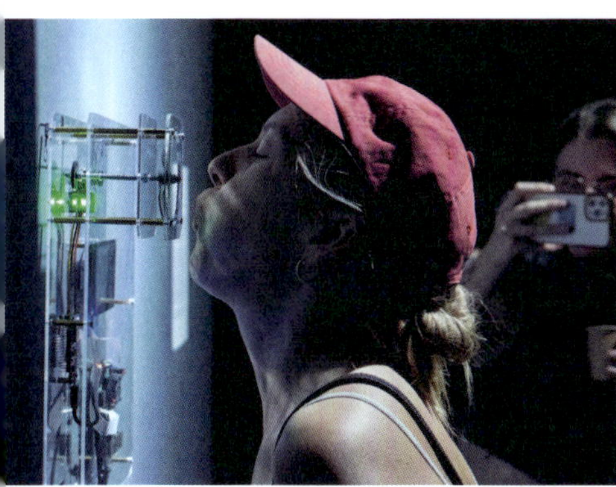

Artist Oksana Pohrebennyk at Asortymentna Kimnata, Ivano-Frankivsk. Photo: Taras Telishchak.

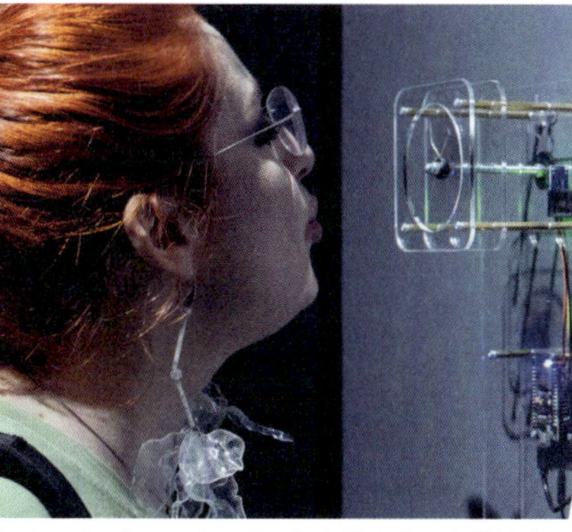

Asortymentna Kimnata, Ivano-Frankivsk. Photo: Taras Telishchak.

During the event, Nataliia Ivanova (director of YermilovCentre), Alona Karavai (co-founder of Asortymentna Kimnata), and Bozhena Pelenska (then director of Jam Factory Art Center) discussed how local art institutions continue their work during the war. They reflected on the ambivalence of safety, sharing their experiences of adapting to challenges such as damaged spaces, power outages, and air raid alerts. They also highlighted their efforts to support local artists, organize exhibitions, and sustain cultural life.

Sense of Safety and Practices of Transformation: How Art Institutions Continue Operating Throughout Ukraine

Discussion

Jam Factory Art Center, Lviv (UA)

Date
13.11.2024

Participants
Nataliia Ivanova (UA)
Alona Karavai (UA)
Bozhena Pelenska (UA)

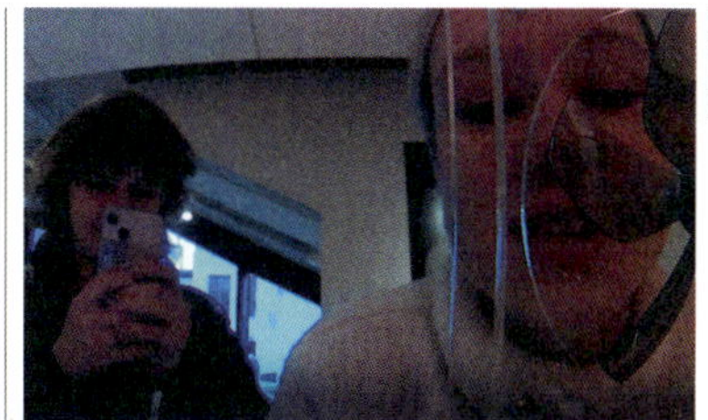

Jam Factory Art Center, Lviv (UA). Livestream screenshot.

bridges of solidarity

Galeria Arsenał maintains longstanding personal and professional relationships with the Ukrainian art community. Within the framework of this support, the gallery hosted three video screening programs based on videoworks from the antiwarcoalition.art platform. The screenings served as a reminder of the ongoing reality in Ukraine and invited the Polish audience to share in presence and empathy. The experience of war became visible within the peaceful space of a cultural institution. Parallel to the event, the space hosted the interactive installation *All That's Solid Melts into Air* by Yulia Kostereva & Yuriy Kruchak.

Screening 1:

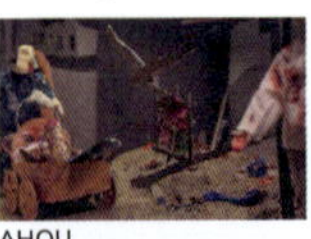
AHOU ALAGHA (US)

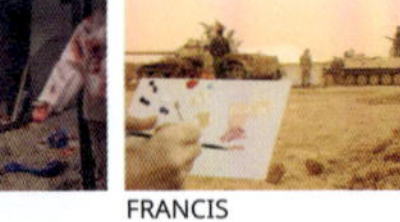
FRANCIS ALŸS (MX)

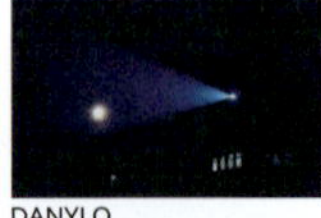
DANYLO HALKIN (UA)

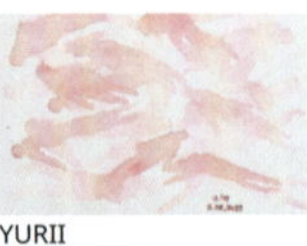
YURII IVANTSYK (UA)

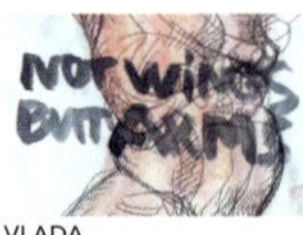
VLADA RALKO (UA)

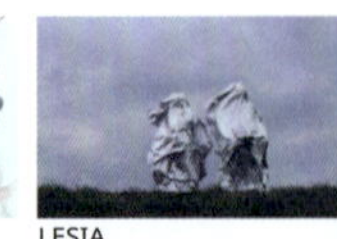
LESIA PCHOLKA (BY)

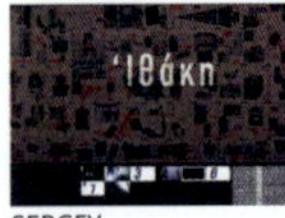
SERGEY SHABOHIN (BY)

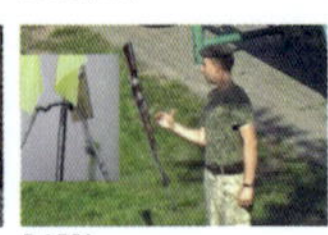
DARIA SAZANOVICH (BY)

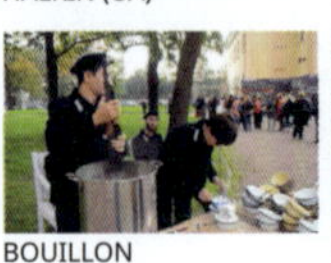
BOUILLON GROUP (GE)

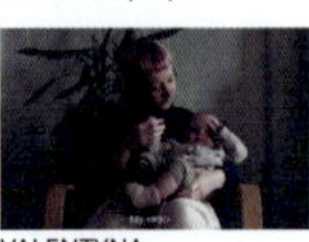
VALENTYNA PETROVA (UA)

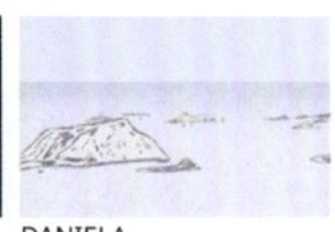
DANIELA WEISS (PL)

AHMET ÖĞÜT (TR)

Screening 2:

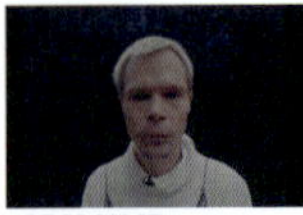
ART PROJECT "REVOLUTION" (BY)

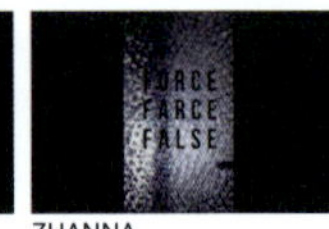
ZHANNA GLADKO (BY)

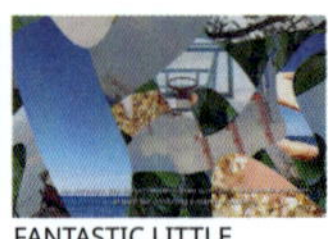
FANTASTIC LITTLE SPLASH (UA)

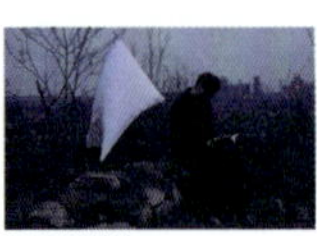
DOBRINYA IVANOV (UA)

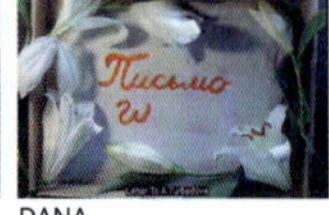
DANA KAVELINA (UA)

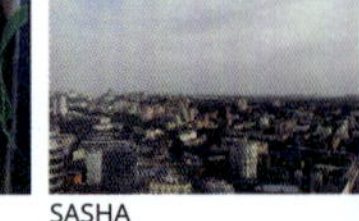
SASHA KURMAZ (UA)

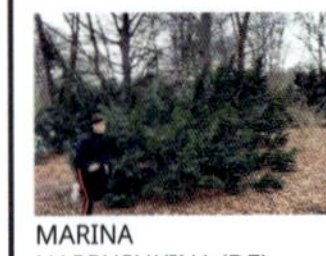
MARINA NAPRUSHKINA (DE)

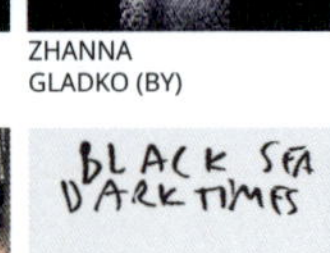
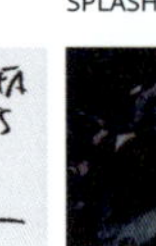
DAN PERJOVSCHI (RO)

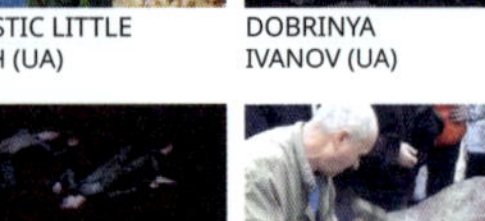
SERGIY PETLYUK (UA)

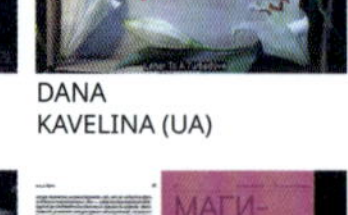
SERHIY POPOV (UA)

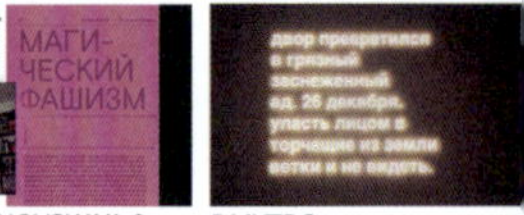
OLIA SOSNOVSKAYA & A.Z.H. (BY)

DMYTRO STARUSEV (UA)

Screening 3:

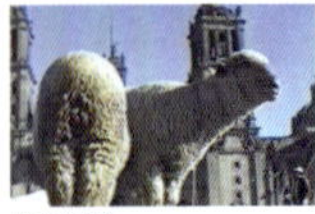
FRANCIS ALŸS (MX)

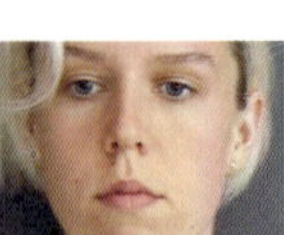
TASHA ARLOVA (BY)

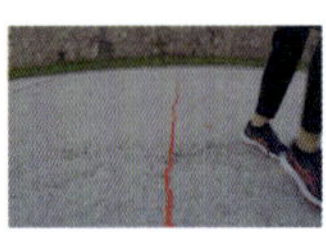
REZZAN GÜMGÜM (TR)

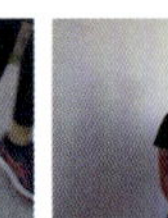
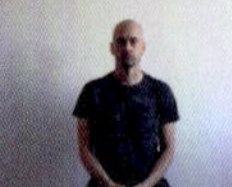
IHAR HANCHARUK (BY)

ULADZIMIR HRAMOVICH (BY/DE)

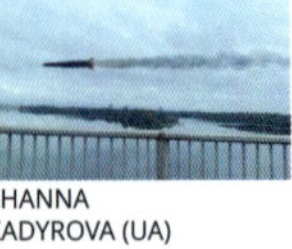
ZHANNA KADYROVA (UA)

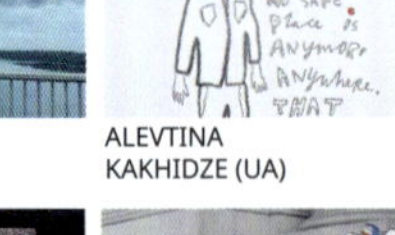
ALEVTINA KAKHIDZE (UA)

ANTON KARYUK (UA)

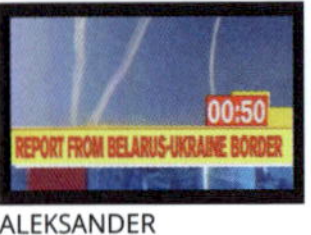

ALEKSANDER KOMAROV (BY/DE)

ELTURAN MAMMADOV (AZ)

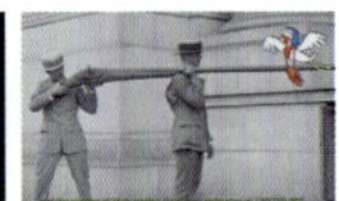
KATARZYNA WOJTCZAK (PL)

Are you here with us?

Series of video screenings, interactive installation

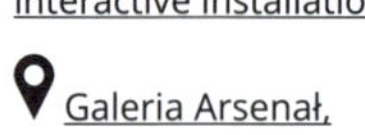
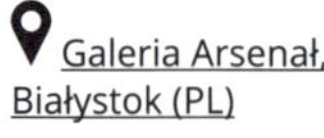
Galeria Arsenał, Białystok (PL)

Date
08, 15, 29.09.2024
02, 09, 30.10.2024
03, 10, 17.11.2024

Curated by
Yulia Kostereva (UA/PL)
Monika Szewczyk (PL)

Film stills from the antiwarcoalition.art platform.

The space Ziegel was initiated by Ukrainian artists and curators from Kharkiv who were forced to migrate to Austria in the wake of the Russian invasion and settled in Graz, where they brought together an international community. The discussion around the project *Sense of Safety* served as a gesture of solidarity and an attempt to restore disrupted ties. Parallel to the event, the space hosted the interactive installation *All That's Solid Melts into Air* by Yulia Kostereva & Yuriy Kruchak.

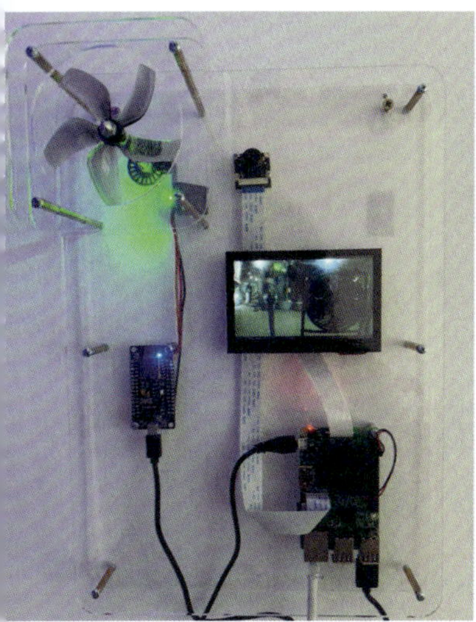

Installation by Yulia Kostereva and Yuriy Kruchak. All photos: Ziegel. Atelier Gemeinschaft ukrainischer Künstler:innen, Graz.

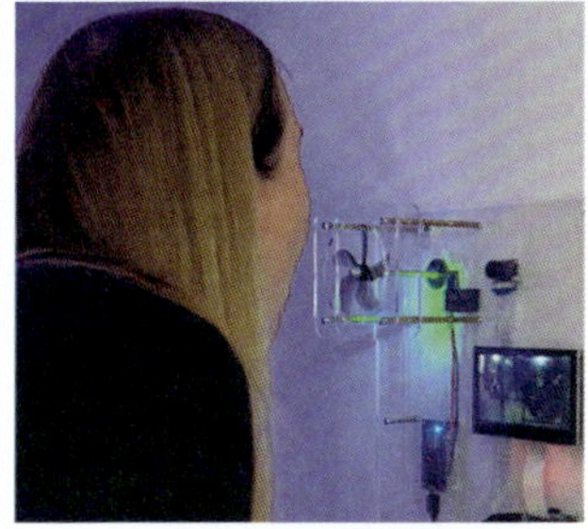

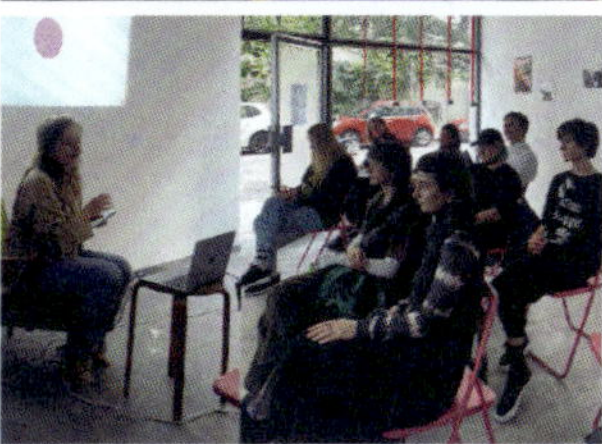

Tatiana Kochubinska giving a talk about the *Sense of Safety* project.

Curator's talk about the *Sense of Safety* project, interactive installation

Ziegel. Atelier Gemeinschaft ukrainischer Künstler:innen, Graz (AT)

Date
18.09.2024

Speaker
Tatiana Kochubinska (UA)

Organized by
Olia Fedorova (UA/AT)
Jura Golik (UA/AT)
Nastia Khlestova (UA/AT)
Anton Tkachenko (UA/AT)

The feminist conception of interdependency as a condition of mutual entanglement and non-isolation lies at the heart of antiwarcoalition.art's practice. Building on the exhibition *Sense of Safety* in Kharkiv, the discussion brought together cultural workers from Georgia, Ukraine, Belarus, and Kazakhstan—regions currently engaged in active resistance to Russian imperial violence. The conversation addressed how war and colonial pressure are reshaping cultural landscapes in these contexts, while also exploring forms of solidarity and mutual support. The discussion functioned as a gesture of trans-local solidarity, emphasizing decolonization as a shared, material, and situated struggle rather than an abstract or symbolic process.

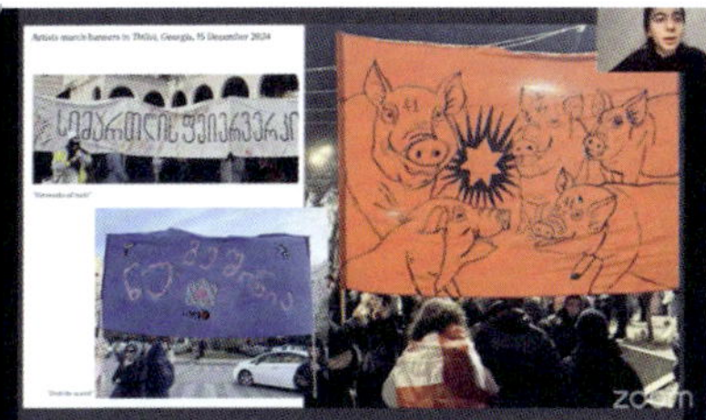

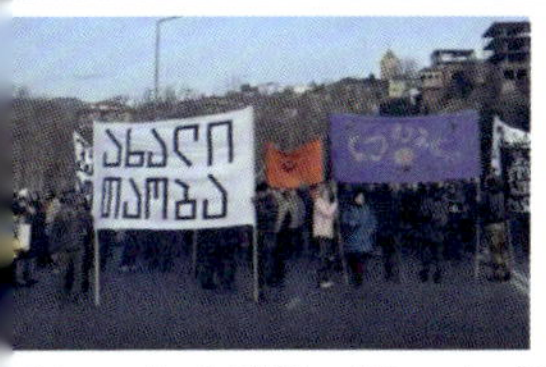

Artists marching in Tbilisi on 15 December 2024. Screenshots from Ana Mikadze's presentation.

Cultural Landscapes in Flux: Artistic Responses to War and Colonialism

Online discussion

Online at antiwarcoalition.art streaming from Almaty/KZ, Graz/AT, Kharkiv/UA, Tbilisi/GE, Warsaw/PL

Date
18.12.2024

Ziegel. Atelier Gemeinschaft ukrainischer Künstler:innen, Graz.

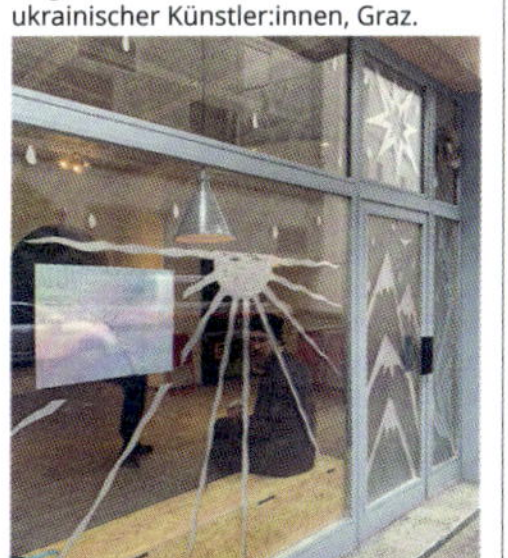

Speakers
Medina Bazargali (KZ)
Nastia Khlestova (UA/AT)
Ana Mikadze (GE)
Lizaveta Stecko (BY/PL)

Moderated by
Antonina Stebur (BY/DE)

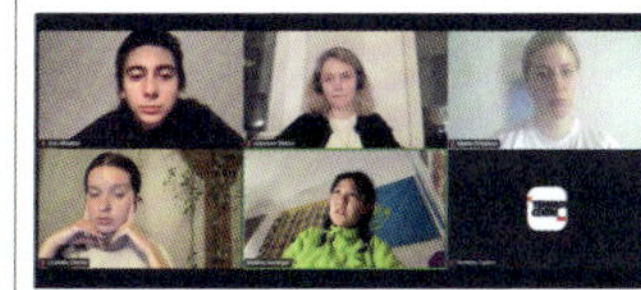

Participants of the online discussion *Cultural Landscapes in Flux*, 2024. Livestream screenshot.

ABA AIR Salon has produced a series of 4 one-hour radio broadcasts connecting Kharkiv and Berlin, providing a space for artistic experimentation where conversation, sound, music, and noise converge. The project fosters collective listening and creative exchange.

Topic 1: Exhibition Opening
The broadcast was created from interviews with curators, artists, and organizers in Kharkiv, offering insights into exhibition concepts, the artists' ideas behind their work, as well as their experiences and perspectives.

Topics 2 and 3: Livestream of *Sense of Safety*
Livestream of *Sense of Safety* from YermilovCentre, Kharkiv to Haus der Statistik, Berlin, which explored artistic experimentation, improvisation, and dialogue between the participating artists, curators, and listeners.

Topic 4: Reading
Special guest: Olga Bubich (BY/DE)
The broadcast featured readings of essays from the *Memory Landscapes* (2023–ongoing) project by essayist, journalist, and artist Olga Bubich, accompanied by electroacoustic music produced by Bomberman. It explored collective and personal memories of traumatic events, as well as issues of censorship and misremembering under repressive regimes.

ABA AIR Salon – Bridge of Solidarity with Kharkiv

Community radio: Freie Radios Berlin Brandenburg (FM: 88.4 Berlin / 90.7 Potsdam)
ABA AIR Salon (DE)

Discussion, livestream, reading

Date
Every Tuesday, from 03.09 to 17.11.2024

Curated by
Aleksander Komarov (BY/DE)
Rosanna Lovell (AU/DE)

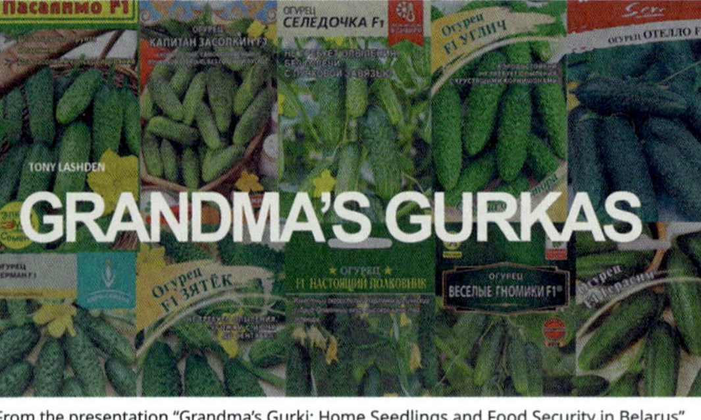

From the presentation "Grandma's Gurki: Home Seedlings and Food Security in Belarus" by tony lashden, nGbK, Berlin, 2024. Courtesy of tony lashden.

As part of Berlin Art Week, the event examined how extractivist practices—whether in relation to land, food systems, infrastructures, or geopolitical domination—are deeply interconnected. Taking the everyday practices of plant cultivation and food production as points of entry, the event demonstrated how colonial dependencies, industrial exploitation, and war-driven destruction reinforce one another across different contexts.

From Soil to Solidarity

Workshop, discursive program, live broadcast

nGbk, Berlin (DE)

Date
13.09.2024

Workshop:
"The Cartography of Home Plants as the Cultural Capital of Childhood Memories" by Taras Gembik (UA/PL) and Marie Manushka (BY/PL)

Discursive program

Presenters
Natasha Chychasova (UA) "Millions of Roses for Nobody"

tony lashden (BY), "Grandma's Gurki: Home Seedlings and Food Security in Belarus"

Moderated by
Antonina Stebur (BY/DE)

Live broadcast of the exhibition *Sense of Safety* from Kharkiv, Ukraine

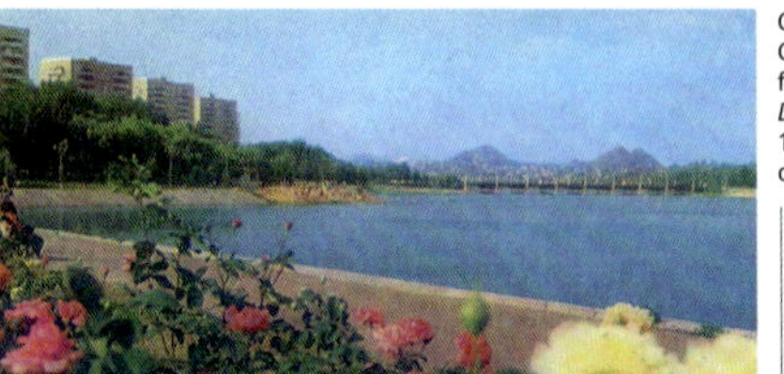
Central Scherbakov Park of Culture and Leisure, Donetsk, from the postcard set *Donetsk — A Tourist City*, 1987. From the archive of Oleksii Fedko.

The event was structured around a multi-channel video stream mixed into a single virtual environment, where participants from Amsterdam, Kraków, and Kharkiv could share the same screen space, as though there weren't borders or thousands of kilometers between them. This environment became a platform for collectively discussing the project *Sense of Safety*, the expansion of artistic space, and the relationship between war, technology, and art. Audiences at *Framer Framed* in Amsterdam joined the discussion, while the livestream was simultaneously available via multiple online platforms, including the project website, and broadcast at YermilovCentre in Kharkiv, where it remained part of the exhibition. The event allowed viewers to engage with creative decisions, ideas, and curatorial strategies, underscoring the role of cultural exchange and solidarity during wartime. This format was enabled by VOID, an Amsterdam-based research project on tactical video and audiovisual publishing. By using livestreaming not only as a tool for documentation but as a means of producing events, VOID connected artists, activists, and researchers across borders, turning the project itself into a platform for collaboration and exchange.

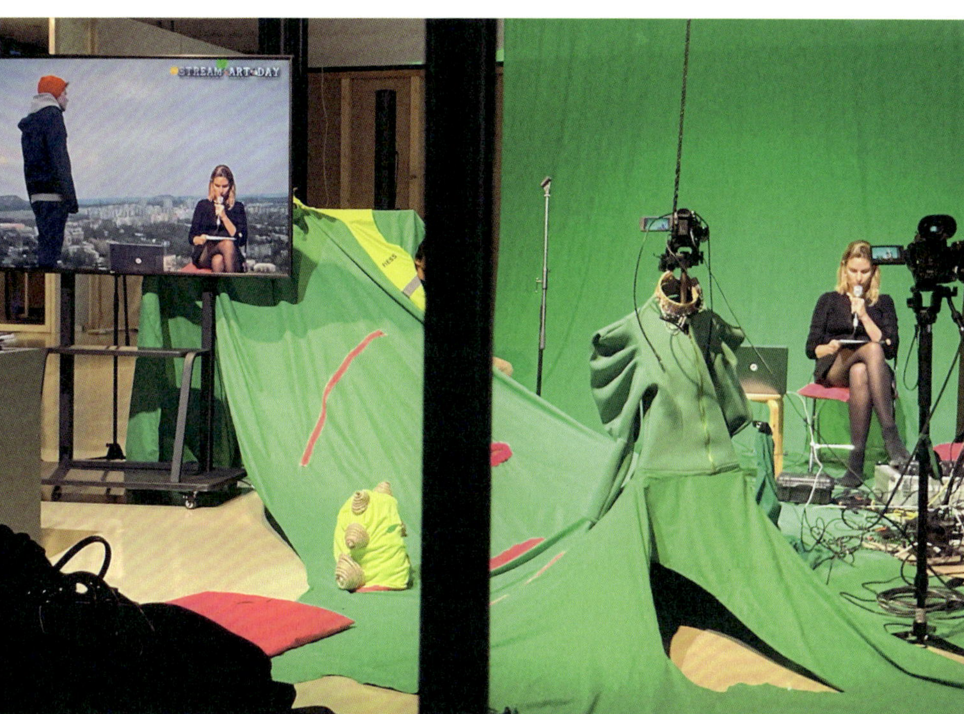

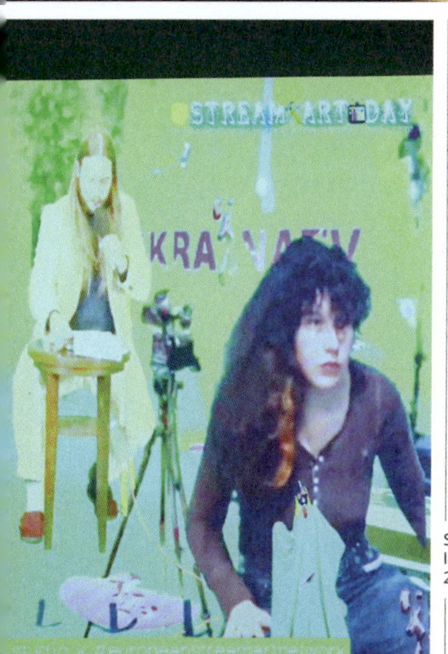

Hybrid streaming event with VOID, UKRAiNATV, and YermilovCentre as part of Stream Art Day at Framer Framed, Amsterdam

Framer Framed, Amsterdam (NL)
Video studio of the V. N. Karazin Kharkiv National University, Kharkiv (UA)
StreamArtStudio, Kraków (PL)

Stills from the event livestream, UKRAiNATV, 2024.

Date
26.09.2024

Participants
Maryna Konieva (UA)
Yelyzaveta Koval (UA)
Giulia Timi (IT/NL)
Maxim Tyminko (NL)

Moderated by
Tommaso Campagna (IT/NL)

Live video mixing
Rom Dziadkiewicz (PL)

Streaming
UKRAiNATV

Science under Shelling

Oleksandr Sorokin

Kharkiv has always been a unique city. Among other things, it is a center of education and science whose influence extends far beyond Ukraine. Thousands of students from across the country and around the world build a living bridge between Kharkiv and the rest of the world. Moreover, the scientific discoveries made in Kharkiv's laboratories have become a cornerstone of international scientific research, laying the foundations of how we understand the world and improve the quality of people's lives. One example of this is the production of crystals known as scintillators, which convert invisible ionizing radiation into visible light. Such crystals are grown at the Institute for Scintillation Materials of the National Academy of Sciences of Ukraine (ISMA). Due to their high quality and unique properties, these crystals are used in the world's most advanced experiments and cutting-edge devices. To give but one notable example, these crystals helped detect the Higgs boson—the so-called God particle—at CERN (the largest European laboratory for high-energy physics) and contributed to research that won two Nobel Prizes.

When Russian invaders attacked Ukraine, they not only sought to rob Ukrainians of their identity and national consciousness, but also to break their close ties with other nations. That's why cultural, educational, and scientific institutions were made into deliberate targets, especially in cities of learning like Kharkiv. All of Kharkiv's research institutions suffered heavy damage, and ISMA was no exception. But despite constant shelling and the hardships of working in a frontline city, scientists made every effort to not only preserve their lives and keep their institutions operating,

INTERDEPENDENCY AND CONNECTIVITY

Interdependency is a concept that draws from feminist theory, where it highlights the sociopolitical dimensions of interpersonal connections, and also from the natural sciences, where it describes the intricate relationships within ecosystems. Focusing on Kharkiv as the assembly point of the whole project, the force field of *Interdependency and Connectivity* foregrounds the city's openness and interconnectedness with other parts of the world via logistical systems of grain supply, labor markets, roads, cables, communication networks, and knowledge transfers. Moreover, *Interdependency and Connectivity* gathers artistic practices related to exchanging experience and knowledge, pulling Kharkiv in and out of the world, organizing bridges of solidarity, and the persistent interconnection of human and non-human agents. This field emphasizes the ambivalence of safety through the idea of transparency as a fundamental condition of interconnectedness.

but also to stay connected with the international scientific community. Some of the ISMA scientists joined the Armed Forces of Ukraine, others went to work at institutes abroad or in safer Ukrainian cities. But most of them stayed. They transformed the underground laboratory premises into a so-called scientific resilience hub, where they set up sleeping areas, a kitchen, and living facilities so that the scientific equipment could continue operating without interruption.

Staff combined their shifts and daily duties with working on an international project under the Horizon Europe program, creating new crystals for CERN while their colleagues, children, and pets lived in the laboratories, sleeping, cooking, and carrying on with their daily routines. Those days showed how ISMA had become not only a workplace but also a safe home for employees and their families, a refuge where humanity and scientific dedication intertwined.

In addition to the scientific results obtained in the underground lab, it was essential to resume the production of various crystals and materials, as it had been suspended with the start of Russia's full-scale invasion.. Local and international partners needed ISMA's unique products, and although they sincerely supported the institute, they worried that the lack of its products would have a negative impact on their activities, leading to the breakdown of longstanding partnerships. Forgoing ISMA's products could lead to a deterioration in the quality of its partners' products (and increase their price) while worsening the results of their experiments.

For example, one of the partners said that in order to fulfill their international obligations in 2022, they had to order crystals from a well-known American company, but they turned out to be of much poorer quality, which significantly reduced the lifespan of their devices. The situation was further complicated by the fact that some of ISMA's equipment was located in an area damaged by missile strikes, which caused the equipment to malfunction. It was decided to move the damaged equipment to a new site with more stable conditions. This task was extremely challenging: due to shelling and a lack of personnel, they had to engage everyone available, including the administrators, scientists, and even their families.

Managers became drivers and couriers, scientists doubled as assemblers and shift workers, so that all the equipment could be transported, assembled, and restarted. Thanks to their joint efforts, they were able to resume crystal growth by the end of summer 2022, and international partners received their first deliveries, despite Kharkiv being shelled daily. By the end of the year, 90% of all orders had been fulfilled, preserving ISMA's reputation as a reliable supplier of high-precision scientific products.

As a result, ISMA was invited to join new international collaborations, including the development and construction of an even more powerful collider planned by CERN.

This episode shows that cooperation between people (or organizations) can outlast the violence of even the worst enemy. Preserving and strengthening these relationships today is not only a crucial scientific responsibility, but also a collective one.

Thomas Hirschhorn **Energy=Yes! Quality=No!**

born in 1957, Bern, Switzerland; based in Paris, France

2024
CRITICAL WORKSHOP PREPARED ESPECIALLY FOR THE EXHIBITION *SENSE OF SAFETY*
WITH THE SUPPORT OF THE GRYNYOV ART COLLECTION

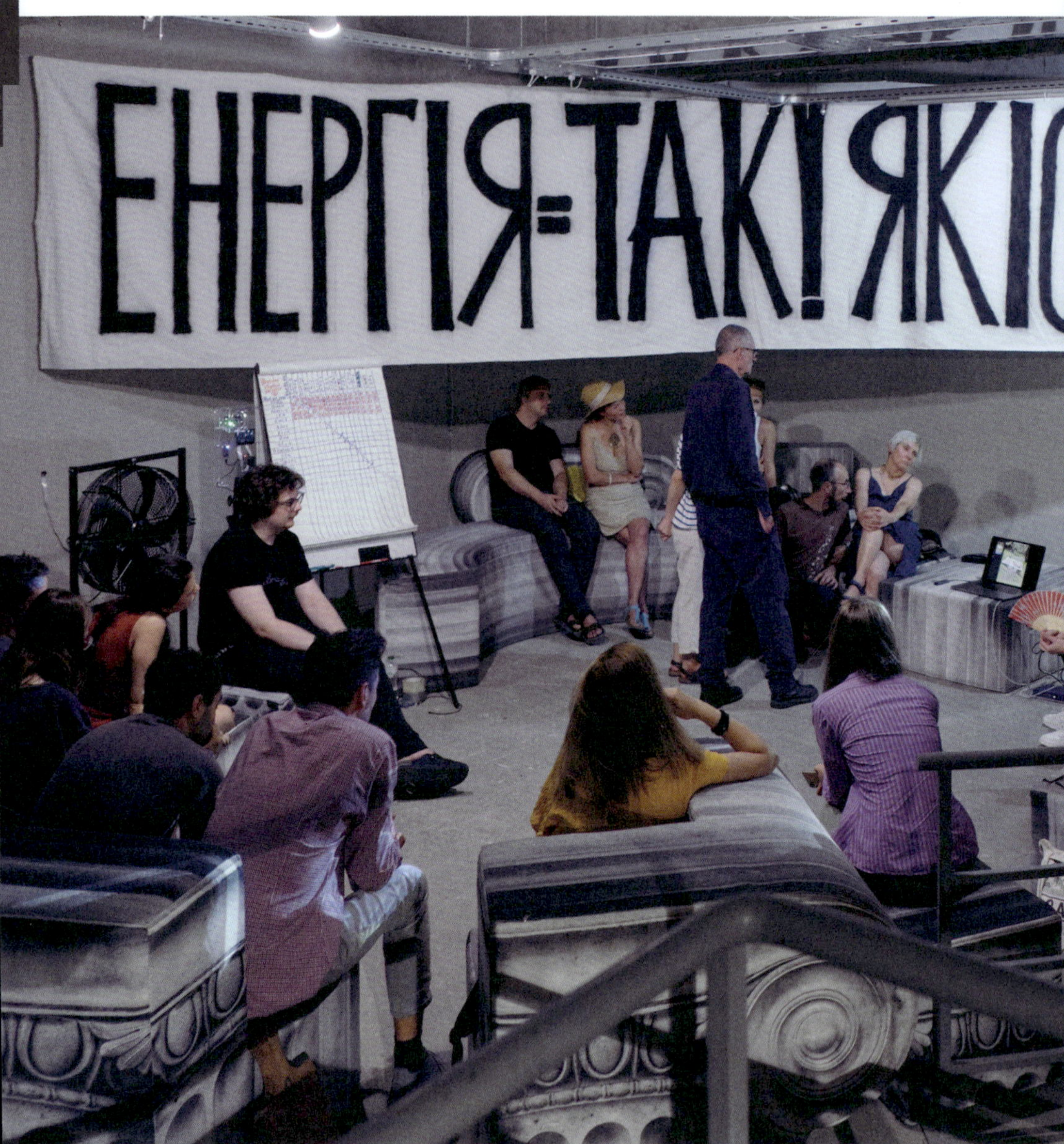

Thomas Hirschhorn contributed to the exhibition with a series of workshops called *Energy=Yes! Quality=No!*, which prioritize the principle of energy rather than exclusive criteria of quality: "Energy is what counts, energy is what I can grasp, energy is what I can share, and energy is what is universal. Energy: Yes! is a statement for movement, for the dynamic, for invention, for activity, for the activity of thinking," asserts the artist.

This concept resonates with Kharkiv, a city known for pioneering the splitting of the lithium atom. Just as splitting an atomic nucleus releases energy, the workshops release energy through the exchange of ideas and discussions; yet this scientific invention has had ambivalent consequences. The workshop's material component is a banner with the slogan *Energy=Yes! Quality=No!* that resonates throughout the entire exhibition. Kharkiv, and especially the YermilovCentre, is a gathering place and focal point that generates a unique energy, which might help resist terror and fuel hope.

The concept of the *Sense of Safety* exhibition emerged from the YermilovCentre serving as a shelter, echoing a theme Hirschhorn has been exploring since the first Gulf War in 1990–1991, by considering the role and necessity of art in times of military conflicts. This idea evolved into his long-term project *ART=SHELTER* (Dubulti Art Station, Jurmala, Latvia, 2022). In Hirschhorn's words, "Art generates a dialogue beyond all borders and all disparities." Art as a shelter brings hope for a new life. Hence, the whole exhibition functions as a shelter of hope, fostering dialogue and encouraging reflection on alternative modalities of living.

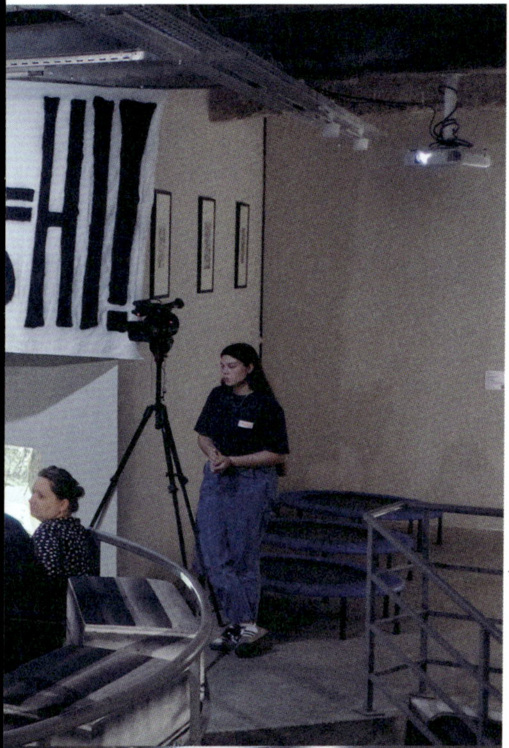

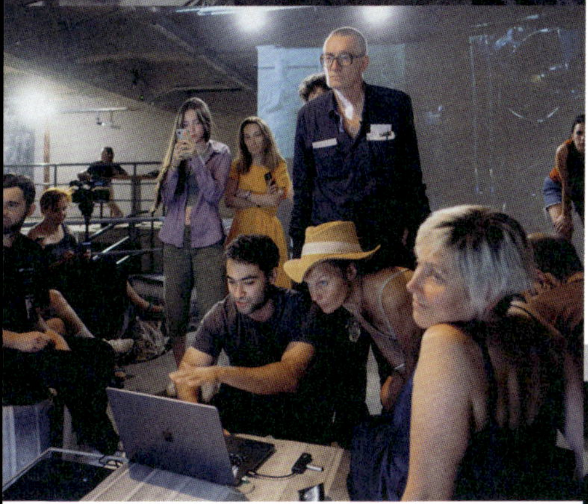

Thomas Hirschhorn during the critical workshop "Energy = Yes! Quality = No!," YermilovCentre, 2024. Photo: Andrei Stseburaka.

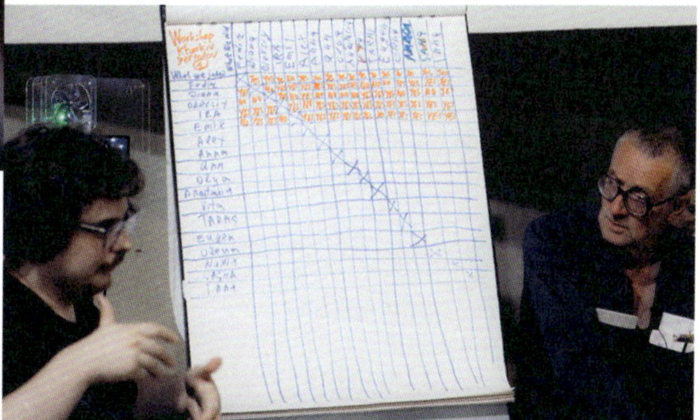

Thomas Hirschhorn's presence in Kharkiv was also a gesture of support for the Ukrainian art community, which made artistic dialogue possible even in wartime. "For me it was clear, and also a commitment to come and to share my work with other artists here and abroad. A short stay in Kharkiv is also an experience that, for sure, I will not forget," Hirschhorn noted. During his lecture, the artist spoke about his practice of working with diverse image sources—from video games and collages to photographs of real destruction—and about forming a unified visual language at the intersection of media. The theme of transitioning between analog and digital space resonated with the project's own format, which combined online and offline events, bridging audiences and geographies.

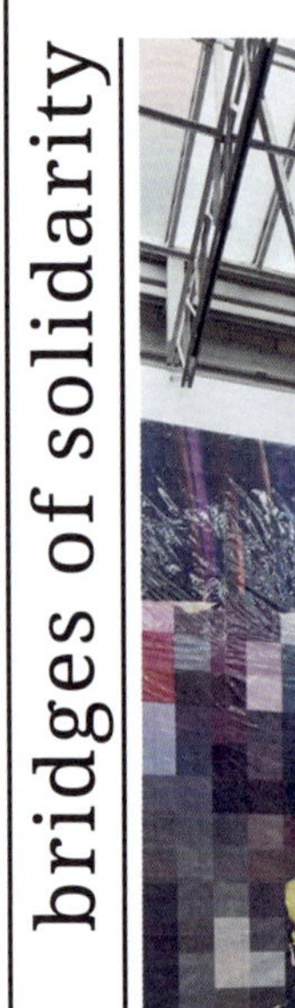

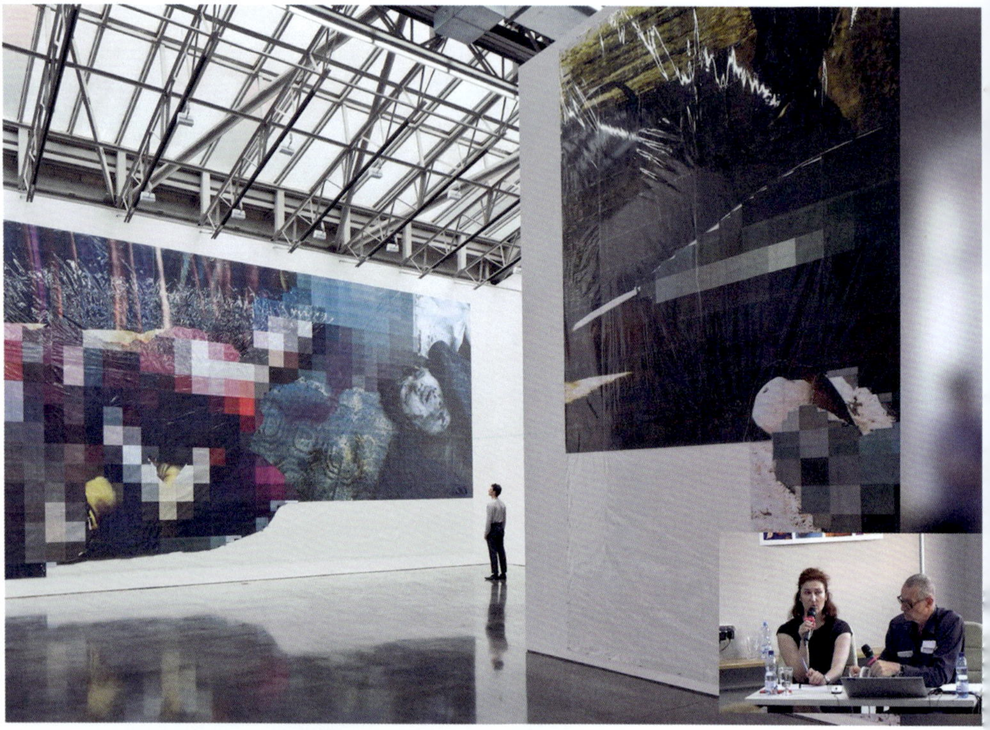

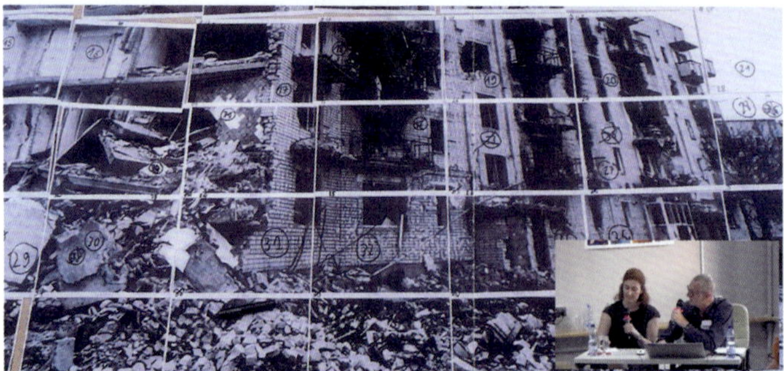

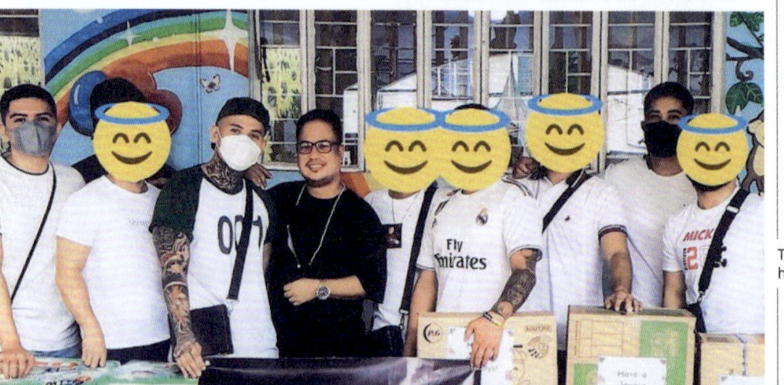

How can the analog exhibition space be combined with the digital world?

Lecture

YermilovCentre, Kharkiv (UA)

Date
30.08.2024

Speaker
Thomas Hirschhorn (CH/FR)

Thomas Hirschhorn during a lecture presenting his work, 2024. Livestream screenshots.

Sergey Bratkov and Eleonora Frolov held a two-day seminar in the Charkiw-Park in Berlin. The park got its name in October 2022 as a gesture of solidarity with the residents of Kharkiv enduring the consequences of Russian aggression, as well as to honor the memory of the victims of the war and support Ukrainian refugees. The seminar participants were displaced people from Ukraine. The outcome of the workshop was their personal creative expressions, presented in the form of video greetings and integrated into the exhibition *Sense of Safety*. Sergey Bratkov, originally from Kharkiv and now living in Berlin, aimed through this event to draw the attention of the European community to the events in Ukraine, support those forced to seek refuge abroad, and simultaneously demonstrate solidarity with those who remain in Kharkiv.

Anna Zviahintseva, *Not Here*, 2024. Documentation of the performance created during the seminar. Photo: Sergey Bratkov.

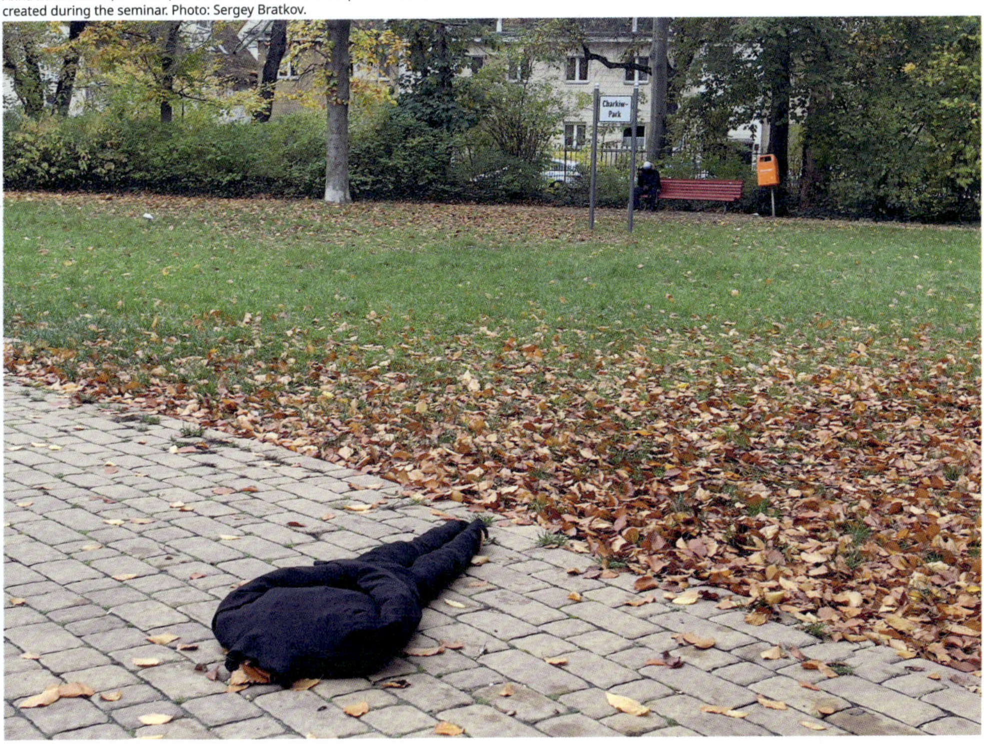

Collage in contemporary art

Live broadcast of greetings from the two-day seminar by Sergey Bratkov and Eleonora Frolov

Charkiw-Park, Berlin, DE
YermilovCentre, Kharkiv, UA

Date
9–10.10.2024

Participants
Sergey Bratkov (UA)
Eleonora Frolov (DE)

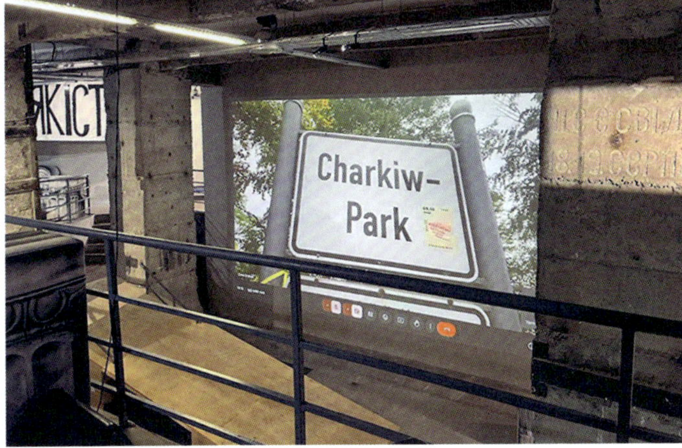

Two-day seminar by Sergey Bratkov and Eleonora Frolov transmitted live from Charkiw-Park in Berlin to the YermilovCentre in Kharkiv, 2024.
Photo: Yelyzaveta Koval.

Sergey Bratkov

born 1960 in Kharkiv, Ukraine; based in Berlin, Germany

Aubergines

2009
VIDEO, 0'43"
COURTESY OF THE ARTIST

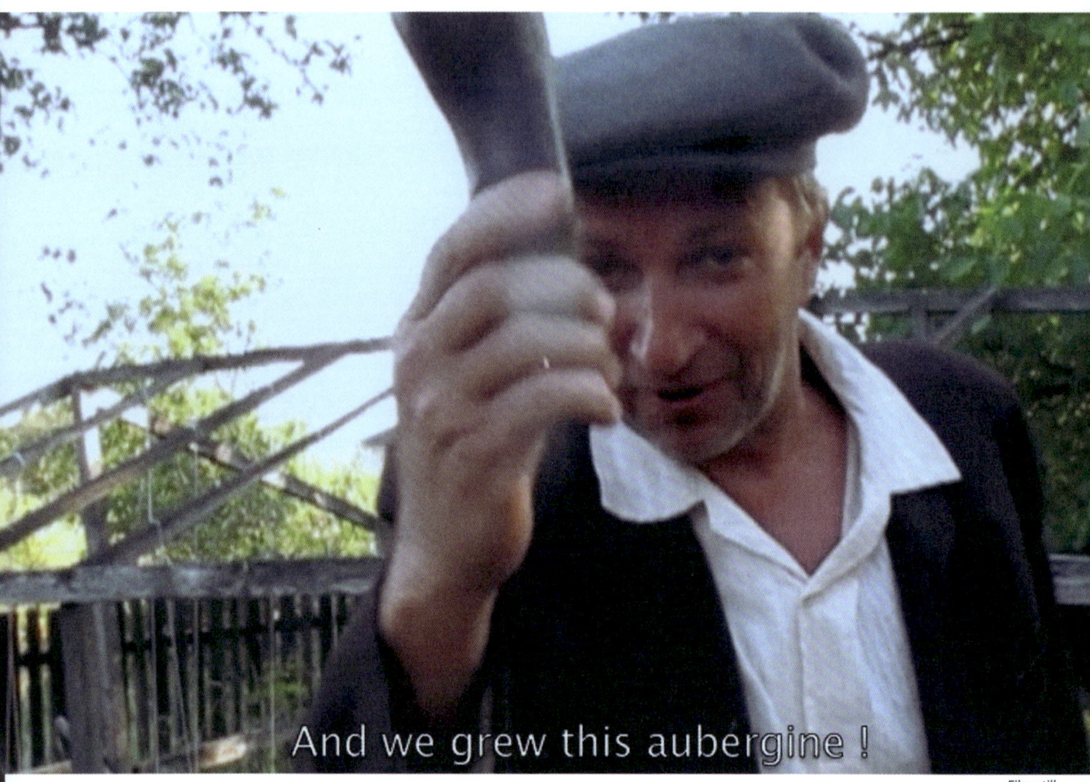

Film still

The humor and self-irony of Sergey Bratkov's videos play an essential part in his multidisciplinary artistic practice. Often co-developed with his brother, the architect Yuri Bratkov, most of these videos feature the artists as scriptwriters, performers, and directors, and were made in the city of Pivdenne in the Kharkiv region. In the self-ironic, grotesque *Aubergines* filmed there in 2009, Bratkov draws on Ilya Repin's painting *Zaporozhian Cossacks are Writing a Letter to the Turkish Sultan* (1880–1891) and highlights humor as a fundamental human value that becomes all the more needed in times of crisis. Laughter, a key element in Repin's painting, allows us to make a bold political gesture of finding our identity, embodying the power of spirit and freedom. Ostensibly following this tradition, Bratkov uses irony as an opportunity to take a ruthlessly honest look at ourselves. Today, this laughter helps us overcome tragic and seemingly hopeless moments in our lives. It becomes an essential tool for finding at least a temporary sense of safety, allowing us to observe things from a certain distance and opening up new perspectives on the neighborhood.

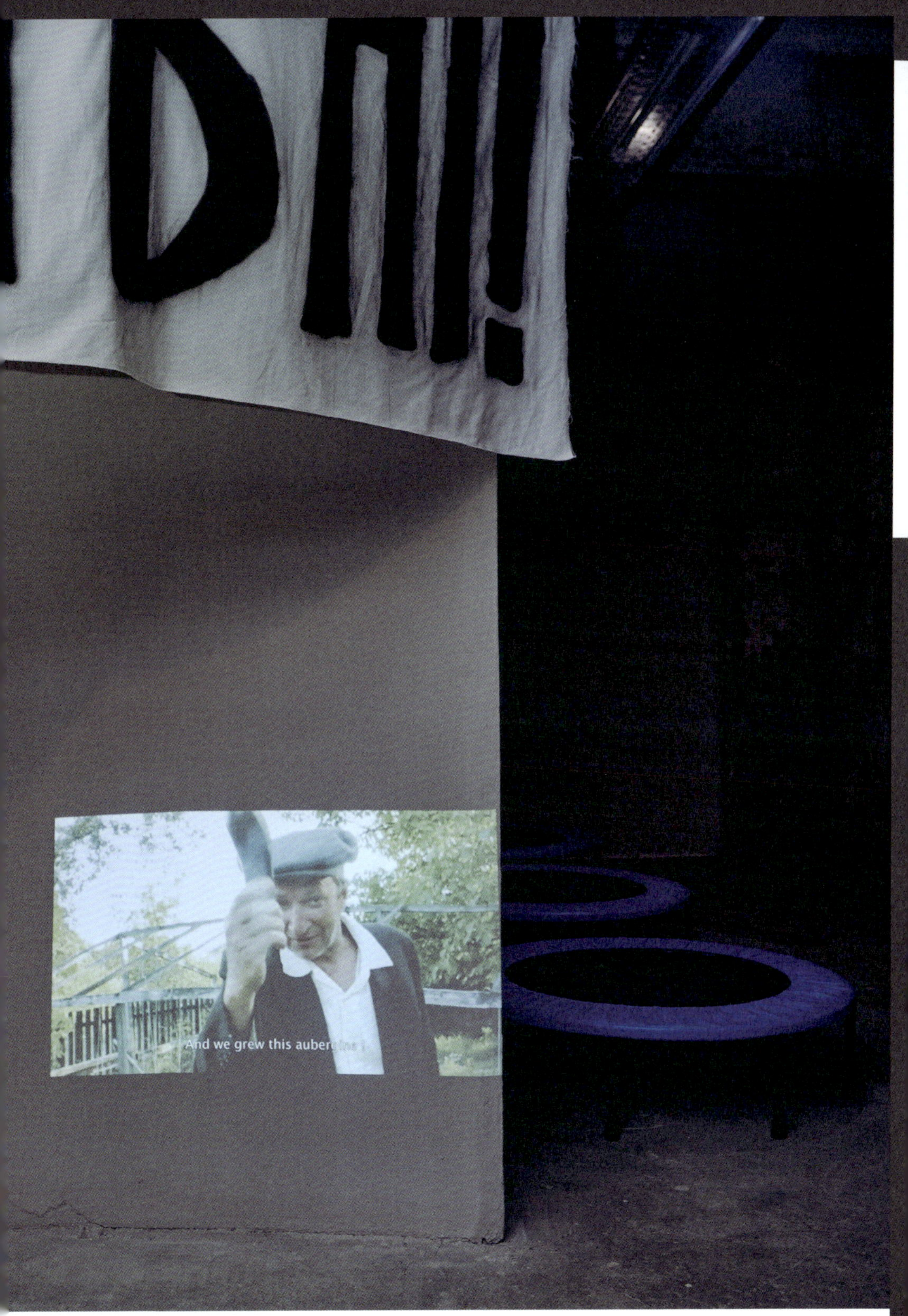
And we grew this auber

Ahmet Öğüt

born 1981 in Diyarbakır, Turkey; based between Amsterdam, Netherlands and Istanbul

2022 — ONGOING
INSTALLATION

2024
EXACT REPLICAS OF ARTWORKS BY:
ALLA HORSKA *THE BRIDE*, 1964, GOUACHE ON CARDBOARD
(FROM THE GRYNYOV ART COLLECTION)
ZOIA LERMAN *FATHERHOOD*, 1966, OIL ON CARDBOARD
(FROM THE GRYNYOV ART COLLECTION)
SERHIY ZHADAN *RED FIRA: FIVE YEARS FROM THE DATE OF FERTILIZATION*, 1996,
COLLAGE (FROM THE KHARKIV LITERATURE MUSEUM)
PRODUCED ESPECIALLY FOR THE EXHIBITION *SENSE OF SAFETY*

Jump Up!

Safe Return of the Evacuated

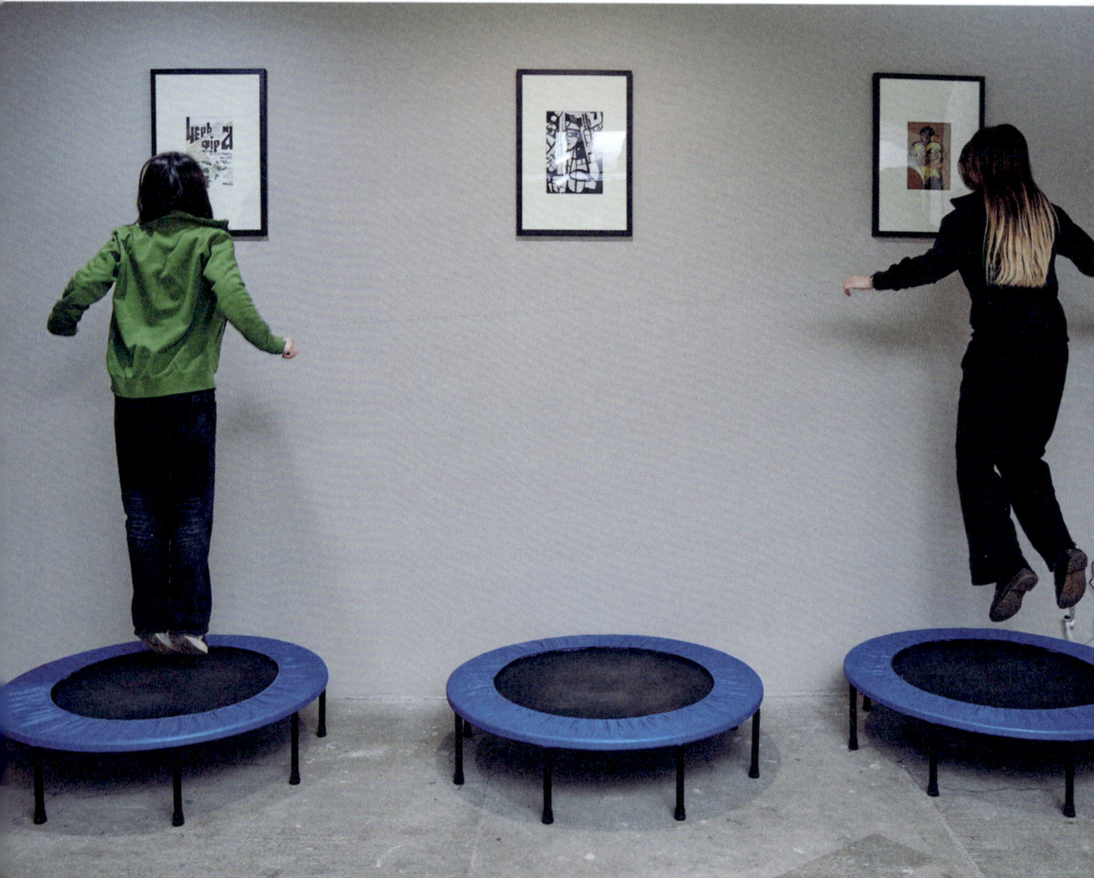

Born to a Kurdish family in the Turkish city of Diyarbakır, which was then ravaged by the civil war, artist Ahmet Öğüt's approach focuses on rethinking art as a tool to create change in oppressive situations. He thinks of art as a political and social situation rather than as an object, shifting his gaze away from Western European hegemony. His works *Jump Up!* and *Safe Return of the Evacuated* continue to reimagine the possibilities of art as a socio-political practice.

The installation *Jump Up!* presents three trampolines that the visitor can jump on in order to glimpse selected artworks. The act of jumping on the trampolines itself emerges as ambivalent: on the one hand, it refers to a childhood experience full of joy, while on the other hand, it literally deprives the viewer of the stable ground under their feet. This impossibility of fixing the act of gazing at a single point is also connected to anxiety, instability, and fragility.

This installation was first realized at the Museum of Contemporary Art Skopje. In 1963, Skopje was hit by an earthquake, and many artists from different parts of the world donated their works as a sign of solidarity. This formed the core of the collection of the Museum of Contemporary Art in Skopje. Ahmet Öğüt's installation *Jump Up!* in Kharkiv bridges the different geographical locations affected by devastating events—the earthquake in Skopje and Russia's full-scale invasion of Ukraine and constant shelling of Kharkiv. The artist creates a profound gesture of solidarity, deeply rooted in the history of contemporary art's response to war and catastrophe, linking contexts in North Macedonia, Bosnia, Palestine, Chile, Ukraine, and elsewhere, once again emphasizing our interdependence and mutual connectedness.

As a gesture of care and solidarity, Ahmet Öğüt's *Safe Return of the Evacuated* presents exact copies of three pieces created by significant Ukrainian artists and public figures—Alla Horska, Zoia Lerman, Serhiy Zhadan—whose political and artistic positions were inextricably linked. The practice of these artists is important for rethinking the history of art, overcoming the centrality of Western Europe, and reinterpreting what a work of art is and can be. For instance, Alla Horska was a central figure in the Ukrainian human rights movement of the 1960s, and Serhiy Zhadan has been a prominent poet and political figure since the 2004 Orange Revolution. He was also one of the organizers of the first big events since the onset of Russia's invasion—a rock concert held in the YermilovCentre that started the revival of public cultural events in the city.

This simple gesture of creating copies of the artworks is particularly important given that most of the art collections have been evacuated from Kharkiv. This act weaves together the sorrow that collections can be evacuated but people cannot, and the concern that these works are not available for public viewing by the people of Kharkiv. Art is much more than a decorative element; it can be the glue of collectivity, emphasized by the fact that Ahmet Öğüt's replicas of these three works will remain at the YermilovCentre until the war is over and the original pieces return home.

Alona Karavai

Happy to Death

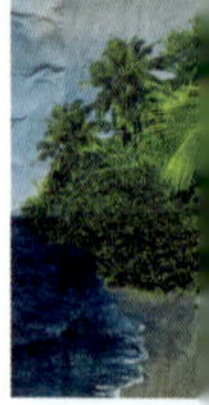

>>> Karina Synytsia p. 38

A Ukrainian woman, an Italian woman, a German man, and a French man board a Ukrainian Railways train.
"Where are you traveling to?" asks the conductor.
"To Kharkiv," they reply somewhat tensely.
"Oh, don't be so worried, everything will be okay, you will survive."

The Ukrainian woman takes out her phone to show a meme she saved the day before. It shows Jesus holding a small dinosaur in his arms, as if it were a human baby. "Don't be scared to death. It's gonna be okay," says Jesus. "Or not," replies the baby dinosaur. Another awkward pause hangs in the air, then everyone laughs nervously.

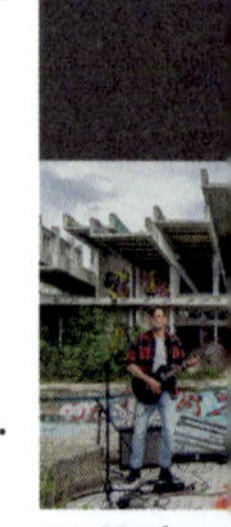

>>> Mark Požlep p. 39

It is late September 2024, and it is hot in Kharkiv—typically hot for the east of Ukraine, unusually hot for some of our guests. Standing on the platform, I take a deep breath. Here, I am close to home, so the air feels familiar—hot, humid, with a hint of machine oil and wormwood. I am embraced by nostalgia and a sense of safety, and in the very next moment I find myself instinctively checking my phone: any alerts? My foreign colleagues have also stepped out of the train and are also busy with their phones—studying the Deep State map and messaging their close ones.

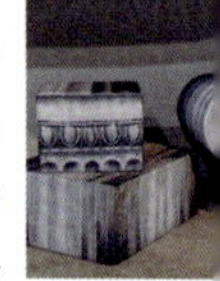

>>> Andreas Angelida p. 42

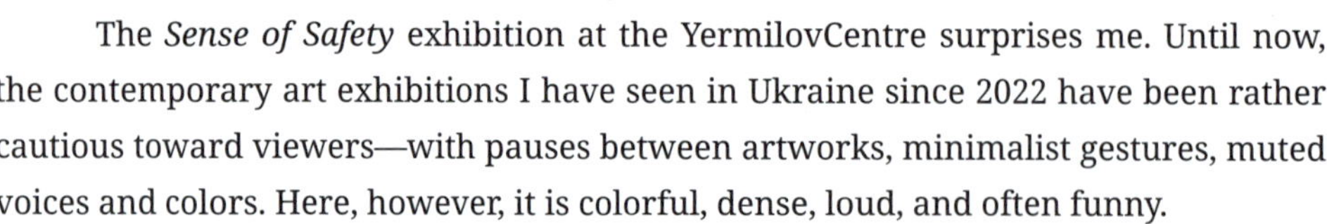

The *Sense of Safety* exhibition at the YermilovCentre surprises me. Until now, the contemporary art exhibitions I have seen in Ukraine since 2022 have been rather cautious toward viewers—with pauses between artworks, minimalist gestures, muted voices and colors. Here, however, it is colorful, dense, loud, and often funny.

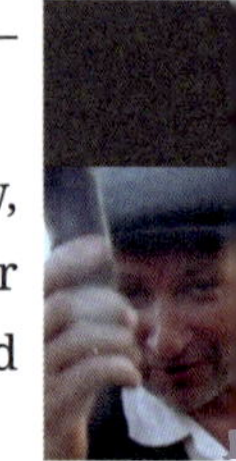

>>> Sergey Bratkov p. 76

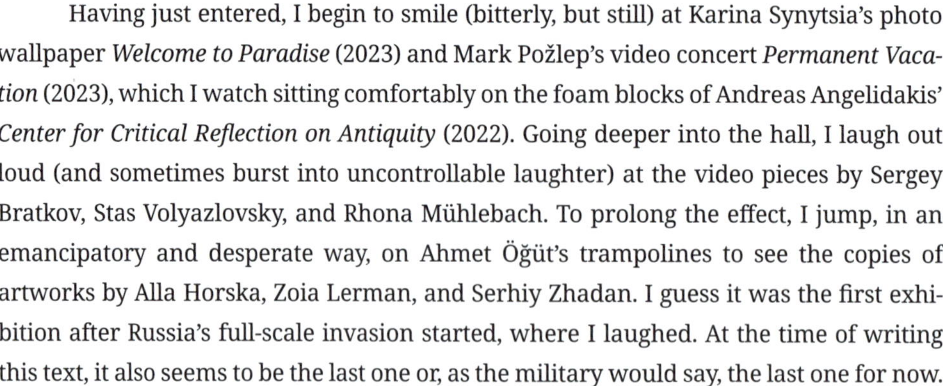

Having just entered, I begin to smile (bitterly, but still) at Karina Synytsia's photo wallpaper *Welcome to Paradise* (2023) and Mark Požlep's video concert *Permanent Vacation* (2023), which I watch sitting comfortably on the foam blocks of Andreas Angelidakis' *Center for Critical Reflection on Antiquity* (2022). Going deeper into the hall, I laugh out loud (and sometimes burst into uncontrollable laughter) at the video pieces by Sergey Bratkov, Stas Volyazlovsky, and Rhona Mühlebach. To prolong the effect, I jump, in an emancipatory and desperate way, on Ahmet Öğüt's trampolines to see the copies of artworks by Alla Horska, Zoia Lerman, and Serhiy Zhadan. I guess it was the first exhibition after Russia's full-scale invasion started, where I laughed. At the time of writing this text, it also seems to be the last one or, as the military would say, the last one for now.

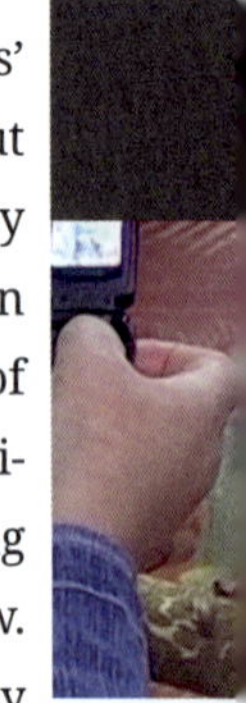

>>> Stas Volyazlo & Max A p. 135

"What an attraction." I share my impressions with my companions, deliberately ignoring the lowest floor of the exhibition, where Katya Lesiv invites us into a claustrophobic space under the stairs for her *Lullaby 5* (2024). The curatorial team deliberately designed the exhibition as an open system where viewers can chart their own routes through different force fields—thematic blocks that form a comprehensive idea of safety. It turns out that (my) sense of safety is formed by a force field of vitality and (dark) humor. It turns out that the best protection (for me) is a dense dome of giggles, cackles, the vibration of trampoline springs, and the shuffling of diary pages. In the latter, which is a participatory project by Kateryna Yermolayeva inviting viewers to share their stories of living during Russia's full-scale invasion, I find, among other things, eight anecdotes and a quote from a poem by Ukrainian diplomat, translator, and poet Yurko Pozaiak:

"No greater joy can you think about
When free from complexes and stress,
Right next to you, jumping around,
There's your pretty friend with a sexy ass!"

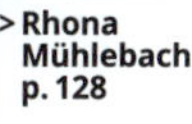

>> Rhona Mühlebach p. 128

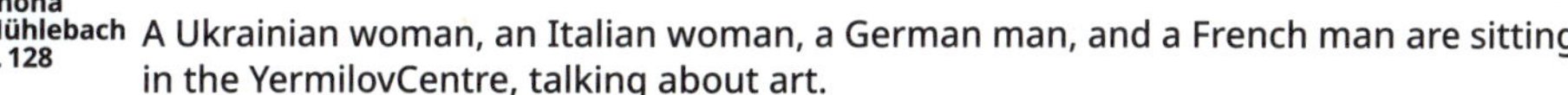

A Ukrainian woman, an Italian woman, a German man, and a French man are sitting in the YermilovCentre, talking about art.
"For me, exhibitions are a safe space for conversation," says the Italian woman.
"Oh, well, it's a basement after all, and the walls are made of concrete. So it's safe," says the Ukrainian woman.

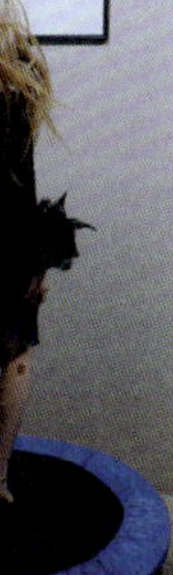

In the early 2000s, I traveled a lot to participate in student exchange programs. I remember almost always finding myself in Balkan groups at various international gatherings. I was attracted to their humor as if by a magnet; it was the most merciless and most understandable to me because it didn't come from abundance but scarcity. My occasional friends from Bosnia and Croatia—I have kept in touch with some of them all these years, while others appeared in my life again after 2022—became my icons of everyday stand-up comedy. For a long time, I couldn't understand how it was possible to communicate as if it were an endless joke. Now I seem to have a better understanding of the nature of this humor and have even learned to do the same.

>>> Ahmet Öğüt p. 78

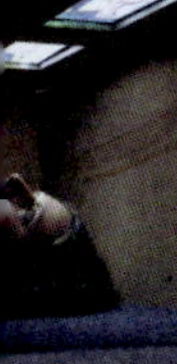

To be honest, humanity knows a lot about the way we use humor. Sigmund Freud, whose father was born in Tysmenytsia and whose mother comes from Brody, discussed the similarities between the macabre and the comical, and also considered humor to be a means of releasing accumulated affect, allowing one to cope with experiences at a "lower cost" than would be possible through suffering. However, despite the substantial volume of anthropological research on humor, laughter, and jokes,[1] the vast majority of studies focus on humor that arises in situations of relative safety. Instead, very little is known about the characteristics of joking during war or other threatening situations. One thing is to mock the outside world, taking an archetypal (and almost always male) position of a lone trickster or clown. Another is to laugh about your own death, standing (or falling) side by side with people like you. These seem to be two very different kinds of laughter, even though they sound similar.

>>> Katya Lesiv p. 132

Based on "peacetime" knowledge, we can assume that the ability to joke during wartime is a way to normalize oneself in an abnormal reality, one of the (rather) ecological coping mechanisms and a sign (rather, or who knows) of a healthy psyche. Here, several mechanisms are activated at once—humor allows one to reduce psychological tension, overcome stress for a short time, and in some cases improve one's mood. Laughing together strengthens social bonds within the community: it is both about the commonality of a cultural code and practicing something unifying together—a mechanism similar to when we eat or dance together. Furthermore, by changing the context through humor, we create distance from the traumatic experience, "freeze" the situation, and thus postpone dealing with the trauma until later—with all the advantages and risks of such a state of postponement

A meme from social media that can be added to various images:
[Top of image] When you're performing a stand-up comedy about the most traumatic event in your life, but your therapist isn't laughing and writes something down in his notebook.
[Bottom of image] He's stealing your jokes.

With the start of Russia's full-scale invasion of Ukraine in 2022, humor became one of the few collective practices that reunited the diverse Ukrainian society and its various communities, which usually do not act in solidarity. More specifically, memes became one such collective creative practice. According to Richard Dawkins, "memes" are units of cultural information comparable to "genes," in that they spread from one person to another.[2] Internet memes, in turn, are defined as humorous pieces of information in the form of text, image, or video that spread quickly online due to their clarity and relevance. Any significant political event—attempts at peace talks mediated by Donald Trump,[3] anti-corruption protests in Ukraine,[4] or Russia's regular threats to use nuclear weapons of mass destruction—triggers a huge outburst of collective creativity in the form of a wave of memes, and the memeification of political life in Ukraine has reached such a scale that every news program—whether television, text, or online—has a dedicated section collecting the most popular memes as reactions to a particular event on social media.

One could joke that in a country with a professional comedian as president, it is hard to imagine any other form of political dialogue during wartime. But, returning to the aforementioned point, I would like to see (more) anthropological comparative studies of how humor functions outside and during times of existential threat to understand the nuances. Because generalizing and speculating—both during wartime and through humor—is too easy. One of the few articles I was lucky enough to find in the library of Humboldt University Berlin was about the anthropology of humor in the island nation of Fiji during the 2000 coup d'état and seizure of parliament, which was followed by six months of violence and chaos. Susanna Trnka, an anthropologist from

New Zealand, describes how a local community, which at other times would be considered rather humorless, burst into a wave of jokes—including sarcastic and racist ones, as well as jokes about violence.[5] Among other things, Trnka draws our attention to the so-called "gallows humor" or "black humor" about extremely serious, tragic, and life-threatening situations such as death, war, illness, and crime. Such humor may be an attempt to "defeat" death or achieve a sense of control over danger because a taboo subject and the negative tension that comes with it are safely released in an alternative way. According to Freud, dreams and jokes are alike in this respect—with the key exception that, to be "activated," a joke must be told to at least one other person.

Memes about nuclear attacks and nuclear apocalypse, morning jokes about death after another (all-)night combined drone and ballistic attack, black humor "just for us" in communities of people with amputations—these widespread types of humor in Ukraine are intended for internal use only and are constantly evolving. It seems that within communities humor is becoming darker and darker, and the boundaries of what is an acceptable joke are increasingly expanding. Any kind of humor is acceptable if you share it with the right people—that is, those with similar experiences.

French journalists and the President of Ukraine are talking. "You used to make people laugh. Do you think you will ever be able to do that again?" a foreign journalist asks the President. [Pause] "It depends on what kind of person I remain inside. I don't know," the President tries to smile.[6]

In Kateryna Yermolayeva's *Collective Diary*, I count eight anecdotes and thirty-seven eggplants. The artist invited the audience to capture their own experiences in the diary, and it is all filled—all 167 pages, including the cover and loose bits of paper on other people's pages. There are many personal stories, many unspoken and painful ones, but there are also anecdotes, none of which can be published in this text, and drawings of eggplants, all of which are dedicated to an eponymous artwork by Sergey Bratkov. Fortunately, anyone can draw an eggplant; it is a very democratic image.

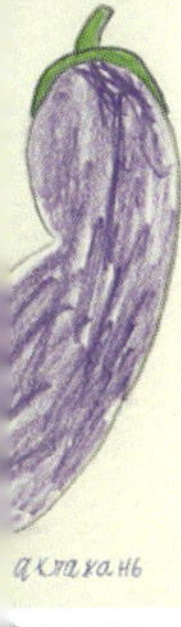

Kateryna Yermolayeva p. 53

Sergey Bratkov's multifaceted art practice generally includes many funny and (self-)mocking videos—he is a postmodern artist after all. The grotesque video *Eggplants* was filmed in the town of Pivdenne in the Kharkiv Oblast with a dedication to Ilya Repin's painting *Cossacks are Writing a Letter to the Turkish Sultan.* In Repin's painting, Cossacks mock the demand of the Ottoman Sultan Mehmed IV to write him a letter of surrender. This historical event took place in 1676, and the painting was created in 1880–1891. In Bratkov's video work, a simple plot involving two eggplants—a smaller one and a larger one—becomes an ironic invitation to mercilessly and honestly laugh at ourselves, and that artistic gesture took place in 2009. In 2024 in Kharkiv, the artwork takes on another layer of meanings—now the viewers laugh at the neighbor's demand to obey, at their sense of self in this stalemate, at the repetition of existential threats, and even at death. Judging by their feedback, this emancipatory act of "overcoming death through laughter" seems to be quite natural for the audience in Kharkiv, bringing them joy and satisfaction.

The Cossacks' letter can be considered one of the first Ukrainian memes, which has been transmitting a certain "unit of cultural information from one person to another" for several centuries now. But what is this unit of cultural information about? Disobedience? Masculine competition? A place of refuge? Collective humor as an act of disobedience?

I like anecdotes. But I'm scared. What if this all ends? And I might not be here anymore. (Entry in Kateryna Yermolayeva's *Collective Diary*, written in Russian)

As I stand in front of the video piece by Stas Volyazlovsky and Max Afanasyev, *In the Museum 2* (2011), I find myself smiling my weirdest smile.

I saw that artwork a few times before the war and remember what it was about and what emotions it was supposed to evoke—the awkwardness of the paradox it revealed, when the "mass" and the "high," the "Soviet" and the "capitalist," the living and the inanimate, the unfree and the once again unfree, caged animals and museum exhibits under strict conservation conditions are all under one roof. This is the kind of awkwardness that makes viewers feel sorry for the people in the video, who, in turn, feel no discomfort whatsoever. It is this multi-layered discrepancy, which gradually unfolds throughout the video, that creates the comic effect of the artwork—but even more so, the unexpected appearance of monkeys in the picture when you watch the video for the first time.

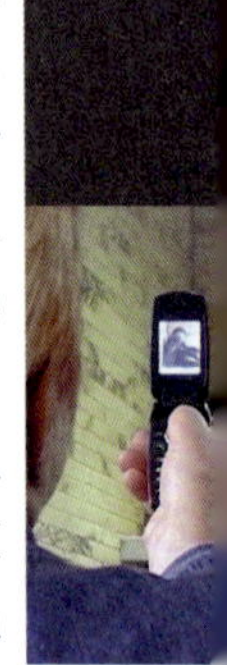

>>> Stas Volyazlo[…] & Max A[…] p. 135

I remember all this, and I remember how I should feel about it, but now, in September 2024, in Kharkiv, I see something completely different in this artwork. I see the unbombed city of Kherson and its undamaged museum, I see many children in the museum, I see Stas Volyazlovsky and Vyacheslav Mashnytsky[7] walking the city streets. I see museum exhibits that were stolen by the Russian army after the occupation of Kherson, which are now, perhaps, being kept in the occupied Crimea. I see a museum that could not cope with its task, neither fifteen years ago, nor during the war. I see monkeys, whose appearance creates a fresh comic effect, as if I were seeing them for the first time. I laugh, and it is a very weird laugh—confused and aware at the same time. Fortunately, humor is designed to integrate paradoxes into the structure of a joke. Fortunately, humor maintains the framework of this reality without simplifying it.

In her video *To Get In Touch With Crows* (2016), Swiss artist Rhona Mühlebach also addresses the issue of the relationship between humans and non-human life forms and, through an imaginary dialogue with a bird, undermines the anthropocentric approach to dialogue, which is structured in human language according to human rules. The video is made in the style of a popular documentary, in which a human narrator observes the lives of animals, but Rhona's piece reverses the perspective—the crows observe people in the park and notice much more (or something else) than we would like to see.

An Italian curator and a Ukrainian curator meet in a bar.
"The zoo is such a powerful image of how the European community views the Ukrainian context nowadays, observing both its suffering and resilience," says the Italian curator.
"We should create a critical curatorial project about this. Let's do it with the Kharkiv Zoo."
The Ukrainian curator drinks silently.

Humor arises in the lacunae within a cultural code, in the gaps between different codes, in the breaks between social norms, in the empty spaces. Humor requires analytical thinking and the observation of paradoxes; humor goes (or leads) beyond the boundaries of everyday life; humor undermines existing boundaries, as does art. In fact, this is why humor and art are so close—close in a similar way that jokes and dreams are. Similar, but not the same.

>> Rhona Mühlebach p. 128

"The epistemic power of humor is, at best, limited to a glimpse of possibility, while art forces and reinforces irreconcilability in an attempt to think differently in one's thinking or something other than thinking in another way of thinking. And while a joke is bold and disrespectful, art is uncompromising and rebellious," writes researcher Mira Fliescher in her book *The Joke of Art.*[8]

In her artwork *Welcome to Paradise* (2023), Karina Synytsia uses a method and visual style that are unusual for her. She paints photo wallpapers that would typically depict idyllic paradise landscapes for relaxation and recovery, which is reflected in the color palette chosen by the artist. However, the artist depicts landscapes of occupied Crimea with scorched earth and ruins. In one of these images, the sky is covered with black smoke, although it appears to be a summer day, judging by the light. Is it smoke rising after an attack by Ukrainian drones? Or is it just clouds gathering before a summer storm that starts fast but passes just as quickly? In this piece, the force field of humor manifests itself in a melancholic irony—the irony of fate, when everything is repeated. First as tragedy, then as farce, if we trust Georg Hegel.

A Ukrainian artist (male) and a Ukrainian artist (male) accidentally meet in Vienna.
"I'm not here."
"And I'm not here either."

It is late July 2025, and the weather in Berlin is cool and rainy—as it usually is in Berlin, where you should never come without a jacket, even in summer (I did not bring one with me again). I have already started writing this text and am on my way to the Berlin Biennale for Contemporary Art now. Its curatorial text refers to artworks as "wild acts of imagination" that are expressed either through fleeting and poetic fugitivity or through humor that "acts as an antidote, thus allowing to reclaim control over a situation." I find stand-up comedy in the basement and a trickster in the attic.

In the basement of Berlin's KW Institute for Contemporary Art, Bosnian artist and comedian Mila Panic has opened a stand-up comedy bar called Big Mouth, which will host six stand-up nights featuring various artists, including one from Russia, throughout the exhibition. The bar displays a series of neon signs by the artist—I read "Hahaha Haha Hahahaha" and "Game was to collect the set. Thanks to me my family is finally together," and "1989–1999" written in charcoal on the wall. I would like to see if I would laugh at this stand-up show, but no such luck.

In the attic, there is an installation by Sawangwongse Yawnghwe entitled *Joker's Headquarters. Gesamtkunstwerk as a Practical Joke* (2025). Sawangwongse was born in Burma—his grandfather was the country's first president, but after a military coup, the entire family was forced to flee. The artist appears as a trickster who explores political, financial, and military connections, "scans Berlin" from under the roof,[9] and communicates with viewers through diagrams on the walls. One of them is called "Forty countries with the highest military expenses in 2023," with Ukraine in eighth place, between Germany and France.

Standing outside, I breathe out slowly. This is my last day in Berlin; I'm going home tomorrow. Or rather, not my last day, but my last day here for now, as some caring people would have me say.

---

1. Mahadev L. Apte, Alexei Yurchak and Dominic Boyer, John Carty and Yasmine Musharbash, Mary Douglas, Alan Dundes, Ralph Piddington, Dr. Philip Irving Mitchell, Dan Rosengren, A. R. Radcliffe-Brown, Marjolein 't Hart, Laurence Goldstein, etc.

2. This definition dates back to 1976—that is, even before the emergence of internet culture and social media platforms such as Facebook and Instagram, where memes are widespread.

3. In August 2025, US President Donald Trump held direct peace talks with Russian President Vladimir Putin, thereby violating the global geopolitical compromise to isolate Putin as long as he wages a war of aggression against Ukraine. The meeting in Alaska did not result in any agreements.

4. In July 2025, a series of mass peaceful protests took place in various cities across Ukraine, opposing significant restrictions on the autonomy of the National Anti-Corruption Bureau. Many young people, known as Generation Z, joined the protests. Parliament subsequently repealed the controversial legislation.

5. Susanna Trnka, "Specters of Uncertainty: Violence, Humor, and the Uncanny in Indo-Fijian Communities Following the May 2000 Fiji Coup," *Ethos: Journal of the Society for Psychological Anthropology*, vol. 39, no. 3 (2011), pp. 331–348, https://www.susannatrnka.com/

6. Interview with Volodymyr Zelenskyy for *Le Parisien*, 18 December 2024, https://youtu.be/d0s0f-dHnck?si=NjSkdlQEvUS2x6FR [accessed 2 February 2026].

7. Ukrainian curator and artist who went missing in occupied Kherson in October 2022.

8. Mira Fliescher, *Der Witz der Kunst: Modelle ästhetischen Denkens* (Zurich: Diaphanes, 2019).

9. A quote from the curatorial text.

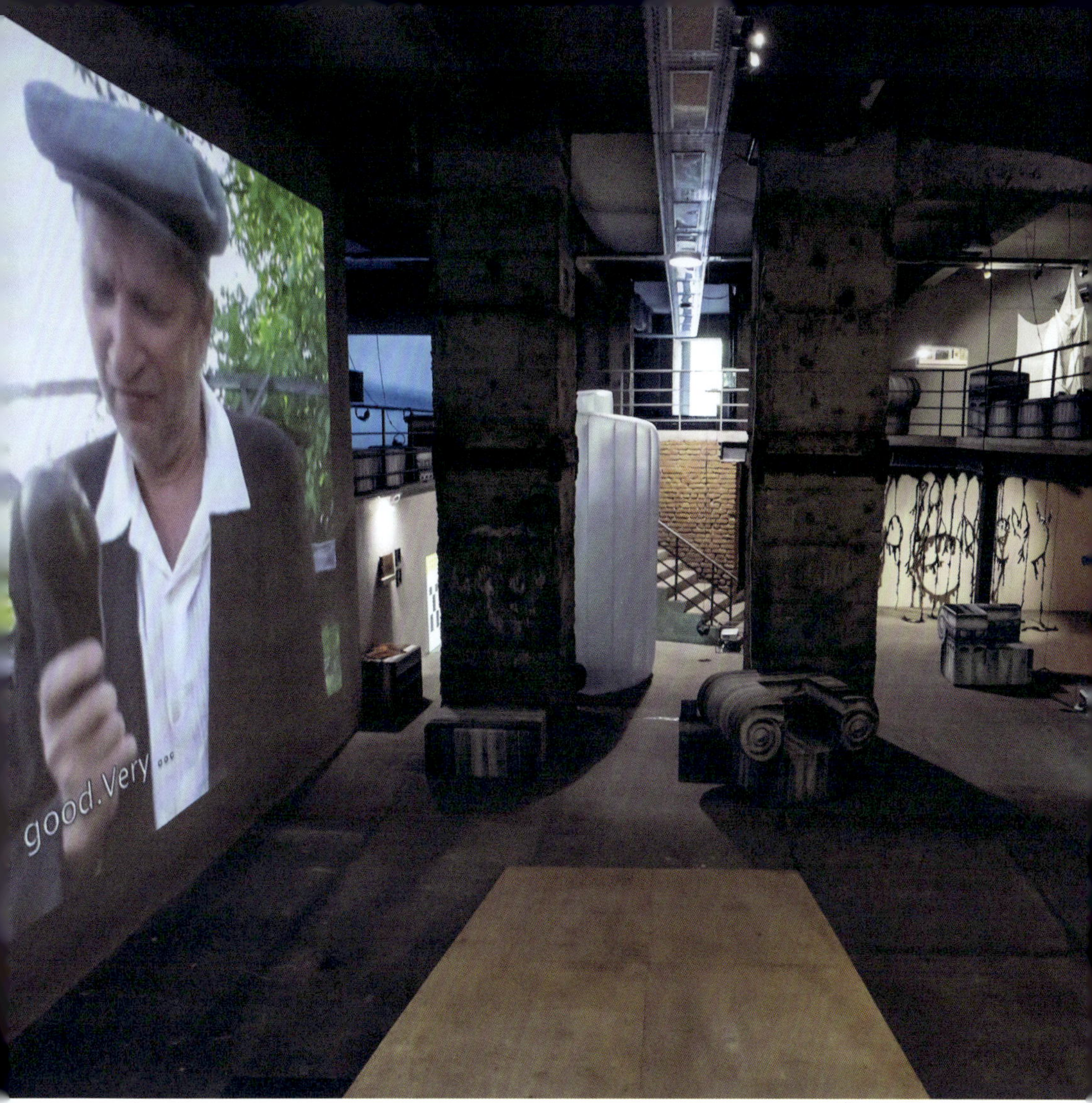

Sense of Safety, installation view at YermilovCentre.
Photo: Oleksandr Osipov.

Visitor inside the *Sense of Safety* exhibition at YermilovCentre, Kharkiv. Photo: Oleksandr Osipov. →

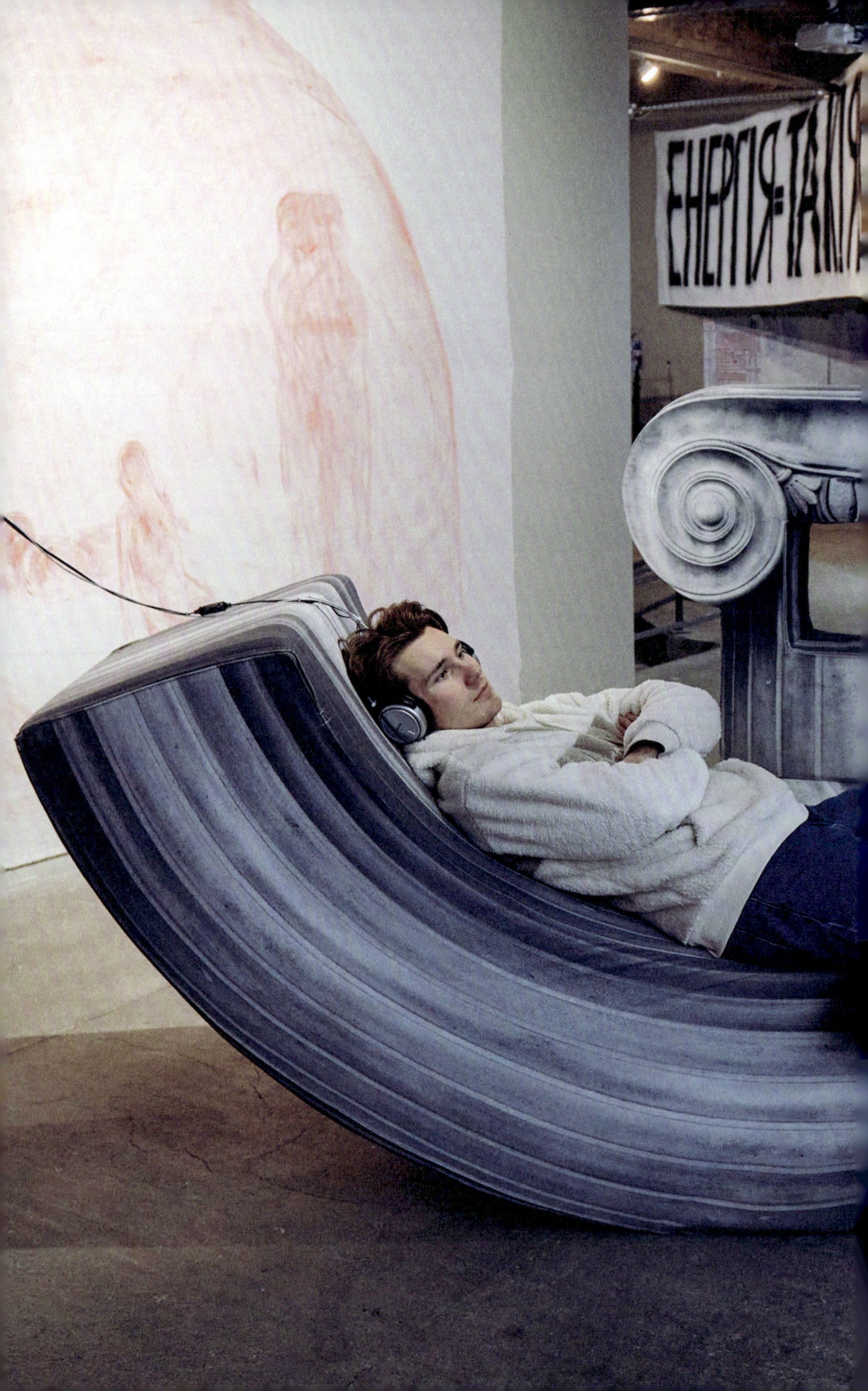
ЕНЕРГІЯ

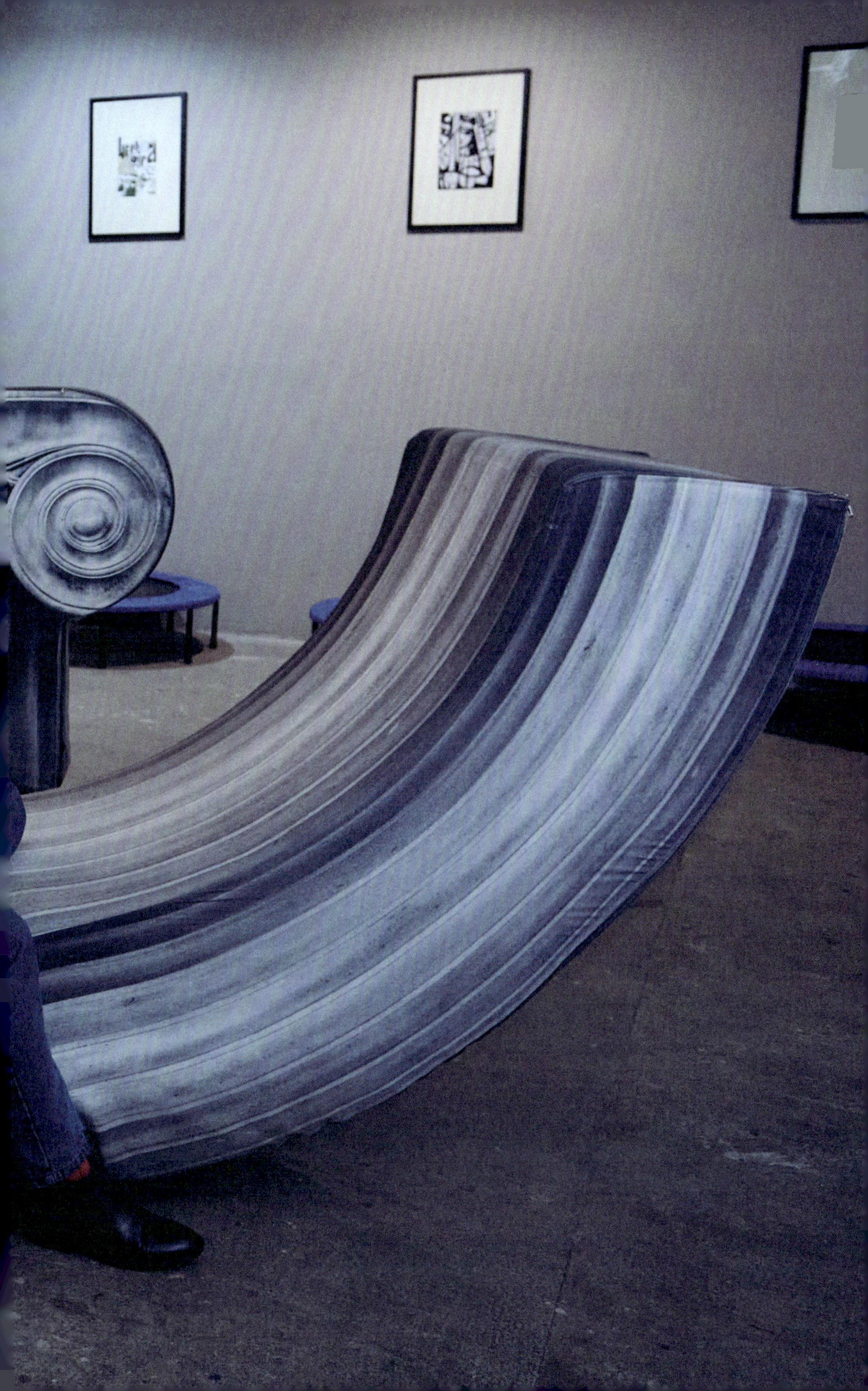

Kateryna Lysovenko

born 1989 in Kyiv, Ukraine; based in Vienna, Austria

The Body of the City

2024
FABRIC, ACRYLIC
PRODUCED ESPECIALLY FOR THE EXHIBITION *SENSE OF SAFETY*
DONATED TO THE YERMILOVCENTRE COLLECTION

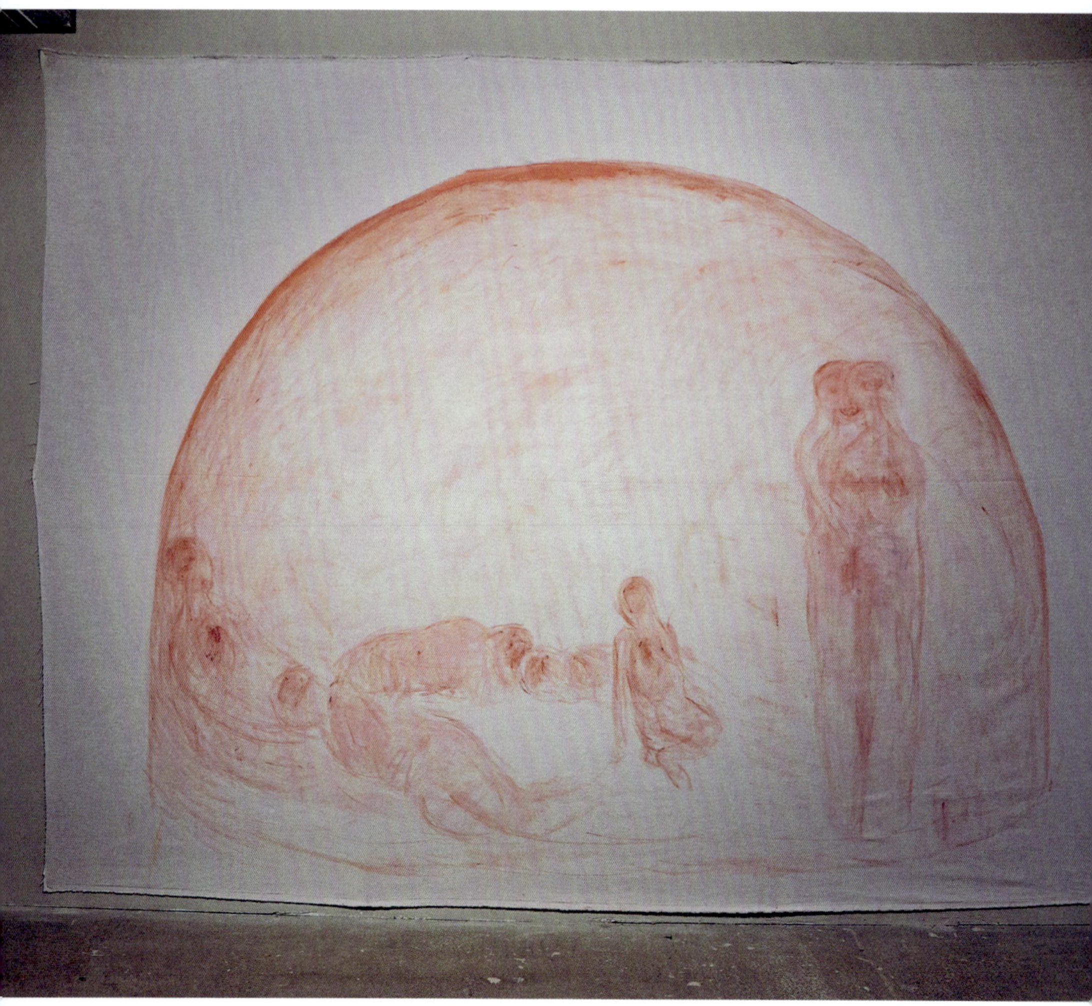

In her painting, Kateryna Lysovenko explores the possibilities of language—how to speak to and be heard by those who are numbed by pain and suffer constant traumatization, exclusion, and various forms of oppression. Her art usually depicts landscapes of bleeding and wounded mythical creatures in various situations—their births and deaths fused into a complex tangle of interdependencies. Her practice creates a space to speak with fragile, vulnerable beings whose existence is often instrumentalized and dehumanized. Kateryna Lysovenko's artistic practice can be described as a praxis of caring, creating a safe but fragile space to represent those whose voices are not heard.

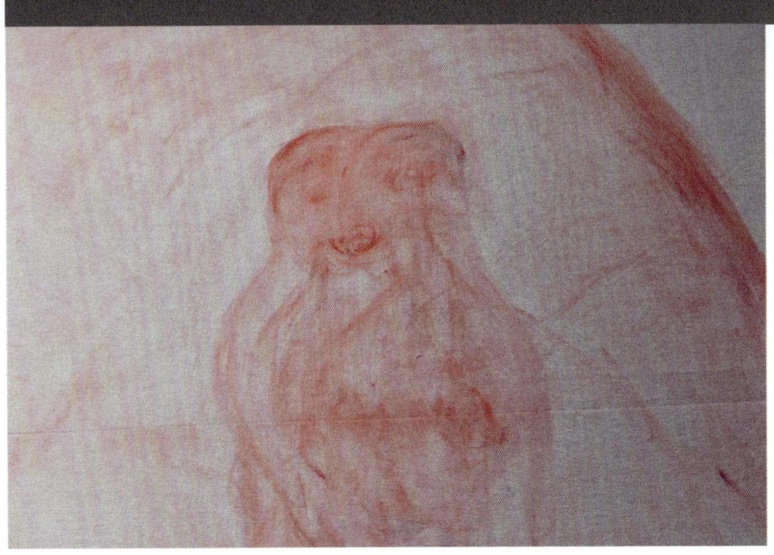

Unlike her previous works, *The Body of the City* does not depict mystical creatures and centers on humans instead. Their bodies are transparent, loosely outlined, but not elaborated in detail. They emerge from the canvas like ancient frescoes or cave paintings. Through this transparency, the artist emphasizes the vitality and fragility of human existence, as well as the permeable, disquieting boundary between human and non-human agents.

Lysovenko's practice is deeply nourished by feminist aesthetics, which has consistently questioned the hierarchical relationship between subject and object as well as the possibility of establishing this boundary. Reflecting on her experience of being in Kyiv during the war and the bombings, the artist stresses the disproportionality of weapons to the human body. In a context where weapons threaten to destroy individual human beings as well as the entire city, the human body and the body of the city merge. The urban area can be grasped as a juxtaposition of human and non-human bodies.

The dome that covers this iconographic group of people highlights the ambivalence of safety: on the one hand, it refers to a pregnant mother's womb; on the other hand, this thin, anxious red line is fragile and unsettling. It requires continuous care and constantly risks disappearing.

Lauren Lee McCarthy

Someone

born 1987 in Boston, USA; based in Los Angeles

2019
4-CHANNEL VIDEO, 44′
COURTESY OF THE ARTIST

SOFTWARE AND HARDWARE DEVELOPMENT: HARVEY MOON AND JOSH BILLIONS
INTERFACE DEVELOPMENT: LAUREN LEE MCCARTHY
FURNITURE DESIGN: LELA BARCLAY DE TOLLY
SMART HOME PARTICIPANT COLLABORATORS INCLUDE VALERIA HAEDO, ADELLE LIN, AMANDA McDONALD CROWLEY, AND KSENYA SAMARSKAYA.

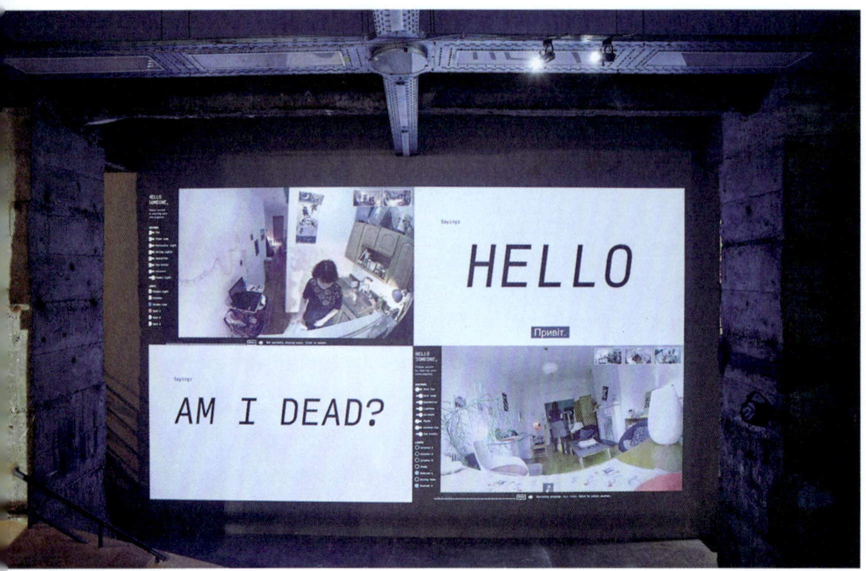

Lauren McCarthy's art installation *SOMEONE* critically explores the implications of home automation and pervasive surveillance technologies for our lives. In 2019, the artist transformed the 205 Hudson Gallery in New York into a command center from which visitors could observe and interact with participants' homes across the United States, which had been outfitted with cameras, microphones, and networked appliances. This interactive experience invited participants to act as human smart home assistants responding to the residents' requests, thus reversing the roles typically played by devices like Amazon Alexa.

The video of the resulting interactions examines the boundaries of privacy and the intrusive nature of smart home technologies. By putting human operators in the driver's seat, it highlights the discomfort and ethical dilemmas posed by such technologies, which often go unquestioned in consumer culture. McCarthy's work draws attention to the increasing encroachment of corporate surveillance under the guise of convenience and connectedness, questioning the trade-offs between privacy and functionality in modern technological interactions.

In this way, the artist questions the ambivalence of security as well as how clear or blurred the boundaries between private and public spaces are. The piece juxtaposes the individual's domestic privacy with public exposure, offering a platform to reflect on how technology shapes our personal and social environments and safety.

Vitalii Kokhan

born 1987 in Sumy, Ukraine; based in Kyiv, Ukraine

2024
TEXT CARVED INTO CONCRETE, SITE-SPECIFIC
PRODUCED ESPECIALLY FOR THE EXHIBITION *SENSE OF SAFETY*
DONATED TO THE YERMILOVCENTRE COLLECTION

Landmark in Exact Place and Time

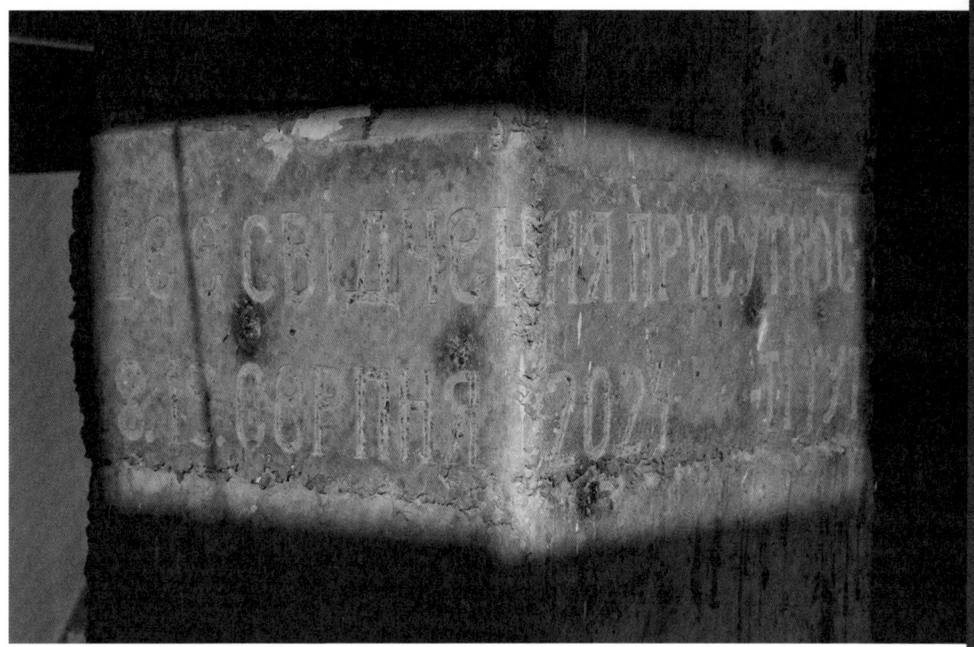

Vitalii Kokhan works across a variety of media while always paying special attention to the properties of his chosen material, whether it's glass, concrete, wood, sand, or even spider webs. The artist explores the potential of each of them, using their natural qualities to arrive at an artistic expression. Vitalii Kokhan's process is marked by quiet meditation and deliberate deceleration. The work created for this project continues his research into the materiality of memory. In the digital world, it is difficult to predict what Internet data will be preserved for our descendants in hundreds of years. History is always rewritten to suit the needs of the present, and the material artifacts of Ukrainian society are being destroyed by the enemy every day. In his work, Kokhan asks: What information is valuable enough to be left to posterity? What material can preserve and transmit information through the ages?

The artist emphasizes the value of the daily experience of life, which can be interrupted at any moment. In search of answers, he turns to the experiences of his ancestors. Like the inscriptions on the walls of St. Sophia Cathedral in Kyiv, the artist carves his messages on the concrete surfaces of the YermilovCentre. Perhaps in a thousand years, archaeologists will find this work and use it to study the history of the Russian-Ukrainian war.

The screening of the film *Dear Beautiful Beloved* (2024) by Juri Rechinsky and the discussion around it took place simultaneously at De Balie in Amsterdam and at YermilovCentre in Kharkiv, as part of the International Documentary Film Festival Amsterdam (IDFA). *Dear Beautiful Beloved* is a delicate and moving story of several humanitarian operations that rely entirely on the dedication of volunteers. In the midst of wartime violence, they supported refugees, accompanied them to train stations, helped elderly people feel at home in shelters, and traveled across the country to retrieve bodies, keep records, and safeguard property. They continued to work tirelessly, bringing moments of light in dark times, even if these moments were often brief. The significance of this bridge lay in the simultaneous screening at the two venues—in Kharkiv and Amsterdam. After the screening, both audiences were able to participate in a real-time discussion, asking questions and creating a shared space of interaction.

Audience at YermilovCentre during the simultaneous screening, live-linked with De Balie. Photo: Lera Borokh

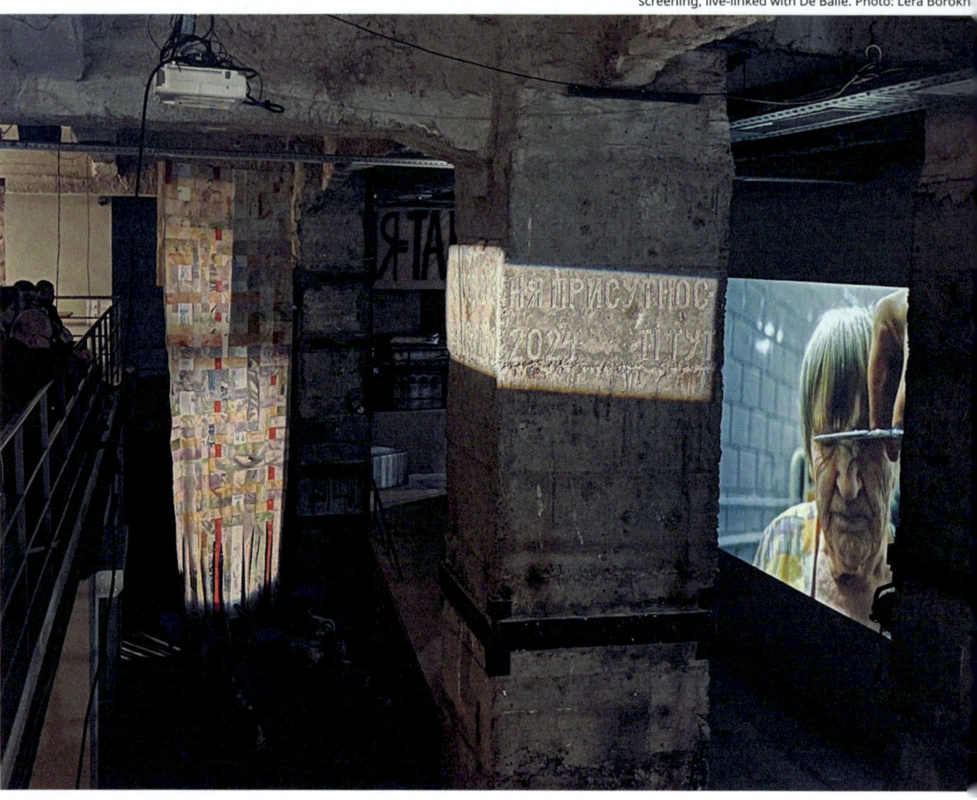

DocTalk "Dear Beautiful Beloved" by Juri Rechinsky

De Balie, Amsterdam (NL)
YermilovCentre, Kharkiv (UA)

Date
17.11.2024

Participants
Juri Rechinsky (UA/AT) in conversation with Tatiana Kochubinska (UA)

Supported by
European Cultural Foundation (ECF)
International Documentary Festival Amsterdam (IDFA)

The discussion continued the conceptual framework of the exhibition *Sense of Safety*, expanding its exploration of the exhibition force field *Asynchrony and the Dream Museum*. Departing from the situation in Kharkiv, where war radically disrupts temporalities of everyday life and memory, the discussion addressed the fragility of archives and practices of remembrance under conditions of war and systemic oppression, where the stable existence of memory institutions is increasingly under threat. Approaching safety not only as a bodily condition but also as the safety of memory, the conversation explored how remembering can be sustained when archival infrastructures are destroyed or denied. Held at the PRADMOVA Belarusian Intellectual Book Festival, the discussion foregrounded contemporary art archives as tools for cultural activism and the decolonization of knowledge. Drawing on practices of queer, independent, and self-organized initiatives, the event examined selective, affective, and provisional forms of archiving that resist dominant historical narratives. In dialogue with *Sense of Safety*, the discussion emphasized archives as unstable yet vital infrastructures, namely spaces where asynchrony, vulnerability, and political imagination intersect.

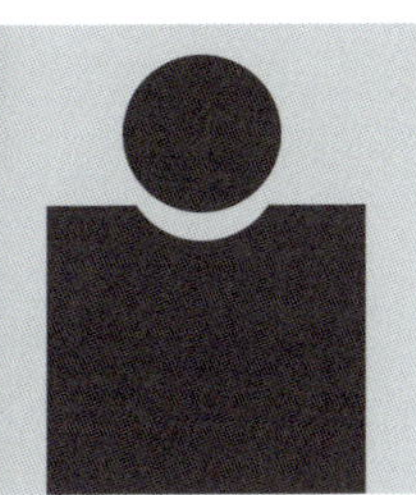

Archives of Contemporary Art as a Tool for Cultural Activism

Discussion

PRADMOVA festival, Poznań (PL)

Date
01.12.2024

Participants
Volha Arkhipava (BY/PL)
Anna Chistoserdova (BY/DE)
Viktoryia Hrabennikava (BY)
Irina Kh (BY)

Moderated by
Vera Zalutskaya (BY/PL)

This discursive event was conceived as a continuation of the exhibition *Sense of Safety*. The lecture and discussion shifted attention to culture itself as a political technology capable not only of mediation and emancipation, but also of legitimizing violence, repression, and colonial domination. Focusing on the historical reception of Polish cultural policy towards the so-called *Kresy Wschodnie*—the territories of present-day western Belarus and Ukraine—the lecture examined how visual art, literature, and education functioned as instruments of border-making, ideological control, and symbolic occupation. The discussion traced how cultural forms became entangled with militarized and repressive regimes, producing narratives that normalized territorial claims and imperial hierarchies. Held within the decolonial research lab Mycelium [Грыбніца], the event placed historical analysis alongside the ongoing war in Ukraine. The conversation reinforced a key proposition articulated by *Sense of Safety*, namely that culture operates within an ambivalent field capable of creating spaces of care and solidarity, while simultaneously serving as a tool of propaganda, colonial governance, and ideological violence.

The Subtle Influence of Culture: Mechanisms of Border Control

Lecture and discussion

The Roma Community Center, Warsaw (PL)

Date
16.12.2024

Participants
Amilia Stanevich (BY/PL)
Marie Manushka (BY/PL)
Antonina Stebur (BY/DE)
Taras Gembik (UA/PL)

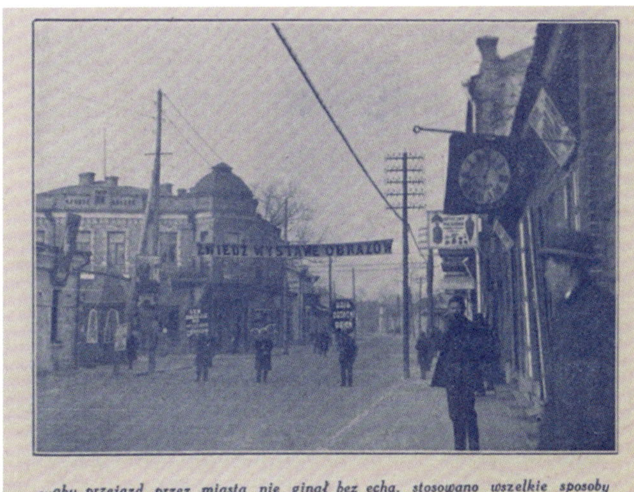

"Traveling Exhibition" (pol. Wystawa okrężna). Advertisement for the traveling exhibition in urban space, 1927. From *Wystawa okrężna. Przegląd ilustrowany*, no. 2, Warszawa, 1928.

The event was initiated by German artist Helmut Schweizer, whose longstanding practice and civic engagement address military conflict, the crimes of the Second World War, and themes of guilt and responsibility. It took place in the stairwell of an art studio building in Düsseldorf, where Schweizer himself works. The site includes a historic Winkel Tower—a kind of above-ground bunker designed by engineer and architect Leo Winkel in the 1930s and realized across Germany to protect civilians during the Second World War. The film was projected directly onto the bunker's wall, which is itself a material testimony to the history of war. Today the structure is surrounded by artists' studios, yet the concrete still "remembers" what war does to people. The screening of the film *Civilians. Invasion* by Daniil Revkovskyi and Andrii Rachynskyi—composed from found footage recorded by civilians during the first months of the Russian invasion of Ukraine—became a symbolic gesture. Testimonies of the current war in Ukraine were brought into a space that preserves traces of a past one. To avoid retraumatizing audiences in Kharkiv, the curators deliberately directed this video "outwards"—that is, into a peaceful Western Europe where the memory of the Second World War is being confronted with the new reality of war unleashed by Russia.

Audience during the screening of the film, 2024. Photo: Maxim Tyminko.

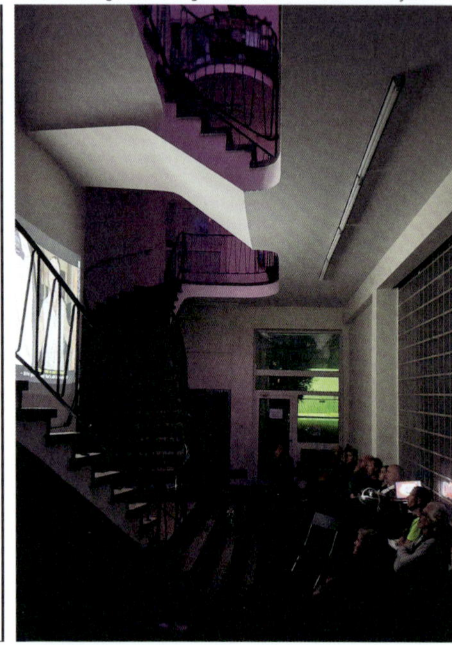

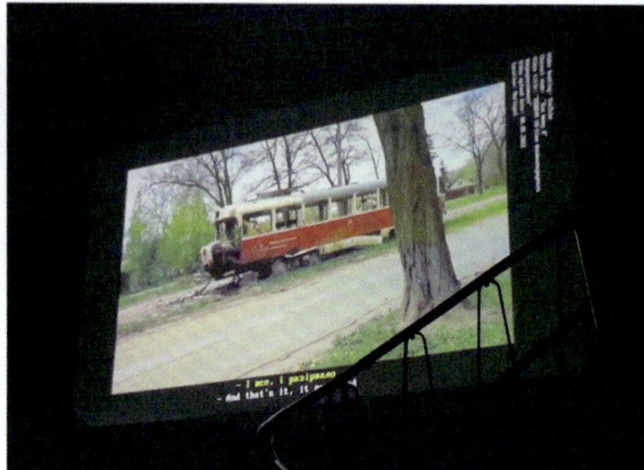

Screening of the film *Civilians. Invasion* (2023) by Daniil Revkovskyi and Andrii Rachynskyi

Discussion with the project's curators Tatiana Kochubinska (UA) and Maxim Tyminko (NL) moderated by Thomas Neumann (DE).

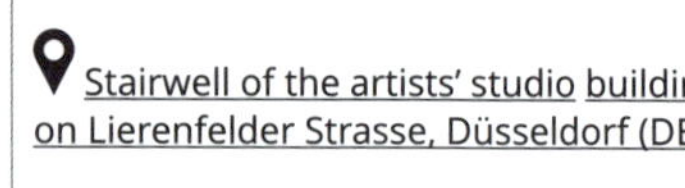

Stairwell of the artists' studio building on Lierenfelder Strasse, Düsseldorf (DE)

Date
20.09.2024

Since three Ukrainian students from the Düsseldorf Art Academy visited my studio on 27 May 2022 and vividly recounted their lives in Ukraine during Russia's brutal war of aggression, I have consistently responded with empathy when Ukrainian colleagues have asked for my support. The bunker wall next to my studio was thus transformed into a fantastic stage for an evening, bringing together Düsseldorf artists who felt connected to Ukraine.

Helmut Schweizer

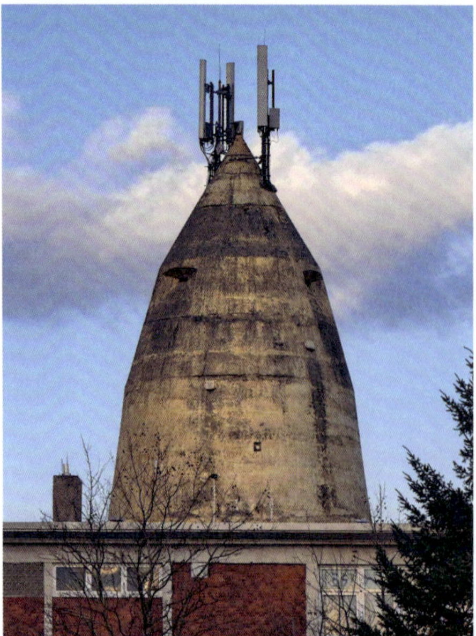

Winkelturm, Lierenfelder Straße, Düsseldorf, 2026.
Photo: Iuliia Bondarenko.

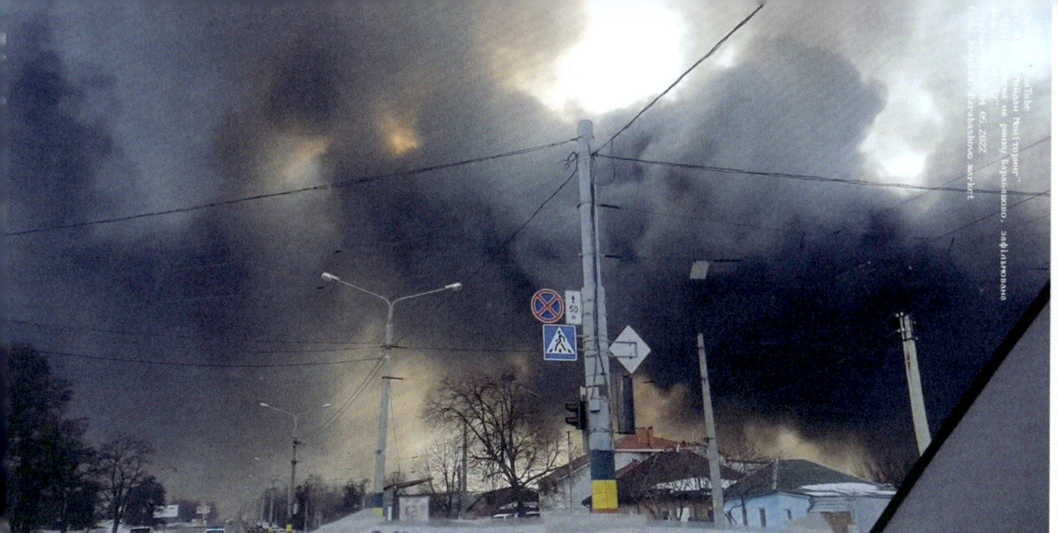

Daniil Revkovskyi and Andrii Rachynskyi, *Civilians. Invasion*, 2023. Film still courtesy of the artists.

Drawing on the history of book illustration, Soviet educational aesthetics, and contemporary gaming imagery, the lecture by artist Uladzimir Hramovich examined how visual languages have been shaped by and have helped normalize militarization in today's Belarus—a state of daily repression and a co-aggressor in Russia's full-scale invasion of Ukraine. The lecture contributed to an ongoing dialogue on the formation of wartime imaginaries and how aesthetic regimes are incorporated into today's wars. The artist revealed how the seemingly non-military sphere of academic drawing and graphic art contributes to the normalization and toleration of war through various infrastructures, such as the industry around the game *World of Tanks*.

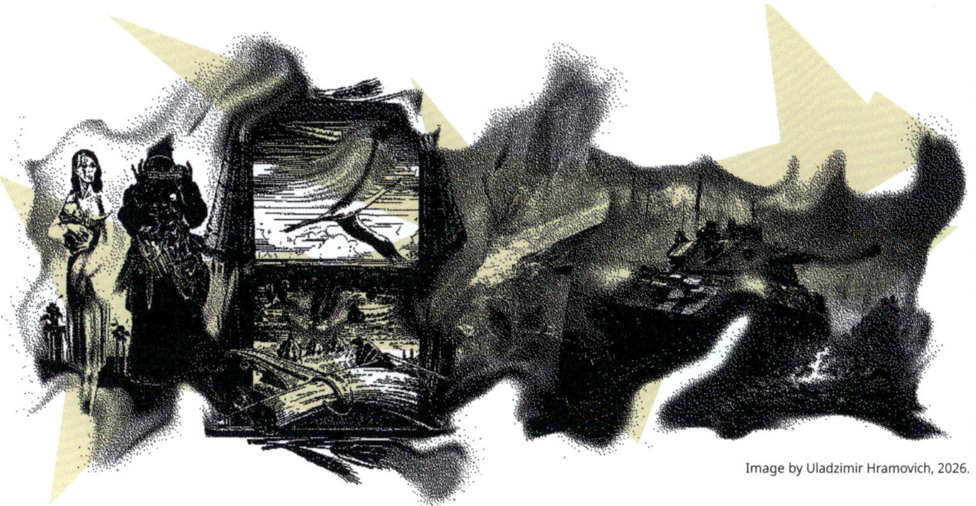

Image by Uladzimir Hramovich, 2026.

rom War to War: Illustration nd Militarization of Visual pace in Belarus

ecture

Uq-Bar-A-Ba project space, erlin (DE)
nline broadcast

Date
27.11.2024

Speaker
Uladzimir Hramovich (BY/DE)

I am interested in the tension between the past and the present and studies of monuments and rituals of memory that are overloaded with ideological meanings and embodied in material objects.

Uladzimir Hramovich.

The event took place after the exhibition at the YermilovCentre was over. At the same time, it demonstrated the continuity of the project itself and the network of interactions it initiated, which continued to develop through institutional partnerships. A key part of the event was the screening of the so-called *Kharkiv Trilogy* by Mykola Ridnyi—a Kharkiv-born artist who has worked at the intersection of art and activism since the early 2000s. The program included his films *Regular Places* (2015 / 2022), *No! No! No!* (2017), and *District* (2023), which document transformations of urban space, everyday experience, and forms of collective memory during periods of profound social and political change in his native city. Taken together, they trace how Kharkiv and its communities have evolved under conditions of prolonged instability—from the Revolution of Dignity in 2013 and 2014 to the period following Russia's full-scale invasion of Ukraine in 2022. Following the screenings, a public discussion took place between Mykola Ridnyi and Napsugár Trömböczki.

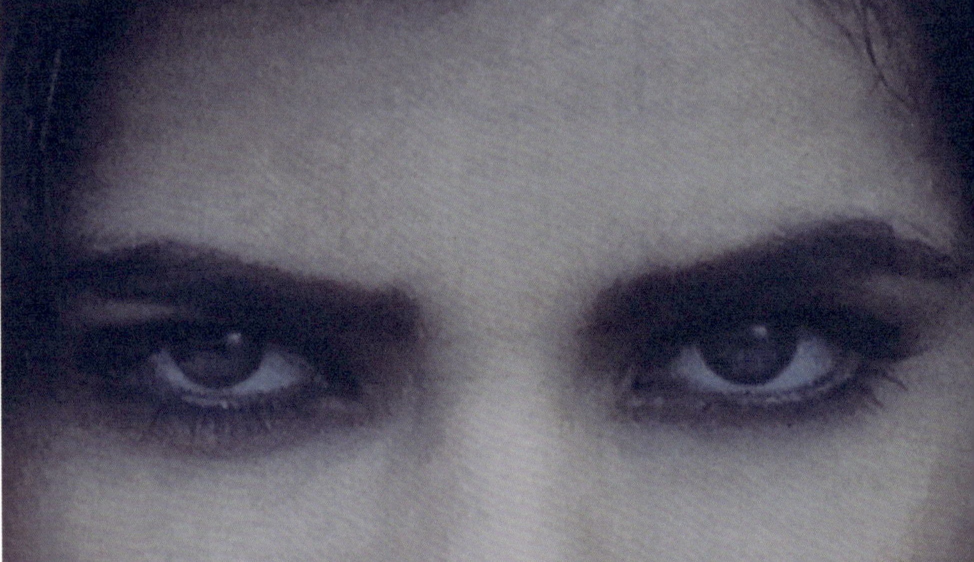

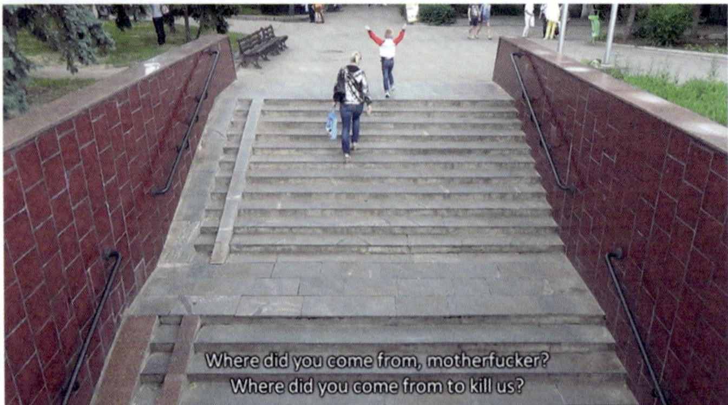

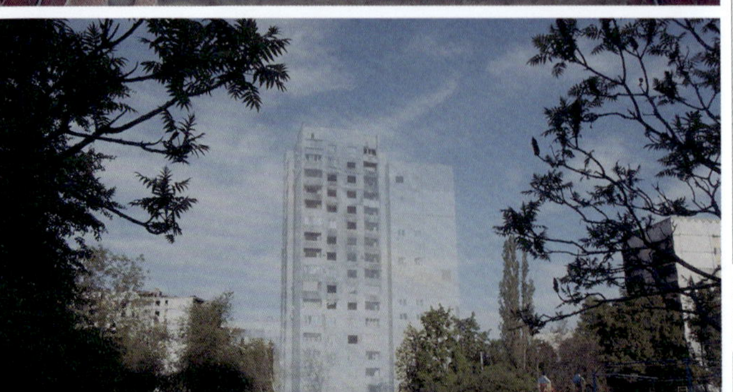

Film screening and a public discussion

PLACCC International Festival of Site-Specific Art and Art in Public Space, Budapest (HU) and Berlin (DE)

Date
25.03.2025

Participants
Mykola Ridnyi (UA)
Napsugár Trömböczki (HU)

Supported by
Nordic Council of Ministers Office in Lithuania (LT)
The Danish Cultural Institute (LV)

Mykola Ridnyi, film stills courtesy of the artist.
Top image: *No! No! No!* 2017
Middle image: *Regular Places*, 2015 / 2022
Bottom image: *The District*, 2023

Echoes of Shelters unfolded as a hybrid performative walk connecting Poznań and Kharkiv through parallel simultaneous actions, narratives, and embodied experiences. Through a psycho-geographical journey, performances, collective readings, and live connections, the walk investigated militarized regimes of space and the ways safety, shelter, and care are produced under conditions of war, occupation, and repression. Moving across underground shelters, cultural institutions, public parks, and temporary gathering spaces, the program traced how infrastructures of protection are inseparable from infrastructures of control, surveillance, and violence. By bringing together testimonies and artistic practices from Poland, Ukraine, Palestine, and other contexts marked by colonial domination and militarization, *Echoes of Shelters* articulated the interconnectedness of different registers of war and repression. In this sense, the walk functioned both as an investigation of militarized space and as a trans-local gesture of solidarity, grounded in material presence and lived experience.

Hybrid storytelling and discussion (Poznań / Kharkiv): reflections on cultural institutions as shelters with contributions from Natalia Ivanova (YermilovCentre, Kharkiv), Maryna Konieva, and Ukrainian artist Olia Fedorova, sharing their personal stories related to safety.
Psychogeographical walk (Poznań): walk through shelters and militarized urban spaces, with simultaneous live participation from Kharkiv.
Playback theater performance (Kharkiv): live-streamed performance by the Nema Playback Theater at the YermilovCentre, exploring experiences of safety and vulnerability.
Movement performance in an underground shelter (Poznań): inspired by the history and contemporary meaning of underground spaces, exploring the relationship between architecture and corporeality. Performers: Tamara Olga Briks (PL), Ada Metryka (PL), Mikita Lewkowicz (BY)
Collective reading of Palestinian poetry (Poznań): reading from the zine *If I Must Die, You Must Live to Tell My Story*, hosted by Julia Niedziejko (PL).
Site-specific exploration of an air raid shelter (Poznań): performative intervention led by Wojciech Mania (PL).
Concert and livestream (Poznań / Kharkiv): performance by the Otucha collective inspired by a trip to the northeastern Luhansk region in 2021. This activity connected Poznań and Kharkiv through shared songs and live transmission. Performers: Agnieszka Bułacik, Mina Đorđević, Magda Jaroszewicz, Kata Kwiatkowska, Agnieszka Kucharska, Julia Legezynska, Doro Michalak, Vlada Rusina, Liene Šilde, Vita Zelenska, Ola Zielinska.

Echoes of Shelters

Hybrid performative walk

ZAMEK Culture Centre (PL)
Poznań Palm House (PL)
Poznań Fortress Days (PL)
Domie, Poznań (PL)
YermilovCentre, Kharkiv (UA)

Date
16.11.2024

Concept and curatorial program:
Lizaveta Stecko (BY/PL)
Zuza Szczepanska (PL)
Katarzyna Wojtczak (PL)

Supported by
City of Poznań

Echoes of Shelter emerged as a method of attuning to the materiality of sound and acoustics across distance. Histories were not only narrated but vibrated through bodies and space. With the rhythm of walking, we moved together across shelters, where movement became a way of composing relations between bodies and landscapes, allowing stories of holding and endurance to unfold. Along the way, we listened to the stories of our compatriots, our neighbors, our grandmothers, and our comrades on the frontlines in Palestine. Working in tandem with YermilovCentre and through our shared presence, we brought into relation cities and institutional spaces in Poznań and Kharkiv. These sites began to shift, collectively becoming shelters and forming a subtle choreography across temporalities of knowledge, memory, and matter.

Katarzyna Wojtczak, artist and anarchist.

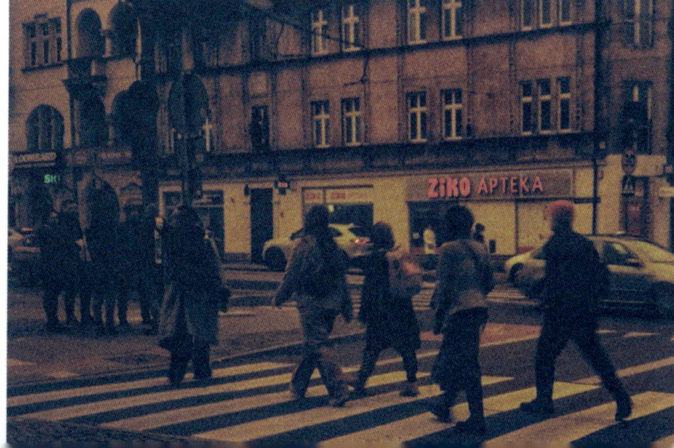

From the psychogeographical walk as part of *Echoes of Shelters*, Poznań, 2024. Photo: Mateusz "Kronos" Stosik.

The Sense …

Tetyana Pylypchuk

ASYNCHRONY AND THE DREAM MUSEUM

Museums are spaces where we come together, share stories, and learn from each other. They keep our memories alive, honor our ancestors, and remind us of the strength to be found in unity and mutual support. Today, each of us is responsible for linking the past, present, and future.
To remember is to resist, while forgetting is like losing life itself.
In times of war, the value of culture becomes painfully clear. When homes are destroyed and one loses personal keepsakes—family albums, mom's old cabinet with the china and crystal, or great-grandma's shirt—the need to preserve what binds us as a community becomes urgent.
Museums capture this connection, reflecting both our break with the past and our hopes for the future. They are spaces where different times and dreams intertwine. After all, a museum is also a place for imagination, where our view of reality and our sense of what's possible are shaped and inspired.

The name of the exhibition, *Sense of Safety*, led me to another name—*Sense of Presence*. This was the title of the first album by the Kharkiv rock band Kalektsiya (2001), borrowed from Taras Prokhasko's eponymous short story.

At the beginning of the full-scale invasion, the Kharkiv Literary Museum evacuated its collection to a safer place, but the museum itself was not relocated. The sense that the collection was safe, in a strange way, coexisted with the sense of our stubborn presence here, in unsafe Kharkiv, the presence of the meanings that our collection embodies. And those meanings—the meanings of our own culture—were actively filling our symbolic space.

The journey of the museum collection to a safer place was full of different coincidences and signs. Or maybe we have just become more sensitive to the symbolic text of reality. Whatever the case, I'll write my travel notes about this later, when times are safer.

Museums are very good at monetizing the past: just think of the queues at the Louvre to see Da Vinci's *Mona Lisa* (1506). Our museum had also been building its activities around "hard" values—the items in our collection. But now our "hard" components are being destroyed. They are disappearing, and we have gotten used to a constant sense of unsafety—in both space and time. This sense forces us to think about the future faster. How far are we able to see?

We can clearly see that museums are no longer just showcases where we display our past through artifacts. As paradoxical as it may seem, the particular situation of Ukrainian museums offers a safe space for contemplating the future of museums in general. We were too attached to illustrating ideas through exhibits. Now deprived of the opportunity to exhibit, we have to work directly with the meanings.

For us today, engaging in unexpected experiments is not an act of bravery but of self-preservation, and thus also about our safety. We have hidden museum collections to protect them from the threat of physical destruction. And we have changed the very concept of museum storage: the more actively we use the information gathered in our collections, the better they will be preserved.

People either throw old things away or donate them to museums. Some things would be a real shame to discard because of their personal or social symbolic meaning. Others are not only meaningful, but also expensive. So what is a museum object? Why is it so important for us to have these "solid" artifacts? How do they relate to our safety? Is it because they carry our shared experience, packed into our memories? The sense of fear—of losing what is most important—is now a constant in our lives, and by throwing us out of our comfort zone, it gives us a different perspective. For example, the main task of museums is not to preserve collections, but to activate them in the present. And not just by creating queues to see expensive old luxury objects.

Museums can give people a sense of belonging to a great history. In fact, this is how the victors' museums work. Museums create an opportunity for individuals to connect their personal lives to a bigger story. And while propaganda only needs to create the illusion of belonging to something greater, museums have another potential: to give people a sense of belonging to their own culture, history, and heritage. Museums can either dissolve a person's subjectivity or strengthen it. Which is safer for us?

Today, when we talk about museums, we talk less about beauty or knowledge and more about safety—not the safety of the museums themselves, but the safety that museums can offer us. Or, conversely, the safety they can take away.

Taras Kamennoy

Is It a Museum

born 1985 in Kharkiv, Ukraine; based in Vysoke, Kharkiv region

2024
C-PRINT, PENCIL ON PAPER
PRODUCED ESPECIALLY FOR THE EXHIBITION *SENSE OF SAFETY*

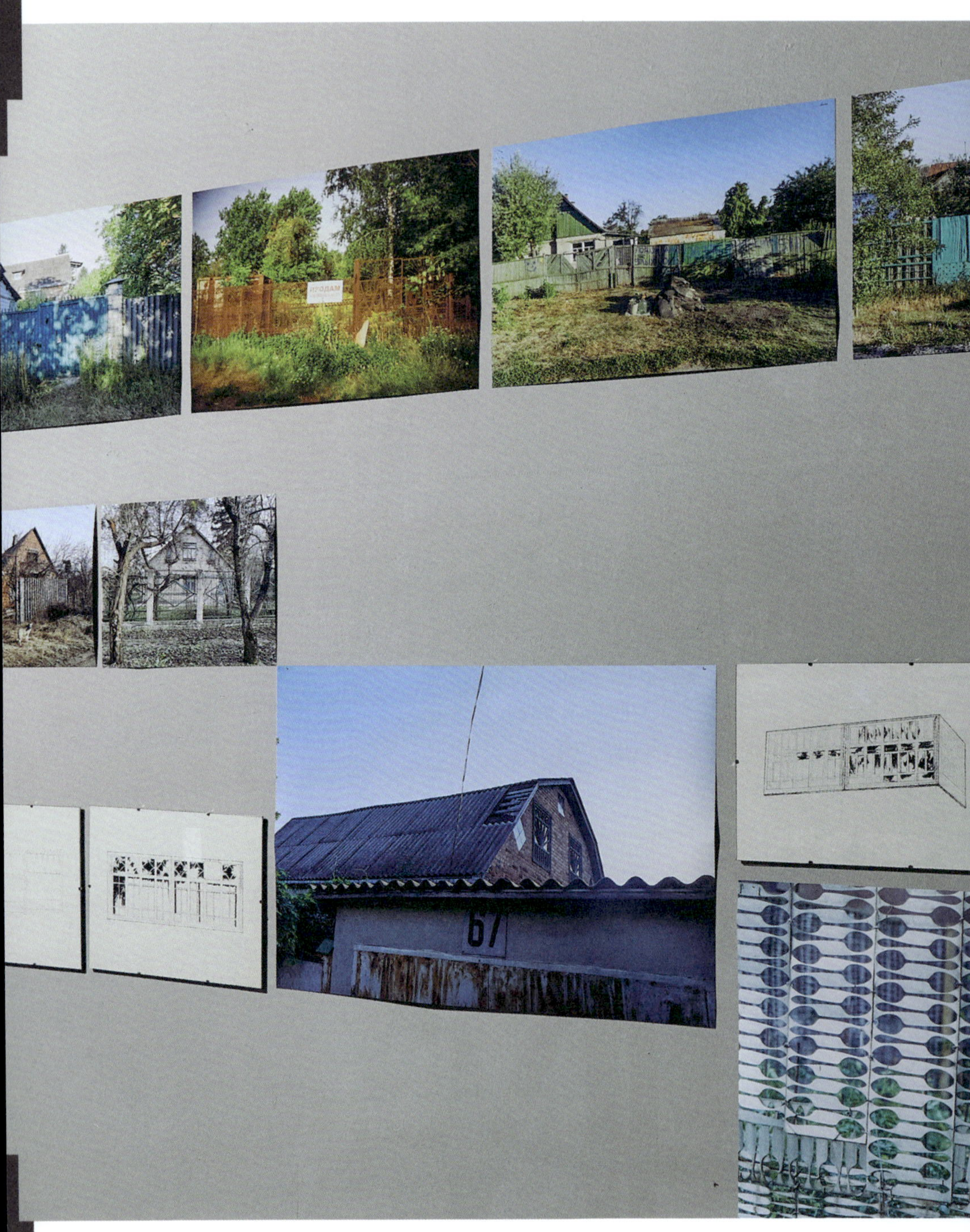

In his artistic practice, Taras Kamennoy often draws on social experiments and investigations, performing in public spaces and organizing exhibitions for workers in sheds. In his critical yet careful studies, the artist analyzes how the environment influences the formation of our political mentalities.

The work *Is It a Museum*, consisting of a series of photographs and drawings, arose from reflections on the role of museums and musealization in times of war. The artist is interested in the parallels between the path of a person and a work of art, as well as reflections on life and death. Getting a work of art into a museum is a way of entering history, but also a kind of death. However, museums also become vulnerable in times of war, and nowadays preserving the life of artworks means putting them into even more remote storage. At the beginning of the full-scale invasion, road signs were famously removed from all the streets, and information about museums was also hidden to protect them.

While living in the village of Vysoke in the Kharkiv region, Kamennoy thought about the memorial room and museum of the prominent cultural figure Hnat Khotkevych (1878–1938) that he last visited during school excursions in the 1990s. Based on stereotypical ideas about the museum and guided by distant memories, the artist began searching for a building that could potentially become the Khotkevych Museum. This process is reflected in a series of photographs and drawings resembling a pseudo-investigation.

In the process of photographing typical architectural structures, Kamennoy is most interested in what he refers to as "folklore"—the desire of people to creatively ennoble their land and own home in order to make it unique. The way the photographs are displayed resembles the boards of a criminal investigation: Kamennoy presents small details and close-ups as substantial evidence, while the general views are smaller. In this investigation, the artist is interested not in the final result but in the process of searching, which becomes a study of architectural form-making and the creativity of anonymously authored structures like fences.

The compositional principle of each photo shows a view through a fence, putting the viewer in the position of a voyeur. The fence becomes an image of a border, a separation, and a symbol of protection and self-defense, something that helps preserve values and prolong memory. Guided by such considerations, Taras Kamennoy's work documents the frontline territory and records a museum of social life during the war.

Pavlo Makov

Bed, Carpet, Brooch

born 1958 in St. Petersburg, Russia; based in Kharkiv, Ukraine

2024
INSTALLATION: *BEDSIDE MAT* (1996),
DIAMOND TARGET (BROOCH, LATE 1990s),
FOUND OBJECTS
COURTESY OF THE ARTIST

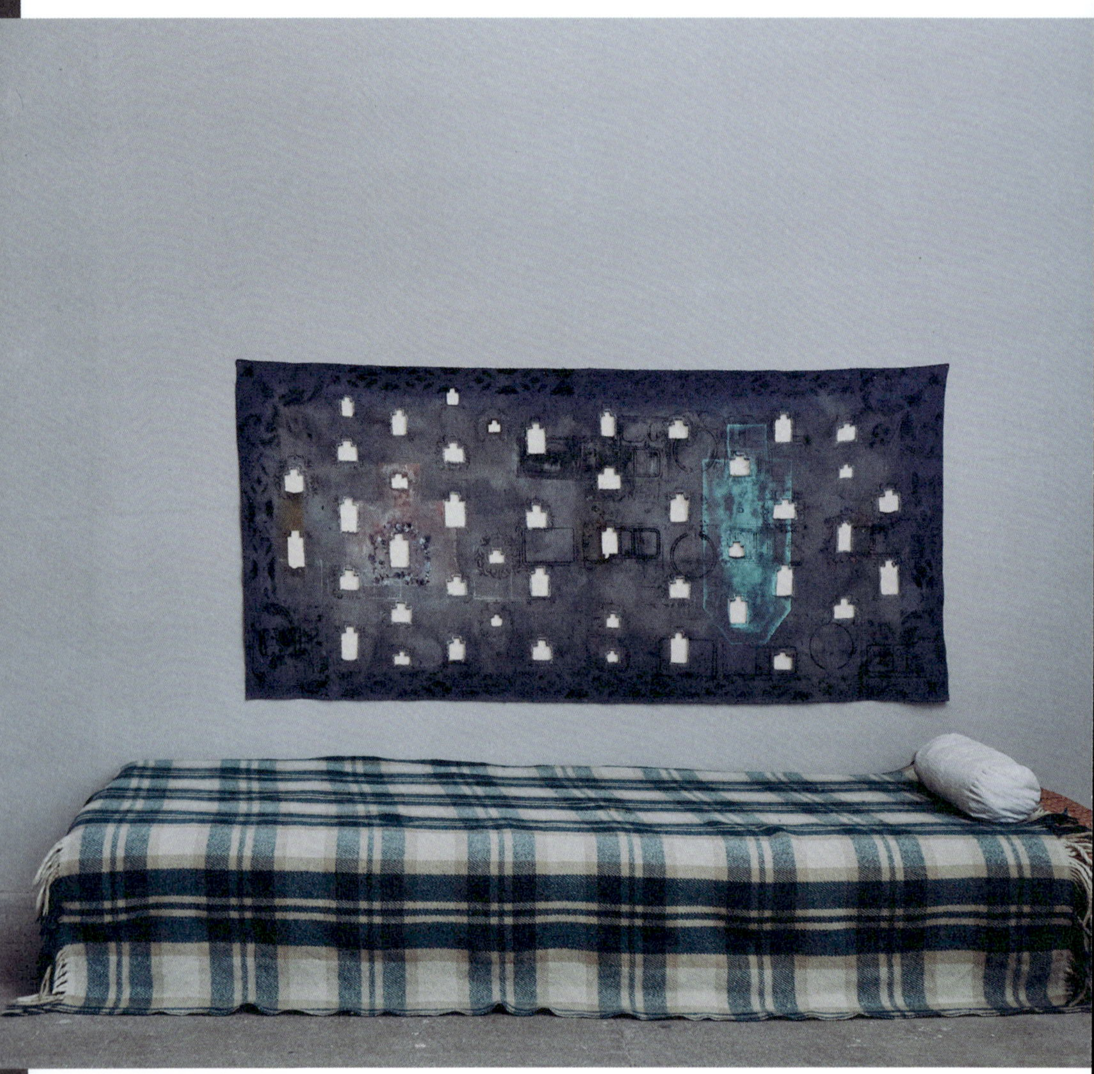

Pavlo Makov has an impressive body of works devoted to targets. The artist worked on them in the 1990s, when he was interested in anonymity and found objects. The starting point for the study was different types of targets collected in schoolyards. Back then, targets symbolizing basic school military training were perceived as an echo of the past. However, on the eve of the third millennium, the real targets and the symbol merged—TARGET became a key concept for millions of people in Yugoslavia, and I realized that it

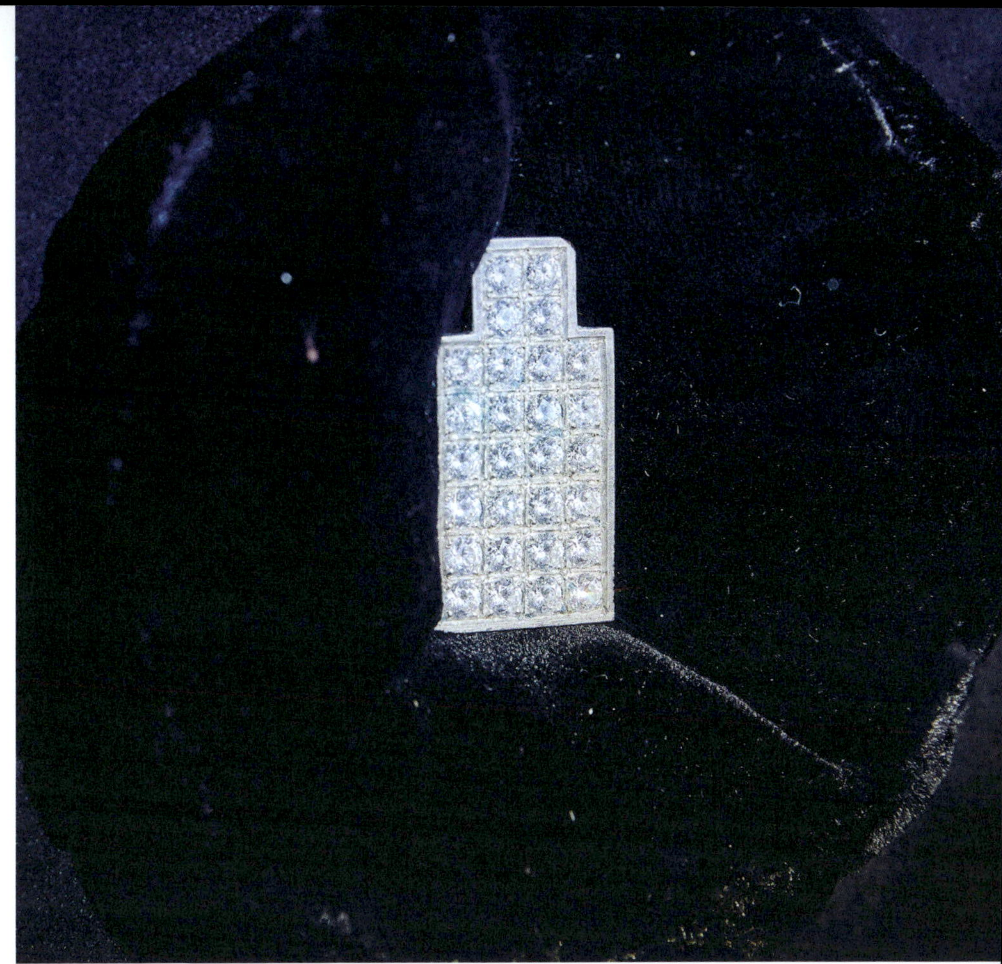

was no longer possible to use it as a sign. Life took it away from art, turning signs into real people," Makov writes in his iconic book *Utopia: Chronicles.* Targets from the past are once again turning into the reality of the present.

In the installation *Bed, Carpet, Brooch*, created especially for the exhibition, Makov rethinks life in fear and danger. The artist refers to his own recent experience of staying around the clock in the YermilovCentre, which served as a bomb shelter at the beginning of Russia's full-scale invasion of Ukraine. The artist transforms this experience into an artistic statement, partly updating his art project from the 1990s, the *Museum of Modern Life*. In that project, the artist sought a vital connection between visual art and everyday life. The new installation—made up of a 1996 bedside rug, a diamond target, and found objects that created a sense of protection and shelter at the beginning of the invasion in February 2022—reflects the traces of our traumatic reality. In this way, the artist creates an updated *Museum of Modern Life*, where reassembled artifacts become tools of self-soothing, shelter-building, and artistic expression, offering a pathway toward a safe space. This is what constitutes post-traumatic growth, which allows us to transform traumatic experiences into opportunities for the future.

Iryna Loskot

Camouflage

born 2001 in Mirny, Yakutia, Russia; based in Kyiv, Ukraine

2024
WOOD, TEXTILE
COURTESY OF THE ARTIST

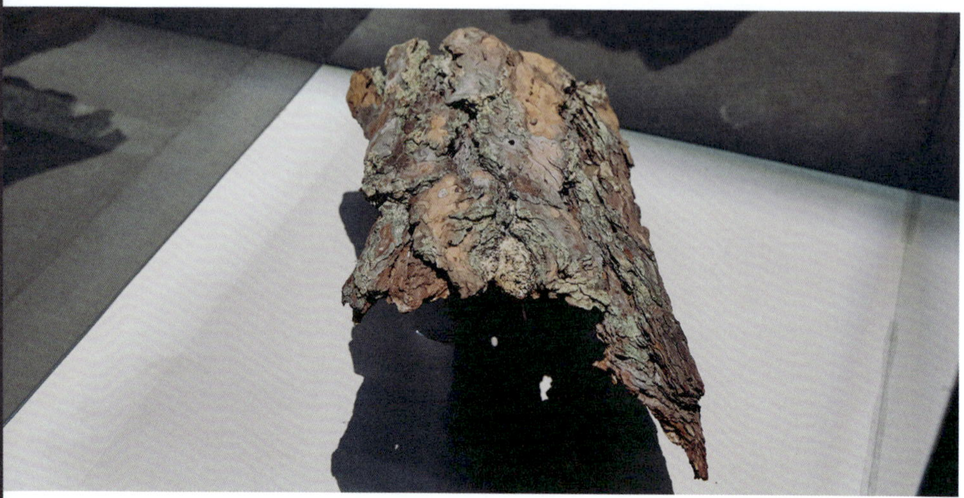

Iryna Loskot's artistic practice explores the interconnection of human and non-human agents, as well as the inextricable entanglements of the personal and the political. In *Camouflage*, the artist addresses the post-traumatic integration of human beings and nature during the war. The artwork features a piece of camouflage fabric on wood bark. Bark as a material acts both as a symbol of safety and a memory object. Iryna Loskot found the bark in her childhood village in the Sumy region, now a frontline territory, where an intensive process of adaptation to warfare is taking place, involving both humans and nature.

The bark is a tree's protective tissue, shielding the plant from damage. A nearly invisible piece of camouflage fabric embedded in the bark reveals the mutational symbiosis between humans and non-humans drawn into this war. But who provides safety to whom: The people restoring nature destroyed by war? Or does nature provide a double layer of camouflage to the soldiers?

The piece of camouflage fabric reminds us that apart from countless human casualties, war also destroys nature. Ukrainian researcher Svitlana Matviyenko characterized this process as a "terror environment," emphasizing that today terror is ecological, turning the living body into a hostage of its own ecosystems. Performance has been a longstanding component in Iryna Loskot's art, and in this sculptural composition performative gestures are inherent to the hidden traces—the search for bark, the transport from Sumy, and the staging of mutation through a piece of camouflage fabric. All these traces reveal the interdependence imposed by the war.

Francis Alÿs

born 1959 in Antwerp, Belgium; based in Mexico

Children's Game #39: Parol

2023
VIDEO, 8'02"
IN COLLABORATION WITH HANNA TSYBA, OLGA PAPASH, EUGENE MOROZ, JULIEN DEVAUX, AND FÉLIX BLUME
COURTESY OF THE ARTIST

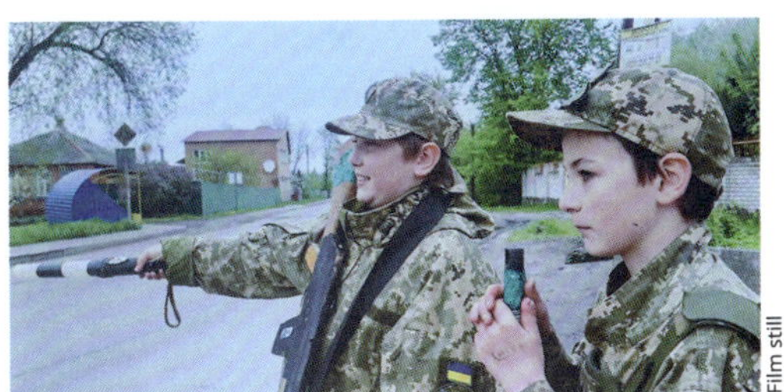

Film still

For over four decades, Francis Alÿs has consistently explored art as a vehicle for witnessing social and political change. Trained as an architect and urbanist in Belgium and Italy, Alÿs moved to Mexico City in 1986, where the rapidly shifting urban context and social dynamics of the late 1980s inspired him to become a visual artist. *Children's Game #39: Parol* belongs to his ongoing project *Children's Games*, which the artist started in 1999 and has since realized in more than fifteen countries. Drawing on Pieter Bruegel the Elder's *Children's Games* (1560), Alÿs explores the potential of games for overcoming the constraints imposed by wars, colonialism, and different forms of oppression.

In order to film *Parol*, Francis Alÿs came to the region of Kharkiv in May 2023. In the video, three boys dressed in military uniforms try out the roles of the adults at the checkpoint, securing their land and families. Passionate about the game, the kids screen cars for Russian spies using a check word, *Palyanytsia*, which means bread in Ukrainian and cannot be properly pronounced by Russians. Most of the adults enthusiastically play along. Yet, the video reflects on the deception of our safety: kids can't really check the cars, and the password is conditional. By creating a simulacrum of the real and transforming the dramatic circumstances around them into a more fictional, ludic world, the act of playing helps those brave boys cope with the traumatic experiences of war. Yet, this is also an action to reassure ourselves of our grip on safety. The video is very human; there is much laughter and love—basic values that ensure the continuation of life, which become especially needed in wartime, when social foundations are crumbling. At the same time, a new foundation of resistance is taking root in these children forced to mature beyond their age.

The video contains subtle and meditative pictorial observations, while an almost unnoticed sunset becomes a backdrop for the game to continue. Here, the game offers an opportunity for society to return to normal, which is one of the principles of safety.

Installation view of *Sense of Safety* at YermilovCentre featuring works by Francis Alÿs and Iryna Loskot. Photo: Viktoriia Yakymenko. →

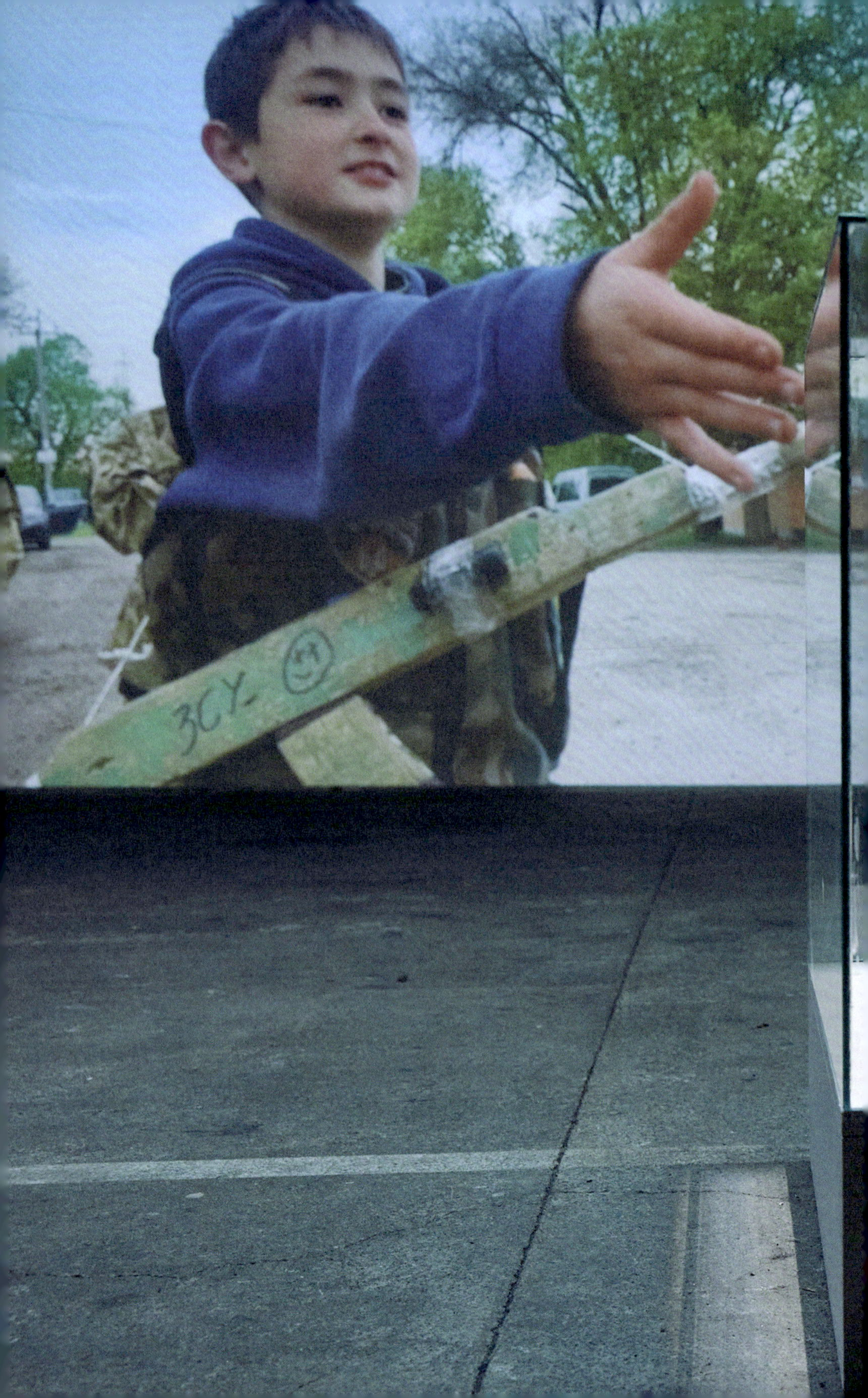
3CY

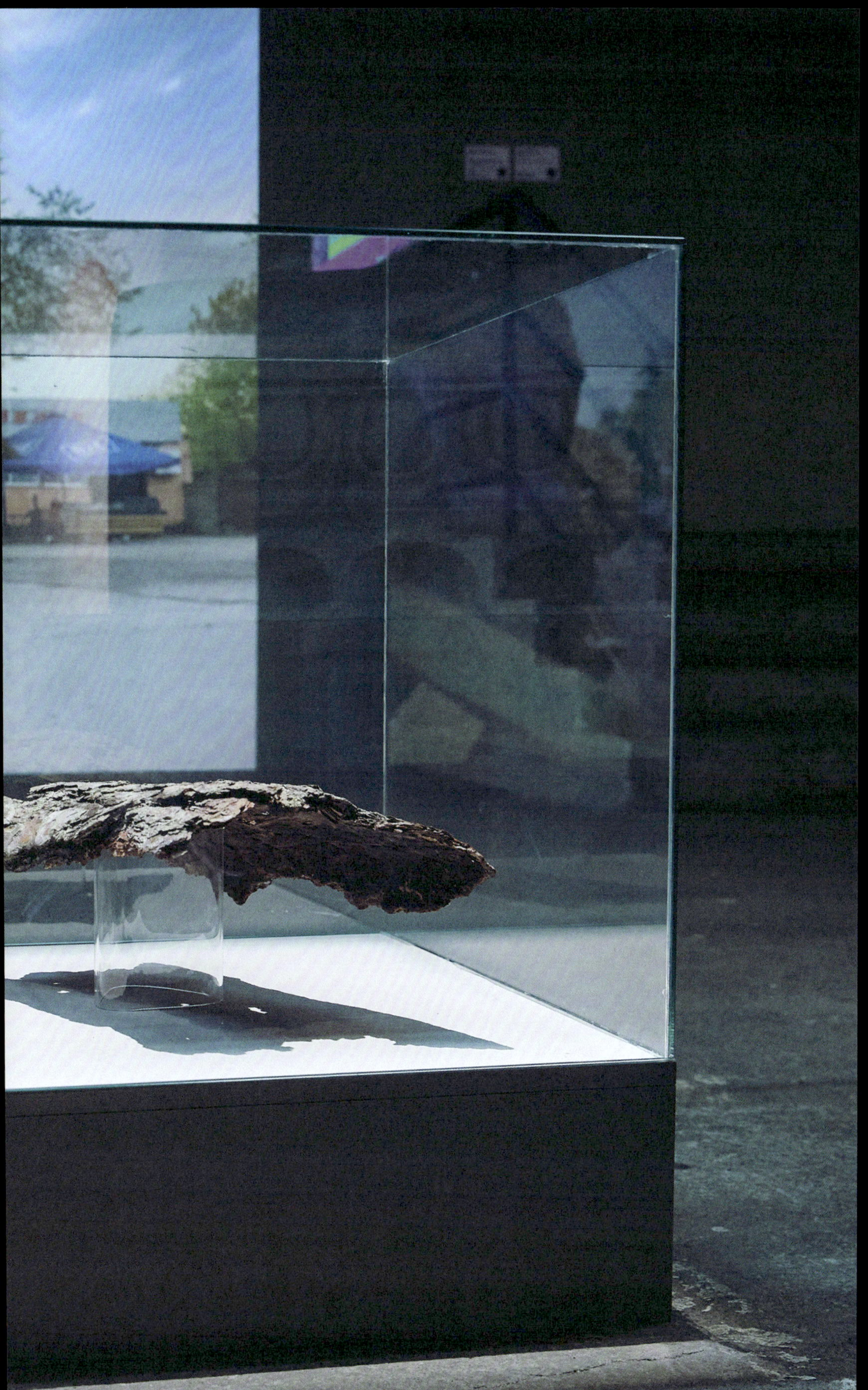

Bojana Piškur

The Art of the Living: Transnational Acts of Solidarity and Resistance

1.

Nowadays the specter of war is everywhere: Ukraine, Gaza, Sudan, and many other conflicts beyond the focus of global media. Old bonds of solidarity have been broken, and new horizons are nowhere in sight. The future looks bleak, while the present is weighed down by unresolved traumas, some stretching back decades, or even centuries.

This fractured reality highlights the urgent need to reimagine and decolonize solidarity, moving beyond inherited assumptions and symbolic performativity to reclaim its transformative power. Although much formal theorization of solidarity has developed within European thought, practices of interdependence and communal responsibility shape cultures around the world, from *sumud* in Palestine and *ubuntu* in parts of Africa to *ayni* in Indigenous Andean communities.

Solidarity is not merely a concept; it is an ethical commitment, a political practice, and an affective force that connects people across communities, struggles, and movements. It entails mutual care, collective action, resistance, and the redistribution of power and resources. These dimensions of solidarity are often most visible during collective crisis, such as war, political, social, or economic upheavals, and the aftermath of natural disasters.

Solidarity is also deeply affective. Affects shape how people act and relate to one another. According to Spinoza, joy increases a person's capacity to act, while sadness decreases it.[1] Political power often exploits sad passions—fear, resentment, despair—in order to uphold hierarchies. Solidarity emerges when these forces are countered by collective joy, which is generated through connection and shared commitment. This strengthens resistance and opens new possibilities for social transformation.

As a radical practice, solidarity demands full participation in the struggles of others, linking local actions to global movements. It takes many forms, including refugee and migrant support, climate justice initiatives and global anti-racist mobilizations, as well as actions in support of those affected by war and occupation. Solidarity also permeates social life, finding expression in art and culture, where artistic practices engage people directly and powerfully.

2.

The connection between solidarity and cultural expression runs deep through history. Artistic practices have long served as a means of articulating collective struggles and fostering shared political imaginaries. This link became particularly pronounced in the twentieth century, when art and politics were often united in the pursuit of utopian models aimed at social and political transformation. As a result, art came to be understood not merely as representation, but as an essential component of resistance movements and revolutionary processes.

Political theorists and philosophers from former colonies in Africa, Asia, and Latin America shared a view that culture served as a form of struggle against colonial domination. At the First International Congress of Black Writers and Artists in Paris in 1956, Léopold Senghor argued that cultural liberation was essential for political liberation. Similarly, Sékou Touré stated at the Second Congress in Rome in 1959 that "it is not enough to write a revolutionary hymn to be part of the African revolution; one has to join with the people to make this revolution."[2] Such positions were closely linked to wider political initiatives, including those of the Non-Aligned Movement, the Afro-Asian-Latin-American Peoples' Solidarity Organization, the Organization of Latin American Solidarity, the Pan-African Association, and others.

Founded in Belgrade, Yugoslavia in 1961, the Non-Aligned Movement (NAM)[3] became a central political and cultural platform for fostering transnational solidarity among the newly liberated and decolonized nations of the Third World.[4] From the Second summit in Cairo in 1964 to the Eighth Summit in Harare in 1986, NAM consistently addressed cultural issues, emphasizing cultural equality and the rehabilitation of cultures suppressed under colonial rule. This period coincided with the movement's greatest political and cultural influence. At summits, the member states articulated strategies to counter cultural imperialism, demand the restitution of looted cultural heritage, and strengthen frameworks for cultural exchange and cooperation.

Various forms of solidarity emerged within the movement: political, economic, and cultural. Cultural solidarity initiatives, however, did not arise spontaneously "from below."[5] Rather, they were organized at the highest state level, primarily through national arts institutions, cultural attaché offices, and committees for cultural exchange with foreign countries. These mechanisms produced an extensive network of exhibitions, biennials, and other programs formalized through intergovernmental agreements. Artists from NAM countries participated in a wide range of international events, including the Alexandria Biennial for Mediterranean Countries, the São Paulo Biennial, the Triennale–India in New Delhi, the Biennale of Arab Art in Baghdad, the Ljubljana International Graphic Biennial, and the exhibitions at the Josip Broz Tito Art Gallery of the Non-Aligned Countries in Titograd (present-day Podgorica). Functioning as instruments of cultural diplomacy, these events operated as forms of soft power, continually negotiating cultural influence in response to shifting geopolitical conditions.

Despite the cultural diversity of NAM member states, these newly established exchanges created spaces for dialogue about the relationship between globally dominant Western culture and other cultural traditions. Artistic practices presented within these frameworks often challenged Western cultural dominance and Eurocentric models of modernity by emphasizing forms of creativity rooted in collective, traditional, and community-based practices. Rather than being positioned as derivative "parallel modernities," such works articulated alternative cultural modes of production.

Within this landscape, naïve and folk art acquired particular popularity.[6] In the former Yugoslavia, galleries dedicated to this type of art were established, such as the Gallery of Naïve Art in Kovačica. Naïve works also entered museum collections, including the solidarity collection at the Museum of Contemporary Art in Skopje and the Josip Broz Tito Art Gallery of the Non-Aligned Countries in Titograd. For many postcolonial societies, these artistic forms represented a rejection of colonial cultural hierarchies and instead drew inspiration from the collective creativity of local communities.

In newly independent states, cultural development was regarded as just as important as economic development. as economic development. Consequently, communities that had previously been denied their cultural heritage began to recognize the emancipatory power of culture. A local-to-local approach was highly promoted, positioning the Third World not merely as an object of representation but as a space from which to speak.

In retrospect, the period from the 1950s to 90s shows how solidarity was closely aligned with state policy and pragmatic political objectives, while also being shaped by a global historical moment marked by struggles for decolonization and emancipation. During this time, artistic and cultural initiatives functioned as tools of political strategy and as spaces for imagining alternative social futures rooted in collective experience.

3.

Such initiatives also took shape through transnational networks that connected artists, audiences, and institutions across Asia, Africa, and Latin America, extending state-aligned and politically driven forms of solidarity beyond national boundaries. Notable examples include the Museo de la Solidaridad Salvador Allende in Chile (1971), *International Art Exhibition for Palestine* (1978), *Artists of the World Against Apartheid* (1980), the Art for the People of Nicaragua initiative (1981), and the *Del Tercer Mundo* exhibition organized as part of the Cultural Congress of Havana (1968). While these projects have been the subject of extensive research over the past decade, the interest in equally important yet lesser-known cases from Eastern Europe had remained largely local until recently.

One example is the 1958 Tashkent International Film Festival,[7] held as part of the Afro-Asian Film Festival (AAFF). Together with later editions in Cairo (1960) and Jakarta (1964), the festival emerged from the political and cultural climate shaped by the 1955 Bandung Conference, which sought to foster Afro-Asian solidarity among newly independent countries in their efforts to assert sovereignty and resist colonial domination.

The 1958 Tashkent edition brought together filmmakers from Asia, Africa, and the Central Asian republics, showcasing works that highlighted national liberation movements, social realities, and the pursuit of self-determination. Films such as *Turang* (Indonesia, 1957) and *Freedom for Ghana* (1957) reflected the festival's commitment to challenging Western-centric narratives, highlighting perspectives rooted in local experience instead of those long imposed by Western frameworks. The festival also contributed to early debates about the political potential of cinema, which would later be more systematically formalized in the 1969 manifesto *Towards a Third Cinema* by Argentine filmmakers Fernando Solanas and Octavio Getino. While the manifesto is often cited as the starting point of Third Cinema, "the essential debates surrounding revolutionary aesthetics and cinema's political role had already been established with the AAFF."[8] Situating the festival as part of transnational networks of solidarity thus allows for a broader understanding of the global history of revolutionary cinema.

In 1981, the Josip Broz Tito Art Gallery of the Non-Aligned Countries was founded in Titograd, Yugoslavia. The gallery reflected ongoing efforts within the Non-Aligned Movement to support cultural initiatives and foster artistic collaboration among countries seeking to assert independent cultural and political identities. Conceived as a space where NAM countries could contribute by donating artworks, the gallery supported diverse artistic practices, promoted transnational exchange, and fostered cultural connections and knowledge-sharing across the non-aligned world, offering alternatives to the dominant Western paradigms. By the early 1990s, the collection had grown significantly, with over 800 donated pieces from 56 non-aligned countries, featuring prominent non-Western artists such as Saleh Rada, Choukri Mesli, Gazbia Sirry, Rabab Nemr, Inji Efflatoun, Rafikun Nabi, Edsel Moscoso, Suresh Sharma, Agnes Clara Ovando Sanz De Franck, Roberto Valcárcel, and Mariano Rodriguez. It also included donations by unknown artists from Indonesia, Palestine, Nigeria, Kenya, Gabon, Iraq, Zambia—works that had once been classified as handicrafts or applied art within the Western art canon but were now being recognized for their cultural significance. Some pieces were also made during artistic residencies at the gallery, such as the sculpture by Bernard Matemera from Zimbabwe or a copper engraving by Kareem Dabbah from Palestine. However, the tumultuous 90s, marked by political upheavals and the breakup of Yugoslavia, had a significant impact on the gallery and its collection,[9] disrupting the networks of exchange and the institutional support that had sustained this ambitious cultural project.

In Skopje, the capital of the Yugoslav Socialist Republic of Macedonia, a devastating earthquake struck on 26 July 1963, leaving much of the city in ruins. The disaster became a focal point for international solidarity, receiving aid from Eastern, Western, and Non-Aligned countries, including cultural and artistic contributions. Out of this effort, the Museum of Contemporary Art was founded in 1964 and opened in 1970. The building was donated by the Polish government, and its collections were assembled through contributions from artists, the Yugoslav Artists' Union, international organizations like ICOM and UNESCO, and museums worldwide. By 1969, the Slovenian newspaper *Večer* reported the museum held 1,737 works, 1,624 of which were donated by 891 artists from 37 countries, including contributions from the Non-Aligned Countries by artists such as Jesus Rafael Soto, Edison Para, Carlos Cruz-Diez, Azza Hachmi, Wifredo Lam, and Roberto Matta.[10] The Museum of Contemporary Art in Skopje demonstrates how artistic initiatives can respond to disaster while fostering international solidarity; a model that would reemerge decades later under very different circumstances in Sarajevo.

During the siege of Sarajevo in 1992 and the war in Bosnia and Herzegovina, the Ars Aevi initiative emerged as an act of cultural resistance. A group of local enthusiasts invited artists from around the world to contribute works in support of the besieged city. Over time, more than 130 works were donated, including pieces by artists such as Michelangelo Pistoletto, Joseph Beuys, Marina Abramović, Mirosław Bałka, IRWIN, and Jannis Kounellis, forming a collection that became both a testimony and a symbolic gesture during the siege. The collection remains in Sarajevo today, exemplifying international collaboration and the enduring role of art in wartime.

Between 1994 and 1998, artistic directors from museums, centers, galleries, and foundations across Italy, Slovenia, Austria, Bosnia and Herzegovina, and Turkey organized the founding exhibitions, presenting works for the Ars Aevi Collection in its early stages. One of the key moments in shaping the project was the international symposium *Living with Genocide*, held at Moderna galerija in Ljubljana in 1996.[11] Participants addressed the genocide in Srebrenica and the war in Bosnia and Herzegovina, reflecting on the art world's limited engagement and its failure to respond politically or generate meaningful critical interventions. The symposium emphasized the ethical responsibility of artists, curators, and scholars to confront historical violence and promote social accountability through art. At the same time, it emphasized that even though these symbolic gestures were meaningful, they remained insufficient without sustained institutional and political support.

4.

Decades after the end of the Cold War, ongoing wars and violent conflicts continue to reveal the unevenness of global responses to suffering. The longstanding occupation of Palestine and the genocide in Gaza show that, despite widespread support and solidarity from movements and civil society, international institutions, particularly in the West, have repeatedly failed to act effectively. This pattern of systemic failure is most clearly manifested through institutional silence. When museums, academic bodies, or cultural organizations that claim to stand for justice and human rights remain silent in the face of mass violence and genocide, that silence is never neutral: it becomes a form of complicity.

Selective solidarity, where some struggles are supported while others are ignored, delegitimized, or even criminalized, as in the case of Palestine, undermines meaningful collective action. Struggles against war, occupation, and displacement cannot be isolated from one another. Ethical engagement demands that these struggles be understood as interconnected, across contexts of political violence, from Gaza to Ukraine, from Sudan to other sites marked by historical and ongoing trauma.

International responses, however, have varied across conflicts. In Ukraine, for example, Russia's invasion prompted rapid mobilization of political, economic, and cultural support. Art has become one of the means to articulate solidarity, share experiences of war, and sustain cultural life under siege, as seen through the project *Sense of Safety* in the YermilovCentre.

During the early stages of the invasion, the YermilovCentre became more than just an exhibition space. It transformed into a shelter where some artists took refuge as the invasion began. In this convergence of art, survival, and political resistance, the distinction between art and life was suspended. Art became life in its most radical sense: the art of the living. In his 1993 short film *Je Vous Salue, Sarajevo* about the war in Bosnia and Herzegovina, Jean-Luc Godard reflects on culture as the rule and art as the exception. He notes that everything speaks about the rule, but nothing about the exception, because art cannot be explained, it can only be filmed, composed, or lived. Sarajevo stands as a crucial historical reference, not only as a site of extreme violence but also as a place where art endured under siege, defying the notion that art cannot exist in wartime. This legacy resonates strongly in Ukraine today.

Taking inspiration from earlier histories of solidarity, Ahmet Öğüt's works *Jump Up!* and *Safe Return of the Evacuated*, presented at the YermilovCentre's exhibition, offer a different approach. Rather than creating new artworks, Öğüt emphasizes preservation and care. His installation features copies of three significant Ukrainian artworks—by Alla Horska, Zoia Lerman, and Serhiy Zhadan—which were evacuated from Kharkiv. Next to them, trampolines invite physical engagement as viewers can only see the works by jumping on them. In this way, the work shifts the attention from artistic originality and symbolic donation towards the ethics of safeguarding cultural memory in times of destruction. Solidarity here is enacted through protection and bodily engagement, rather than remaining merely declarative.

An earlier version of *Jump Up!* was first shown and specifically conceived for the Museum of Contemporary Art in Skopje alongside the museum's solidarity collection. The trampolines introduce an element of play that is neither escapist nor innocent. Drawing on Giorgio Agamben's notion of the "invasion of life by play,"[12] the work suggests that play can interrupt and accelerate time, disrupting the steady progression of violence. Through play, people can free themselves, if only temporarily, from the constraints of regulated time: from the time of war, trauma, and repetition. In this sense, play becomes a political act, offering a fragile yet vital reprieve from the totalizing force of violence over life.

By reactivating *Jump Up!* in Kharkiv, Öğüt forges connections between contemporary Ukraine and previous sites of artistic and cultural solidarity, linking local acts of preservation to transnational histories of resistance and care. His work embodies the ethical and affective dimensions of solidarity discussed throughout this text. It acknowledges past struggles, interconnects communities across time and space—from Gaza to Skopje, Sarajevo to Kharkiv—and demonstrates that art can function as both medium and practice of resistance. In doing so, Öğüt shows that solidarity is not merely symbolic; it becomes a lived, participatory, and transformative experience, connecting memory, imagination, and action across historical and contemporary contexts, making tangible the radical potential of the art of the living.

---

1. Baruch Spinoza, *The Ethics*, Part 3, trans. R. H. M. Elwes, *Project Gutenberg* (1997), https://www.gutenberg.org/cache/epub/948/pg948-images.html [accessed 13 December 2025].
2. Sékou Touré, speech at the Second Congress of Black Writers and Artists, Rome, 1959, quoted in Frantz Fanon, *The Wretched of the Earth*, trans. Constance Farrington (New York: Grove Press, 2004), p. 145.
3. The Non-Aligned Movement was a coalition of small and medium-sized states, mostly former colonies and developing countries from the Third World. Yugoslavia was one of its founders and key members. At the first Summit in Belgrade in 1961, there were 25 participating countries, and by the 1986 Summit in Harare the organisation had grown to 101 members.
4. The term historically carried emancipatory and anti-colonial connotations, implying a struggle for political independence, economic development, and cultural self-determination. Today, it is considered outdated, and Global South is generally preferred.
5. See Bojana Piškur, "Southern Constellations: Other Histories, Other Modernities," in *Southern Constellations: Poetics of the Non-Aligned* (Ljubljana: Moderna galerija, 2019), pp. 9–24.
6. International Association of Art Critics (AICA), General Assembly, Yugoslavia (Zagreb, Ljubljana, Belgrade, Dubrovnik), 1973. At this meeting, one of the main discussions was a polemic around Eurocentric modernist approaches versus naïve art. Oto Bihalji-Merin, a Yugoslav art historian, advocated for naïve art as bridging folk traditions and contemporary art.
7. See for example the project by DAVRA, "Friendship of Peoples: Tashkent Film Exchange," https://davra.ca/creating/friendship-of-peoples-tashkent-film-exchange [accessed 13 December 2025].
8. Elena Razlogova, *Cinema in the Spirit of Bandung: The Afro-Asian Film Festival Circuit, 1957–1964*, 1st ed. (New York: Routledge, 2014), p. 9.
9. For more information and history on the NAM collection, see *Odjeci nesvrstanih: darovi i uzvraćanja = Nonaligned Echoes: Gifts and Returns* (Podgorica: Muzej savremene umjetnosti Crne Gore, 2024), Natalija Vujošević, pp. 12–15. The collection is part of the Museum of Contemporary Art of Montenegro. When the Laboratory of the Collection of the Non-Aligned Movement was established in 2022, the collection underwent a revival, featuring new exhibitions, research projects, and international collaborations.
10. The Archives of the Moderna galerija contain a folder entitled "Skopje," which includes Yugoslav newspaper clippings about the artists and their donations to the "Museum of Solidarity" in Skopje.
11. *Living with Genocide: Art and the War in Bosnia* (Ljubljana: M'ARS, Moderna galerija, 1999).
12. Giorgio Agamben, *Infancy and History: On the Destruction of Experience*, trans. Liz Heron (London: Verso, 2007), p. 76.

A Culture of Support

Maryna Konieva

10.03.2022, 19:50

Maryna, hi! How are you? Have you left?

Hi! No, I'm in Kharkiv How about you?

I was in Kyiv, and we left the day before yesterday. Which neighborhood are you in? Don't you want to leave? Can't you?

I'm near the train station.
But I don't plan to leave.
I'm volunteering a bit, saving art a bit))) lots of things to do))

Okay, Maryna.
Take care.

Thank you, you too))

I heard about some vacancies in Dresden museums, including the Albertinum. I thought you might be interested.

Thank you, but I've decided to stay for now.

Okay.
I understand.

We don't know each other very well, but could you text me sometimes? I'm really worried about what's happening, especially in Kharkiv.

From correspondence
with Tatiana Kochubinska

Those few caring messages to someone I barely knew started a long and sincere conversation full of understanding and support, which grew into a friendship and later a collaboration on the *Sense of Safety* project.

INFRASTRUCTURE OF CARE

By channeling a vision of human existence as fragile, bodily, and vulnerable, the force field *Infrastructure of Care* emphasizes the fact that safety is not just an individual emotion or experience. It is first and foremost a collective practice, supported by a complex system of infrastructures. This force field shifts the focus from those who experience safety or unsafety to those who create, maintain, and support safety, often at the risk of their own lives and well-being. *Infrastructure of Care* brings together various artistic practices of care, from the collective to the intimate, that organize temporary or long-term care structures. The effects of these infrastructures go beyond aesthetic perception, encompassing gestures of solidarity, hospitality, and sharing.

When the full-scale invasion started, it definitely mobilized the whole cultural community, which by then had a longstanding network of connections and mutual support. Very quickly, that system adjusted to the new challenges. Helping with evacuations, finding safe places to stay, searching for places to store art, delivering food and money, and even just asking a simple but super meaningful question: "How are you?"

During those first days, representatives of the Kharkiv art community received messages and phone calls from colleagues in other cities, as well as from virtually all of their international partners with whom they had ever collaborated, offering shelter or simply asking: "How can we help you?"

Almost instantly, the professional network transformed into an extensive infrastructure with a common purpose: to help.

03.04.2022, 20:12

Marisha, hi! How are you, girl? Well, Yaroslava told me about your situation. And you probably know about mine...
Thank you for helping out tomorrow.
Here are some more helpers:
I talked to Kokhan and Kalashnik—they'll come tomorrow to help with the artworks if they need to be moved from the storage room upstairs...
You have Vitalik's phone number, don't you?
And Kolomiets is ready—I couldn't reach him, but Les talked to him.
He/Kolomiets can also come to help—he's available until 1 pm. Kokhan promised that they would take another look at the situation with the windows and doors and maybe come up with something.
Thank you!
Take care, and stay strong!

Thank you! Yeah, I was also thinking about Kokhan, Kalashnik, and Hamlet. But we need to check it out first. If there's no water, the paintings will be safer in the storage room than upstairs. We'll see depending on the situation...
And yeah, we need to figure something out with the windows.
We'll get through this! Hugs)[1]

From correspondence with Tatiana Tumasian regarding assistance for the damaged Municipal Gallery[2]

Everyone had their own inner reasons to take the first step and get involved. For some, it was an impulse of self-defense, for others it was a need to stay connected to reality or just a logical consequence of their own professional ethics. This is how Vitalii Kokhan explained his decision to volunteer: "When you are somewhere outside and see what is going on, you have a better grasp of the situation than if you just read the news while sitting in a basement." For some people, the motivation came from the simplest everyday situations. Oleh Kalashnik recalled that people reached out to him simply because they knew he had a car and, therefore, he was able to help. In peacetime, these same contacts worked quite differently: fellow artists would call him to ask him to transport their artworks from their studios to a gallery, deliver materials, or help install an exhibition. When the full-scale war began, the network of artistic mutual aid almost imperceptibly shifted its focus—now the same people were asking to evacuate their relatives, deliver medicine and food, and so on.

Similarly, the functions of cultural institutions have changed. Galleries, which until recently gathered visitors for exhibition openings, became spaces of support: windows were boarded up, shelters were arranged, and people helped each other to survive—both physically and professionally. The artistic infrastructure, which had been working to exchange ideas and visual solutions, was transformed into a system of care. And this also demonstrated the power of community: the ability to maintain connections, reconfigure them, and make them useful in circumstances that no one could have predicted.

07.05.2023, 20:46

Maryna, hi!!! You ok?

Hey!)) Yeah!)) How are you?

oh well... we have 7 tons of humanitarian aid, some of which has already been transported to Kherson, but now it's so dangerous to go there... And my friends are going back and texting me that it's crazy out there, but they're going back.
Our people are invincible)

I have a tiiiiiiiny creative request for you)

could you tell me what you did during the blackouts? what did you do in the dark?

Should I write it here?

Yeap

I'm currently doing a little research on how artists experienced all that. And then it will become an art book by Max and me—we started it during the blackouts.[3]

From correspondence with Olena Afanasieva

Each of us dealt with the experience of encountering war in our own way. What seemed ephemeral and distant suddenly became our common everyday life, changing our pace, our perspective, and the way we manage our inner resources. Psychologists identify three ways of responding to a sudden threat: fight, flight, or freezing. Within the art community, these reactions were particularly vivid.

Some people literally froze: they could no longer work with the material, reconnect with the canvas, pick up their musical instrument, or return to the text. Others, on the contrary, tried to capture every action, every piece of news, every soundbite and headline——as if they were trying to keep sane with the help of art. For many, creativity became a way to balance the chaos and maintain their presence in events.

Later, when the first shock had passed, the art community began to form its own strategies for action. New projects, new interaction formats, and new institutions emerged—either temporary or with a longer-term perspective. Artists with quite separate practices were uniting around tasks that went beyond the aesthetic: to support, explain, witness, preserve, and help ...

As Ukrainians defend their cultural heritage—from archives to museums, from books to frescoes—the art community itself has become part of a broader support infrastructure. Because art is not just about images and forms; it is also a way to support society, reduce its vulnerability, and create a space where people can breathe, speak, and be heard.

The war continues, and we are adjusting and preserving everything that matters.

1. Vitalii Kokhan, Oleh Kalashnik, Mykola Kolomiets, and Hamlet Zinkivskyi are representatives of the Kharkiv art community who have been involved in volunteer work since the first days of the full-scale invasion.
2. Tatiana Tumasian is a gallerist and founder of the first Ukraine Municipal Gallery (1996). In early March 2022, the gallery space was damaged due to the bombing of a neighboring building.
3. The artbook *Blackout* (2023) by Max Afanasyev and Olena Afanasieva was part of the exhibition *Sense of Safety*.

Asia Tsisar

On Solidarity: In Bold Italics at the End of the Section

As I sit down to write this text, I think about time and space—the distance between me and this exhibition, between the exhibition and you who are reading about it. How many kilometers, languages, and borders separate you (us) from the point in space-time that produced this exhibition? From what temporal distance, and under the shadow of which war—this one or another; global or intergalactic (as I write this, belief in any peace feels fragile)—are you opening this catalogue? What is it that you want to understand through it?

In another text, I will write about a textbook—a textbook on solidarity that our generation never received. The meanings and practices of solidarity in this war, as in others simultaneously unfolding elsewhere, have had to be written on our knees. A textbook would give us a clear formula: 2 + 2 = 4. Writing on our knees, we instead grope through objects in a dark room, trying to imagine what a "4" might look like. This, dear readers of the future, is what the search for an answer to the question "what is solidarity?" looks like on the eve of a Third World War. Those of you (us) who work in art, scattered across the world, ask this question as a strategy of survival. We want to believe there is still time. We hope there are not many objects left in the room.

This text is not a textbook. But I would like it to become part of one. At school, I remember that after each theoretical chapter there were always a few pages set in bold italics. They told a story—from life, from a newspaper, or from a diary—meant to show how theory worked in practice, how events shaped the lives of those who lived through them.

In an explosion, there is a moment when the blast has already happened but the ground keeps shaking, distributing the force of impact. The shockwave has passed, and the struck object is suspended in silence. Debris thrown into the air freezes for an instant, then slowly begins to drift back down, guided only by gravity. Objectively, this only lasts seconds—an interval as brief as the full-scale invasion might come to seem within the flow of world history. But time is subjective, and subjectivity is never simple. For those close to the epicenter of the explosion, time becomes thick, bodily. They must push through every millisecond, respond, adapt. For those watching from afar ... yes, subjectivity again, never simple. Proximity to the epicenter is not a bad framework for forming a community. The farther away you are—physically and metaphysically—the more that framework dissolves, the more room there is for subjectivity. Somewhere within these suspended seconds, the exhibition *Sense of Safety* took place. We are still in the second after the explosion. The fragments of time torn apart years ago are still suspended in the air.

My subjectivity in relation to the epicenter has thrown me to a point neither obvious nor expected. Physically, I am far away. Mentally, I live in the past of a place that no longer exists. "Kharkiv stands"—you have likely read this in news reports or texts by those who dare to come despite everything. These short visits often produce stories about culture blooming under bombs, about heroic people who earn Kharkiv the name "reinforced concrete." As you read this, keep nearby, or at least in mind, all the sharp edges and soft mental cushions that such romanticization contains. As for me, when I step into this city, I know I am a guest in my own home. The Kharkiv I knew shattered into splinters after a direct hit by a cruise missile on 1 March 2022 (subjectivity—never simple). Since then, those who were close to the epicenter, and those who later arrived, have reshaped the space according to their needs and the reality they found themselves in. I was not there. I did not change alongside them. And although I can still walk these streets with my eyes closed, I no longer know the city I return to. This feeling is a hollow pain bordering on an overwhelming, sunlit gratitude. It hurts like I am a lost button, or an old sweater left behind because it did not fit into a hastily packed suitcase. At the same time, I am grateful to everyone who cares for, defends, and fills my home with life when I am not there. To those who stayed. To those who came. Thanks to you, there remains a point on the map to which we can return—a space not consumed by Russian darkness. From this place of pain and gratitude—as a reluctant observer of my own home—I write this text. I no longer have the right to speak on behalf of Kharkiv, but I can act as a conductor. Not a guide, not a narrator, but a material that does not resist, like metal carrying an electric current. I can try to transmit, across distance and time, the city in which *Sense of Safety* took place.

In the unexpectedly warm and gentle autumn of 2024, I sit on Andreas Angelidakis' fabric-covered soft ruins inside the YermilovCentre—a space I visited countless times before the full-scale invasion, and which I am entering for the first time since. Everything is exactly as I remember it, and entirely different at once.

I know these concrete walls and slabs, the heavy metal doors, the low windows. When the YermilovCentre opened in March 2012, they felt like the architecture of a contemporary art institution the city had long deserved. In the years that followed, this demanding concrete felt like an obstacle: mounting exhibitions here was difficult because the space always dominated. Now none of that matters. The cubic meters of concrete surrounding me are a direct marker of safety. This is not a metaphor about art as a safe space for dialogue. This safety is literal. This concrete can protect my body from a missile that flies faster than the air-raid siren turns on.

Here are people, a few of them I still know, with whom I began working in art decades ago. Here are faces that seem familiar: when I left Kharkiv, you greeted every third person on the street and knew every second one indirectly. And here are people

I am meeting for the first time. When I left, they were schoolchildren. Now they are students—second or third year. They are not visitors here, but staff: the small team that keeps the YermilovCentre alive. These children are here instead of us, those who left. And this, then, is a story of institutional continuity.

Do all of us who left feel ashamed? After all, by fleeing we were exercising our right to safety, a right enshrined in international conventions and in the biology of the human body. And yet, why does this right feel like a legal paradox in wartime? To exercise it means to escape responsibility toward one's country, city, or place. And if no one owes anything to anyone, if this debt is only imagined, why do I feel like a thief when I look at these prematurely grown-up children?

Among the faces, I single out one I know best: Maryna Konieva—curator, art historian, the person who once taught me, with sheets of drawing paper and colored markers, how to draft my very first exhibition; co-curator of *Sense of Safety*. Maryna smiles at me, and I, trying to fit my emotions into socially acceptable patterns, ask:

— How is the exhibition? How was the opening?

— The opening? You know ... it was like before. Everyone came.

People, especially people who work in art, had been leaving Kharkiv long before the full-scale invasion. The city took offense. Art here was always the work of individuals: artist-people, institution-people, people as schools and movements. In such a human-centered world, institutions, styles, and schools do not outlive their creators. They pack their suitcases with them, burn out with them, rediscover themselves or settle into the comfort of stories that take the place of Kharkiv's history of art. There were better times, worse times, but the city's rhythm was never broken. Every autumn, several hundred thousand new people flooded the streets: students, young people arriving from the east, north, and south. Newcomers inhaled the spores of old stories and caught their inspiration. Life went on in the anthill.

The full-scale war paralyzed not only Kharkiv, but also the network of routes that crossed through it. East (Luhansk and Donetsk), North (Sumy), South (Zaporizhzhia, Kherson, Mykolaiv)—all of them, like Kharkiv itself, turned into combat zones. Kharkiv, once a central hub where all routes converged, became a dead end. Now people come for a day or two in search of compelling stories: about war, about culture blooming under bombs, about heroic individuals. These stories are recorded and quickly taken away, beyond the Dnipro, across borders, perhaps even across oceans, to tell the world about a city the world has left alone.

You might say: instructive, interesting, but this is an exhibition catalogue after all, and surely one would like to read something about the exhibition itself. Yet solidarity is a practice that falls into the blind spot of photo and video documentation.

It gets lost at a distance from the explosion and disappears when the debris finally hits the ground. *Sense of Safety* is the first international exhibition in Kharkiv since the beginning of the full-scale invasion, but its importance lies not in the list of names or works. It matters because, instead of taking something from the city, this project chose to give something back. For the duration of *Sense of Safety*, Kharkiv once again became a center—a node that connects people. And even if this feeling is only an illusion, like a blanket you hide under during an explosion, it gives strength to endure the moment. That is already more than enough.

Of course, Maryna and I will never say any of this out loud. No one in Kharkiv ever will. The war may have changed the city, but it has not taken away its self-respect. Kharkiv has never known how to ask or complain; it has never felt the need to explain itself. Short phrases like "everyone came" and "it was like before" are enough. Our small talk continues. I ask:

— Tell me about the works.

Maryna walks me through the exhibition. In an instant, I become a guest again in a home I have only just rediscovered. The fragile thread of understanding between me and Kharkiv snaps. I do not understand these works, their selection, the connections between them. The sense of safety woven from the words "like before" turns out to be unreliable. I fall. I catch myself in a toxic, paternalistic position. I know most of these works, especially the archival ones and those created at the beginning of the full-scale invasion. Beyond the Dnipro, abroad, across the ocean, each of them has long acquired a set of established interpretations, and none of them work here. Before me is a rebus made of images, signs, fragments of words. Once again, I am a lost button, unable to see the connections needed to solve this puzzle.

To find meaning, I need not time but another conversation—not with those I have known for years, but with people I am meeting for the first time. Sonia, Lera, and Vlad are students, mediators of *Sense of Safety*, prematurely grown-up children now here instead of us. They are the ones explaining the exhibition to me, an adult, a curator of sorts, a lost button who does not know how to read this display. Sonia, Lera, and Vlad say that the exhibition attracts many visitors; the YermilovCentre has not seen so many people in its halls for a long time. These visitors—locals, internally displaced people, soldiers, those whom the war has turned into Kharkiv residents—spend hours here. They ask questions, share thoughts, and say thank you. It does not matter that I cannot locate myself within this exhibition. It is not about me. It is about them. Art-historical theories and conceptual frameworks, the entire apparatus of high-minded contemporary art, becomes secondary here and is (fortunately) instrumentalized to create what art and solidarity should be in essence: a situation in which viewers find themselves, and find answers to questions they may not have known they had. The safety of this project is also a space where locals can reflect on their feelings and find words to better understand their experience of frontline Kharkiv. And it does not really matter whether this makes sense to anyone outside.

Together with Liza, a manager at the YermilovCentre, we step into the courtyard. Liza is only a year older than the exhibition mediators and is preparing to defend her bachelor's thesis. Like them, this is her first experience working on a major international project. Since the beginning of the full-scale invasion, only one person from the YermilovCentre team remained working in Kharkiv—its longstanding director, Nataliia Ivanova. Liza first came as a visitor and, after one event, simply asked Nataliia: "Do you maybe need some help here?" We talk about preparing the project, correspondence with artists, transporting works from abroad, logistics, long curatorial discussions, and installation. *Sense of Safety* began when the team of antiwarcoalition.art called Nataliia Ivanova to ask: "What do you need? And surely an exhibition is the last thing you need right now." To which Nataliia replied: "Oh no, an exhibition is exactly what we need."

What can an international exhibition offer a frontline city left on its own? Lofty meanings or, quite simply, jobs. Something that is taken for granted in cities far from war: opportunities for young people to gain experience, build CVs, acquire skills, and grow professionally. It is a simple gesture of solidarity, one that is not immediately obvious.

Among those feeling their way through objects in a dark room are people who rely on intuition and those who draw on experience, their own experience of political repression, war, and forced displacement. They search for solidarity through a set of questions: How would we want to be addressed in a situation of existential threat? What did we need in that moment but were never asked about? How do we avoid confusing solidarity with charity? What forms can solidarity take in a dialogue between equals, when inequality of resources between those who express solidarity and those who need it is the starting point of the conversation?

A “documentary witness” performance unpacked the cycle of life and nonexistence in the context of wa emigration, and human relationships. It served as a method of reflecting on and transforming the harsl realities that seize hearts and minds. In a world where everything unfolds simultaneously and is difficult t grasp as a whole, the performance initiated a process of “digesting” these experiences through artistic prac tice. Structured around personal monologues, the performance brought together different actors who eacl addressed a complex and urgent topic, including war, emigration, and relationships. The music was created i real-time, complementing the stage with live sound reflecting shifting emotions and moods. The performanc combined bodily and verbal experiences to foster a sincere dialogue with the audience.

Digestion, performance, 2024. Photo: Mykhailo Protsenk

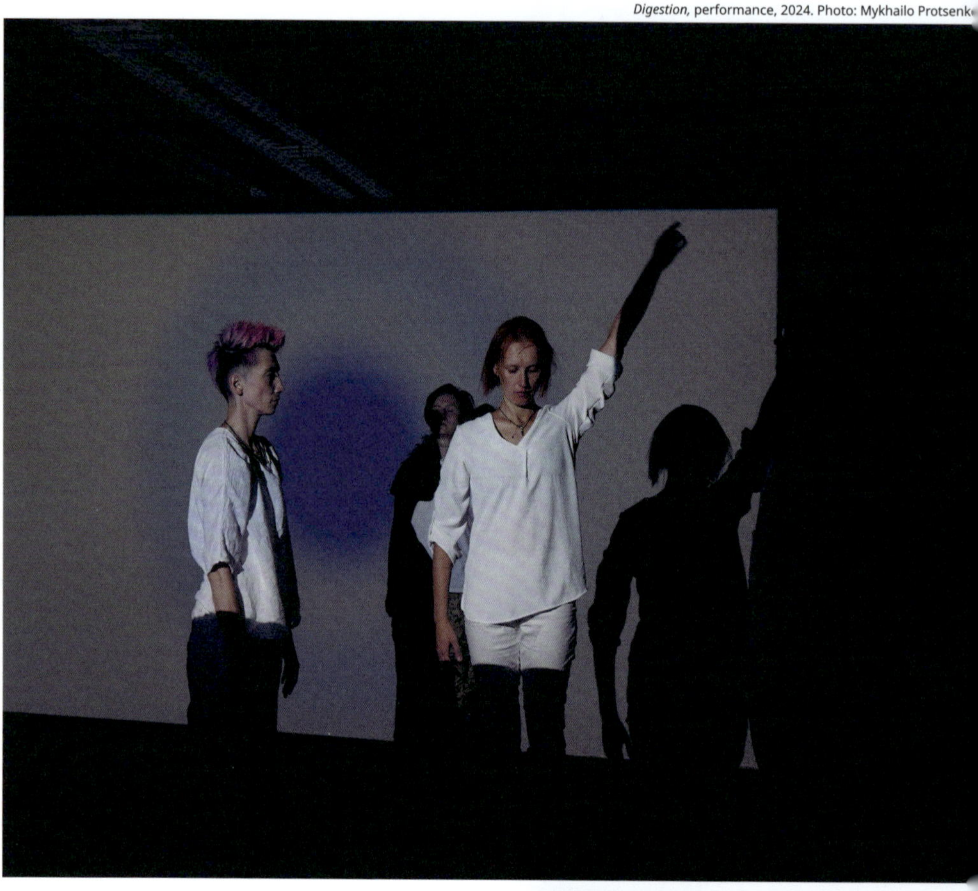

Digestion

Performance

 YermilovCentre, Kharkiv (UA)

Date
07.09.2024

Participants
Kateryna Berezovska (UA)
Kostiantyn Ivanov (UA)
Anna Pohoryelova (UA)
Kateryna Radushynska (UA)
Alisa Volkova (UA)
Olena Yermishkina (UA)

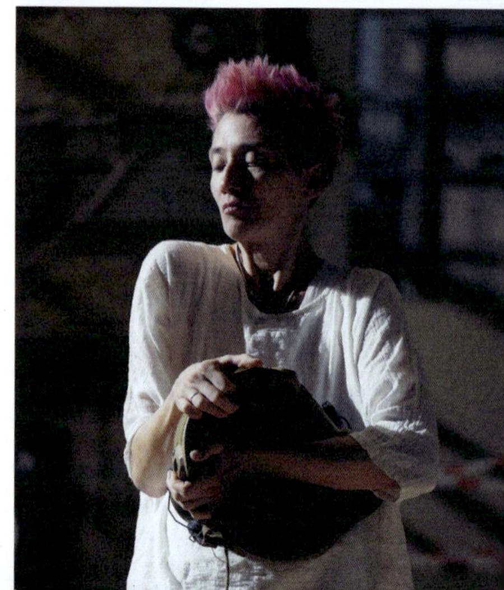

The event took the form of a livestream broadcast from the studio of UKRAiNATV in Kraków, mixed with video streams from YermilovCentre in Kharkiv and further disseminated, creating a synthesis of different streams that generated a sense of presence within a multichannel media environment. The final stream integrated the exhibition at the YermilovCentre, forming a live audiovisual bridge between different geographical and political contexts. In addition to the live audiovisual connection to Kharkiv, the event resonated with the entire *Sense of Safety* project's hybrid presence and ideas of expanded space. It aligned with the central mission of UKRAiNATV as an experimental cross-sector media project that combines internet television, a streaming hub, and a "glocal" network under the conditions of war.

tills from the event livestream, UKRAiNATV, 2024.

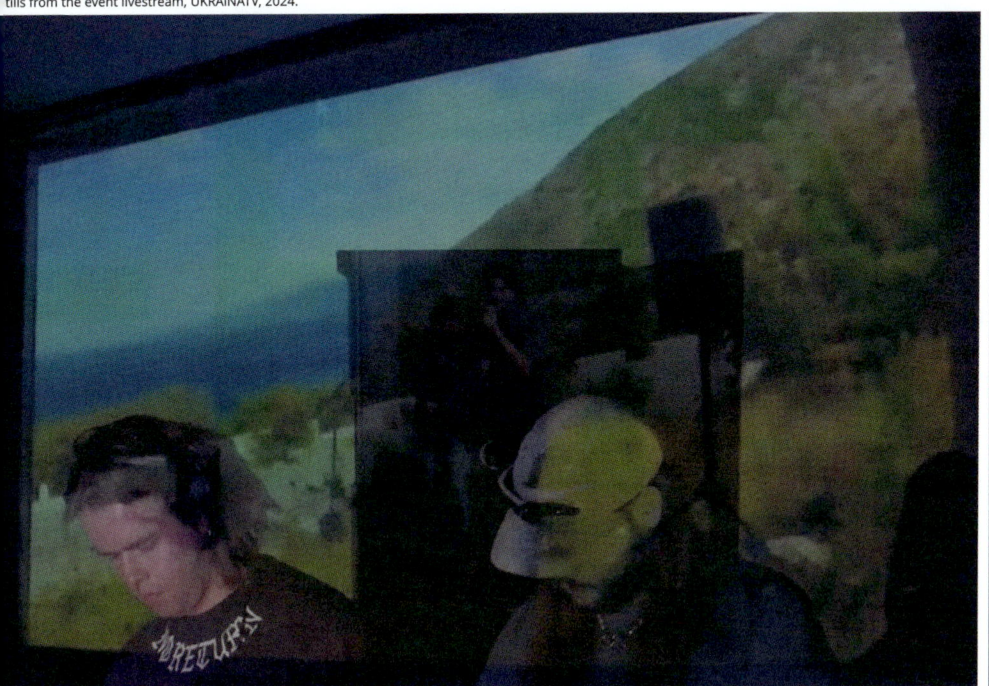

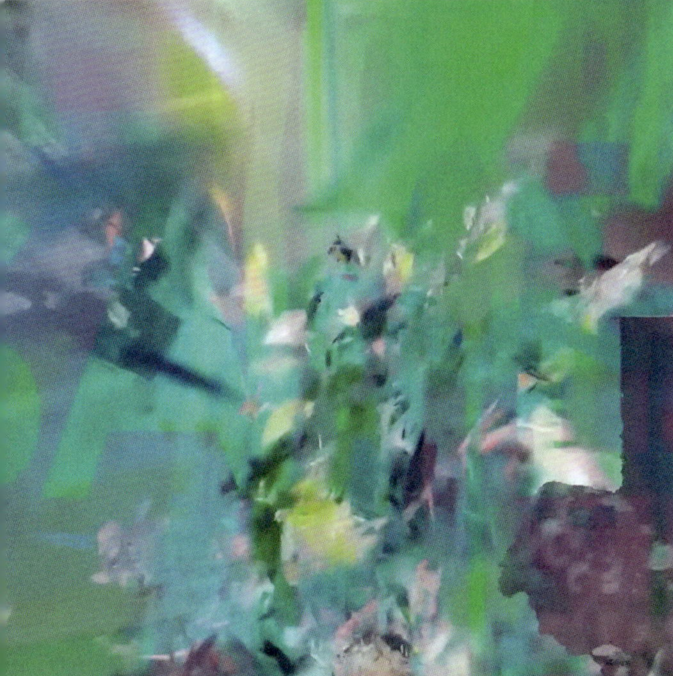

UKRAiNATV stream

Hybrid event and stream

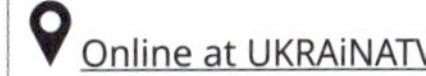
Online at UKRAiNATV

Date
05–06.09.2024

Participants
Timothy Maxymenko (UA/UK)
(r)Hlib Dovzhuk (UA)
Sofiia Reznichenko (UA)
Rom Dziadkiewicz (PL)

Rhona Mühlebach

born 1990 in Zurich, Switzerland; based in Glasgow, Scotland

2016
VIDEO, 6'23"
COURTESY OF THE ARTIST

To Get In Touch With Crows

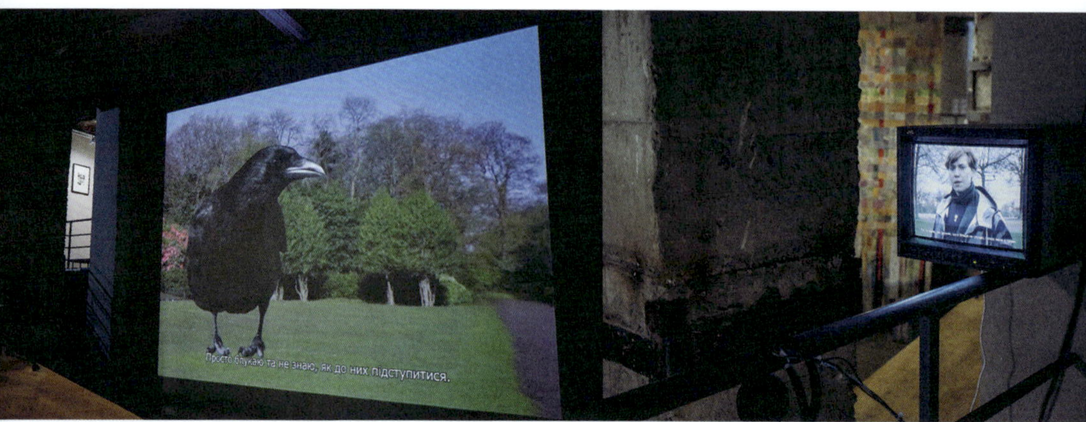

Rhona Mühlebach's artistic practice explores the gap between humankind's desire to humanize nature and nature's inability to match our expectations. Humans regularly seek to endow nature with qualities like cruelty, kindness, humor, sadness, or sympathy, though often in vain. Yet through her dedication to engaging with non-human agents, Mühlebach shows that this experience can also be compassionate and existential, where the attempt to connect with nature may be more meaningful than the final result.

In her video *To Get In Touch With Crows*, edited images and cawing, overlaid with a human voice, create a disquieting form of language that the artist uses to highlight the impossibility of dialogue through humanization, revealing the ambivalence of communication as a site of safety. The artist goes to Queen's Park, where she attempts to establish a relationship with crows. The video references the format of popular nature documentaries, where the world of animals and birds is portrayed in terms of human feelings and social relationships.

This seemingly serious narrative devoid of redundant details ironically shows the failure of the anthropocentric approach, as it maintains clearly hierarchical boundaries between subject and object. Here, the only possibility for the object, i.e. nature, to be "heard" is when it corresponds to the expectations and norms of human society. When watching animals, people seldom consider that humans, too, are being observed, and that the gaze of animals reacts to our actions, though we can only understand their perceptions on a very rudimentary level. In the context of the exhibition, Mühlebach's video opens a new "door" to the realm of imagination, a place where you are never alone and where "non-human others" are always present.

*foundationClass

In My Embrace

founded in 2016; graduation class of 2024, Berlin

Participants: Anna Dmytrenko, Katerina Andriuscenco, Oksana Dmytriienko, Nikitenko Nataliia, Sasha

2024
ACRYLIC, OIL, INK, GOUACHE, PASTEL ON CANVAS
PRODUCED ESPECIALLY FOR THE EXHIBITION *SENSE OF SAFETY*
DONATED TO THE YERMILOVCENTRE COLLECTION

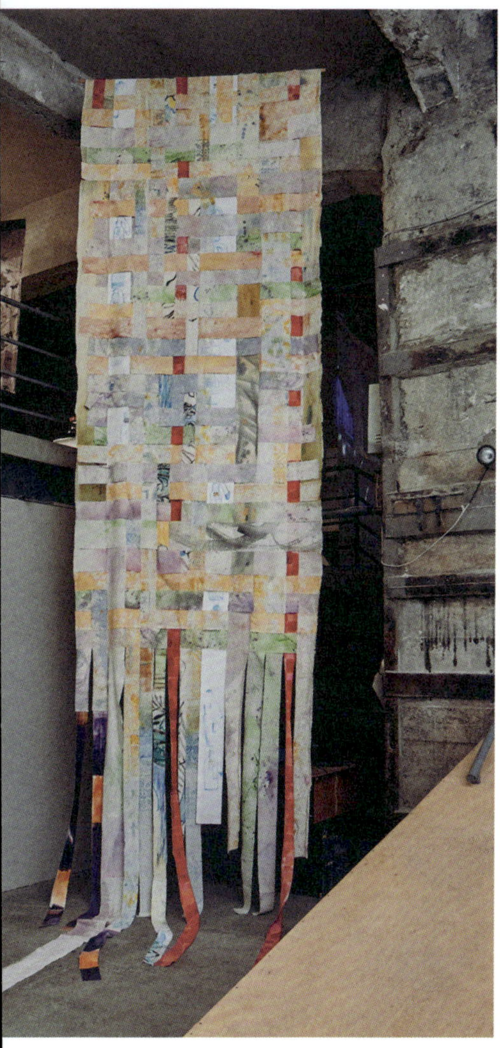

*foundationClass is an activist and educational art initiative founded in 2016 at the Kunsthochschule Weißensee in Berlin as a platform for mutual support and exchange. It promotes access to art academies for cultural workers who have fled to Germany from war and political repression. Nearly every academic year *foundationClass assembles a new group of artists with refugee experiences to help develop their professional practice.

The 2024 graduating cohort of *foundationClass was invited to participate in the exhibition in Kharkiv. They set aside their individual practices to create a large patchwork-like piece titled *In My Embrace*, symbolizing togetherness and solidarity. The collective weaving of a single cloth, which acts both as a protective shield and refers to traditional female knitting practices as well as to the children's game of making a blanket into a shelter, links the idea of safety to collective practices of care. The materiality and performativity of this work emphasize that safety is fragile and needs constant solidarity, care, support, and maintenance.

The gesture of forgoing and literally transforming individual practices into an intertwined canvas, where distinct artistic voices form seams and junctions rather than merging into a homogeneous smooth surface, highlights the principle of connectedness and interdependence. The work is also informed by an ecological perspective: much like a good household trying to minimize waste, *foundationClass uses existing materials to create new artwork.

Karina Synytsia

born 1999 in Sievierodonetsk (now Siverskodonetsk), Ukraine; based in Kyiv

2022
ACRYLIC ON PAPER
COURTESY OF THE ARTIST

Fast, Easy Memory Transfer

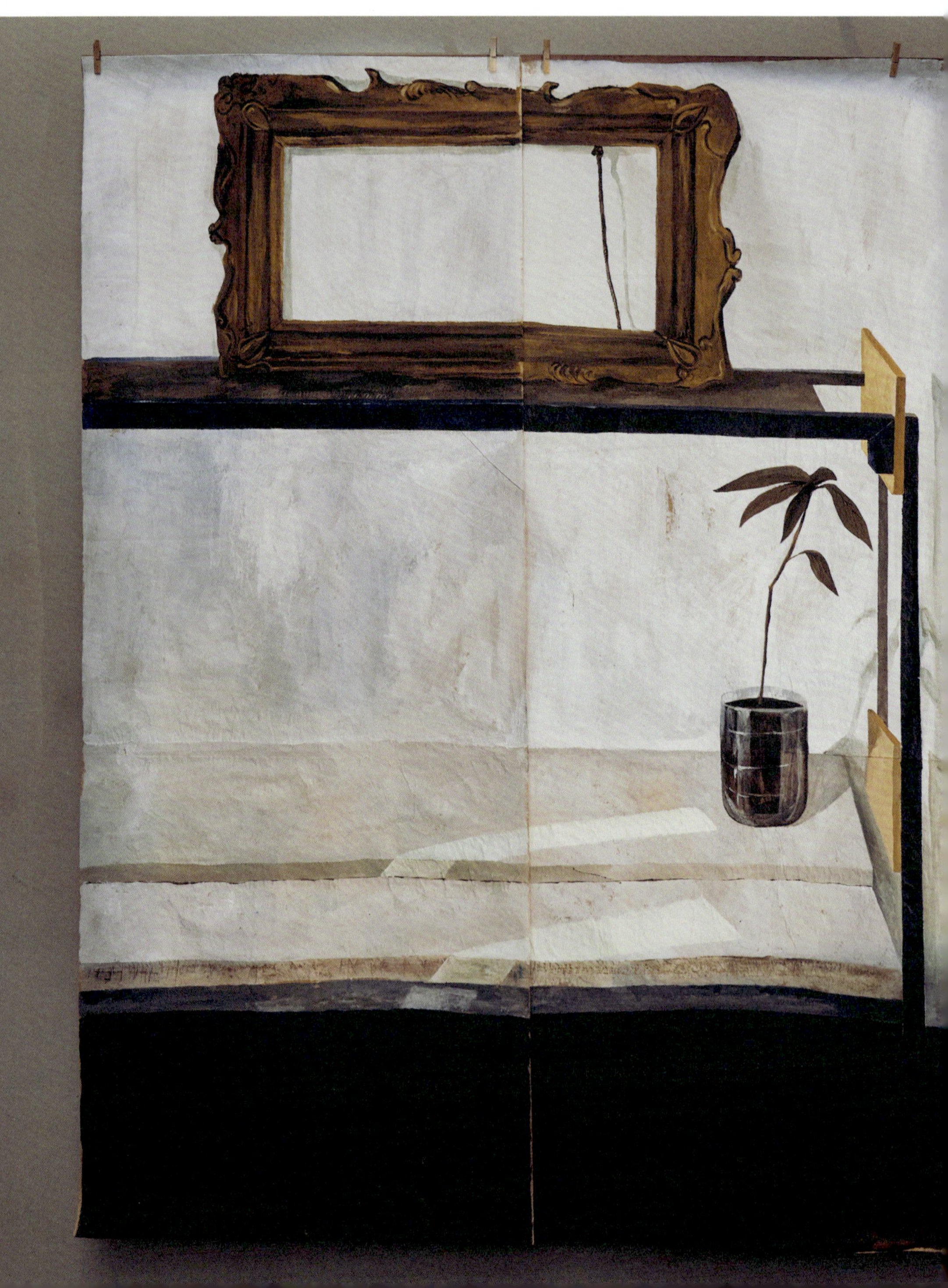

Karina Synytsia's artistic practice is deeply rooted in studying the interaction between humans and their environment. She strives to convey inner experiences and psychological aspects of life through her work. Here, the artist uses her own feelings, memories, and observations as reference points in the process.

The work *Fast, Easy Memory Transfer* is based on the experience of helping friends evacuate artworks at the beginning of Russia's full-scale invasion of Ukraine. This prompted the artist to look for lighter and more compact materials for her artistic practice. The work on paper could be easily rolled up and moved to another room if necessary. The painting depicts a fragment of the interior of the dormitory room where the artist lives. Thanks to the mobility of the material, Synytsia was able to create a work that easily adapts to changing circumstances. Thus, she is able to recreate her native space as an island of stability and safety in a new place. The artist emphasizes the importance of details like the room's interior, which not only reflects her memories but also points to the broader perception of space.

This work is a means of exploring and visualizing the sense of loss that accompanies the process of environmental change. Her work becomes a metaphor for the search for new forms of safety and comfort in the face of instability, which is especially relevant in the context of forced displacement.

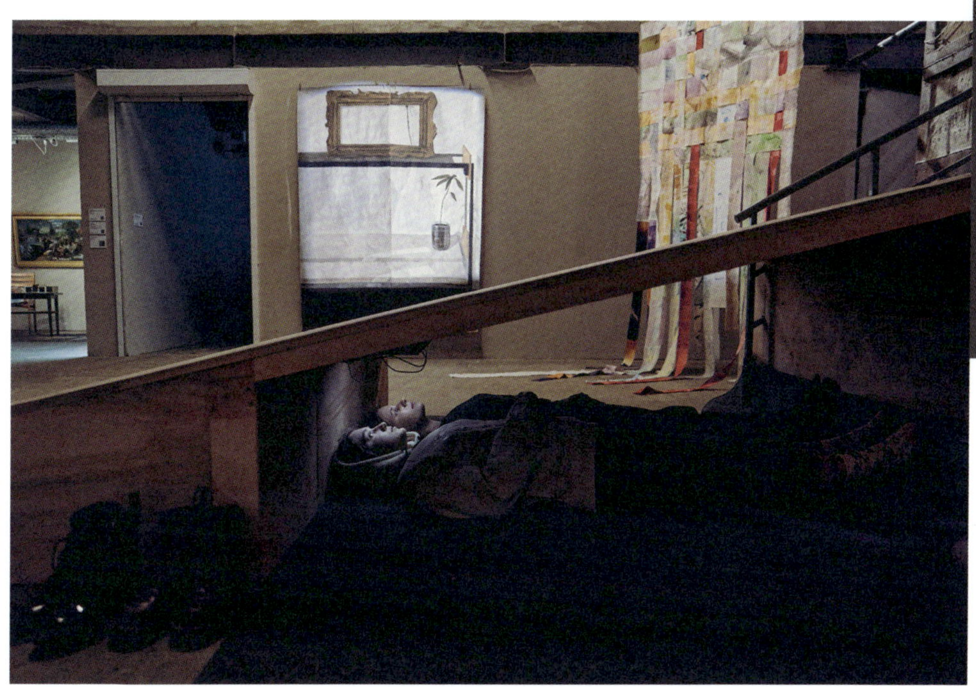

Katya Lesiv

Lullaby 5

born 1993 in Khmelnytskyi, Ukraine; lives and works in Kyiv and Helsinki, Finland

2024
SITE-SPECIFIC INSTALLATION, PLYWOOD, LOOPED VIDEO
PRODUCED ESPECIALLY FOR THE EXHIBITION *SENSE OF SAFETY*
TECHNICAL DEVELOPMENT: VIKTOR DVORNIKOV

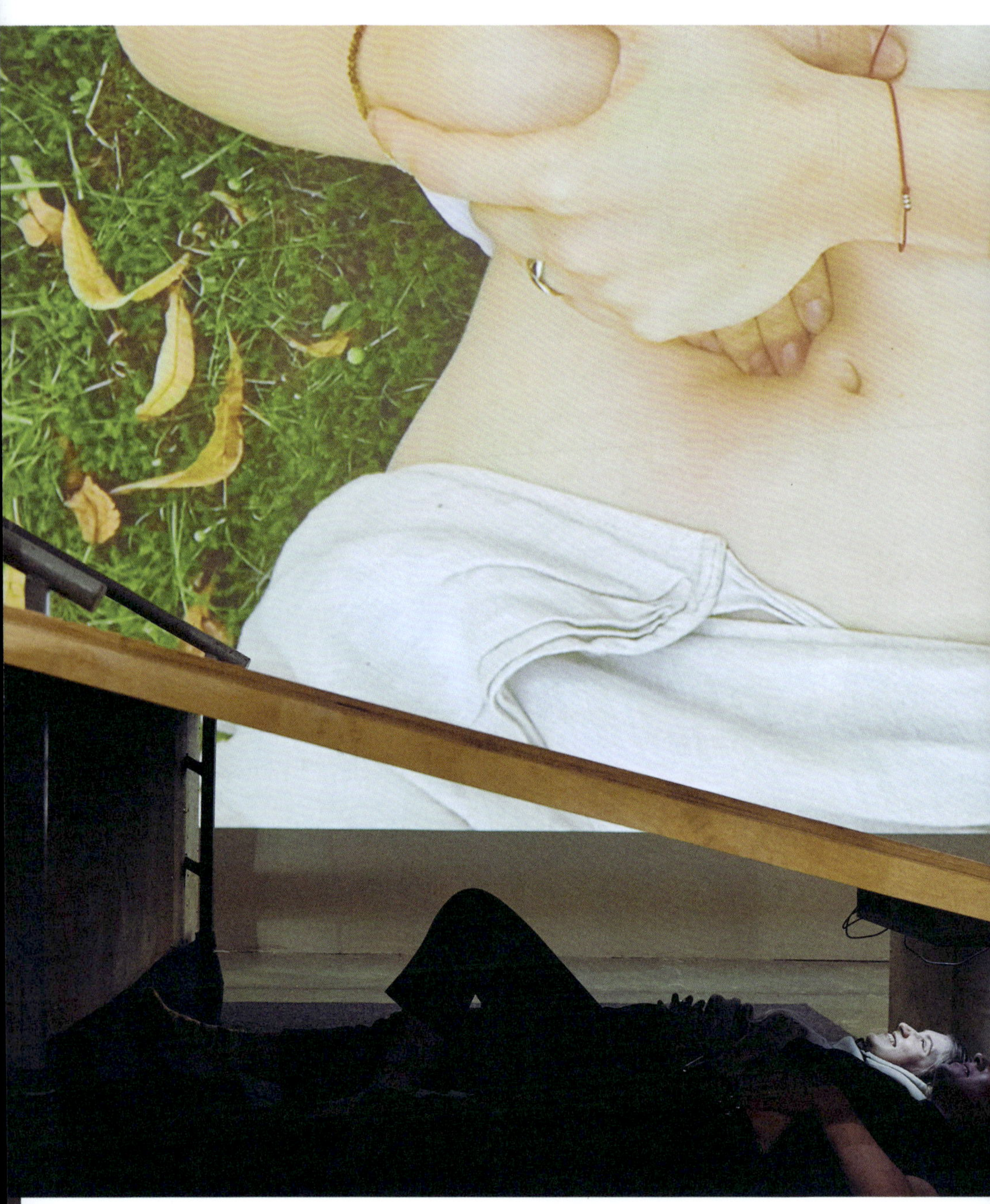

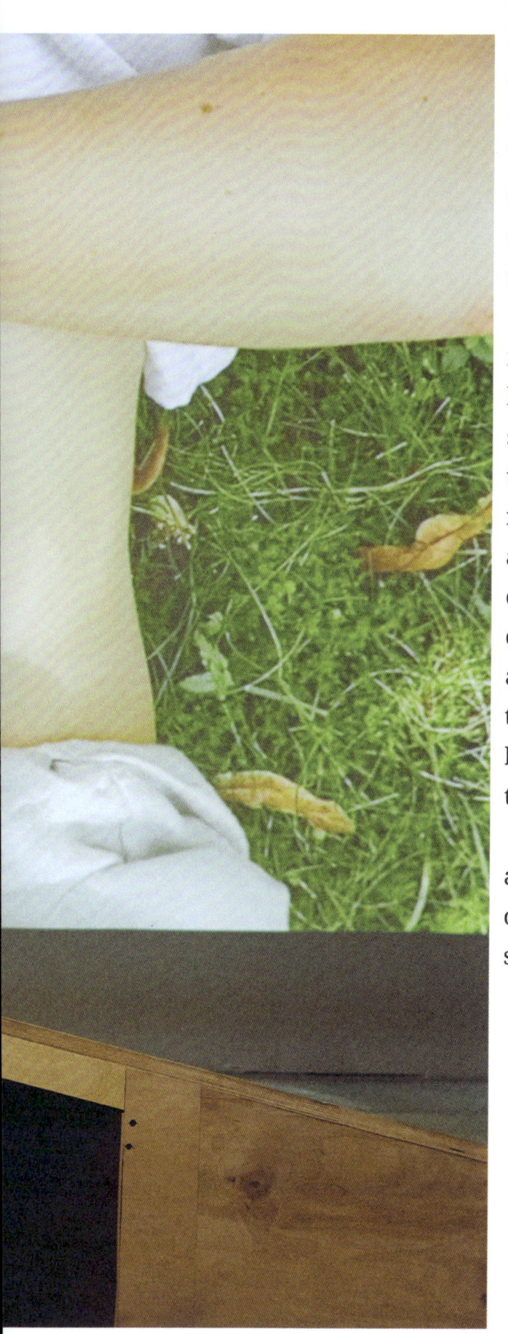

Katya Lesiv works with cyclicality, physicality, and visceral experiences. In her artistic practice, she focuses on the sense of presence through the materiality of various media, including photography, artbooks, installations, objects, text, drawings, and video. Her performative method, often based on domestic or personal rituals, is a way of completing and sharing an intimate experience without violating the boundaries of personal space. With her installation, *Lullaby 5*, the artist transforms the exhibition space of YermilovCentre and creates conditions for the viewer to interact with the work.

Lesiv's object covers the stairs without impairing their practical function of helping visitors move between floors. Under the changed conditions, a space for a person appears between the floor and the object. This cramped hideout could be seen as a reference to children's "shack" constructions built as a safe, controlled space. But inside the object, the claustrophobic descent from above and the sound of footsteps overhead can also trigger a sense of anxiety, danger, and hopelessness. The sound of the video can be heard from outside the structure, but the video itself can only be seen by lying inside the object.

Regardless of one's own associations, interactions with the artwork can be guided by curiosity and physical engagement, both of which are signs of safety and trust.

Vladyslav Krasnoshchok

born 1980 in Kharkiv, Ukraine; based in Kharkiv

House-Museum of Vladyslav Krasnoshchok

2010–ONGOING
MIXED-MEDIA INSTALLATION
COURTESY OF THE ARTIST

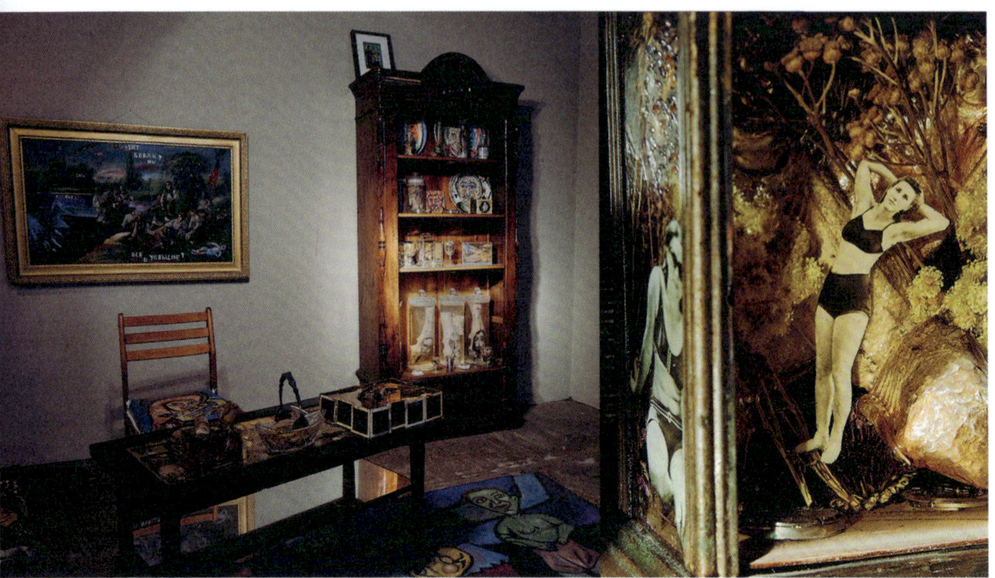

Vladyslav Krasnoshchok is part of the Kharkiv School of Photography and co-founded the art group Shilo in 2010. Alongside his versatile artistic practice, he also continues his medical career, which often influences his artwork. In addition to the photographic series specifically devoted to the daily routine of an oral and maxillofacial surgeon, his medical experience also manifests in the method of his artistic practice. Fascinated by a new technique, the artist carefully explores its possibilities until he feels he has mastered all its facets. Working with assemblage, street art, collage, tattooing, or coloring vintage photographs, the artist seems to dissect existing images, breaking them down into their parts then stitching them back together according to his own aesthetic preferences.

For a long time, Krasnoshchok labeled his photographs with the inscription "museum," emphasizing the value of the works and their prospects of being included in a world museum. In 2017, the artist created a museum of his own works in his childhood home. For the *Sense of Safety* project, the author installed his interior items and artworks, thus recreating a part of his home museum in public space. The artist emphasizes that with the outbreak of a full-scale invasion, he feels the need to surround himself with familiar and valuable objects that contribute to his emotional peace. He thus demonstrates one way of creating self-support and self-stabilization.

Stas Volyazlovsky

1971–2018, Kherson, Ukraine

Max Afanasyev

born 1971 in Kherson, Ukraine

In the Museum – 2

2011
VIDEO, 7'01"
COURTESY OF THE GRYNYOV ART COLLECTION

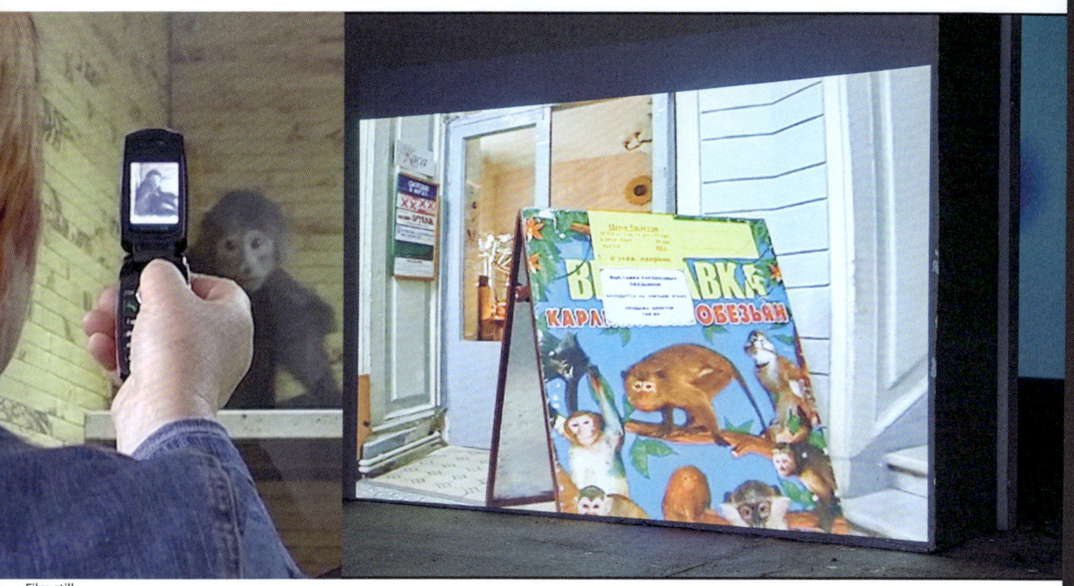

Film still

In his artistic practice, Stas Volyazlovsky drew on mass culture, art brut, the visual language of prisons, and the everyday routines of Kherson's residents. The artist addressed important social, psychological, and political issues through hyperbole, sarcasm, and provocation. Volyazlovsky worked in various media and described his work as "chanson art." He often collaborated with other artists, which was typical of the Totem artist union, of which he was one of the most prominent members. In recent years, he collaborated with the artist Semen Khramtsov as part of the hip-glam band *Rapany*.

In the video, Volyazlovsky and Afanasyev emphasize the absurdity of a situation where the Kherson Art Museum hosted an exhibition of live monkeys. Within this supposed temple of art, artworks recognized as national heritage collide with a form of mass entertainment that uses imprisoned animals. This contrast emphasizes the deep social contradictions and problems in the fields of culture and morality. After Russia's full-scale invasion of Ukraine, the work gained a further layer of meaning.

None of the works documented in the video have been preserved and were stolen by Russian occupiers after the capture of Kherson. This event adds another aspect to the understanding of the work, emphasizing the issue of preserving cultural heritage in the face of war and occupation.

Alina Kleytman

Po-domashnemu

born 1991 in Kharkiv, Ukraine; based in Turin, Italy

2024
MEDICAL PLASTIC, CORPSE BAGS
PRODUCED ESPECIALLY FOR THE EXHIBITION *SENSE OF SAFETY*

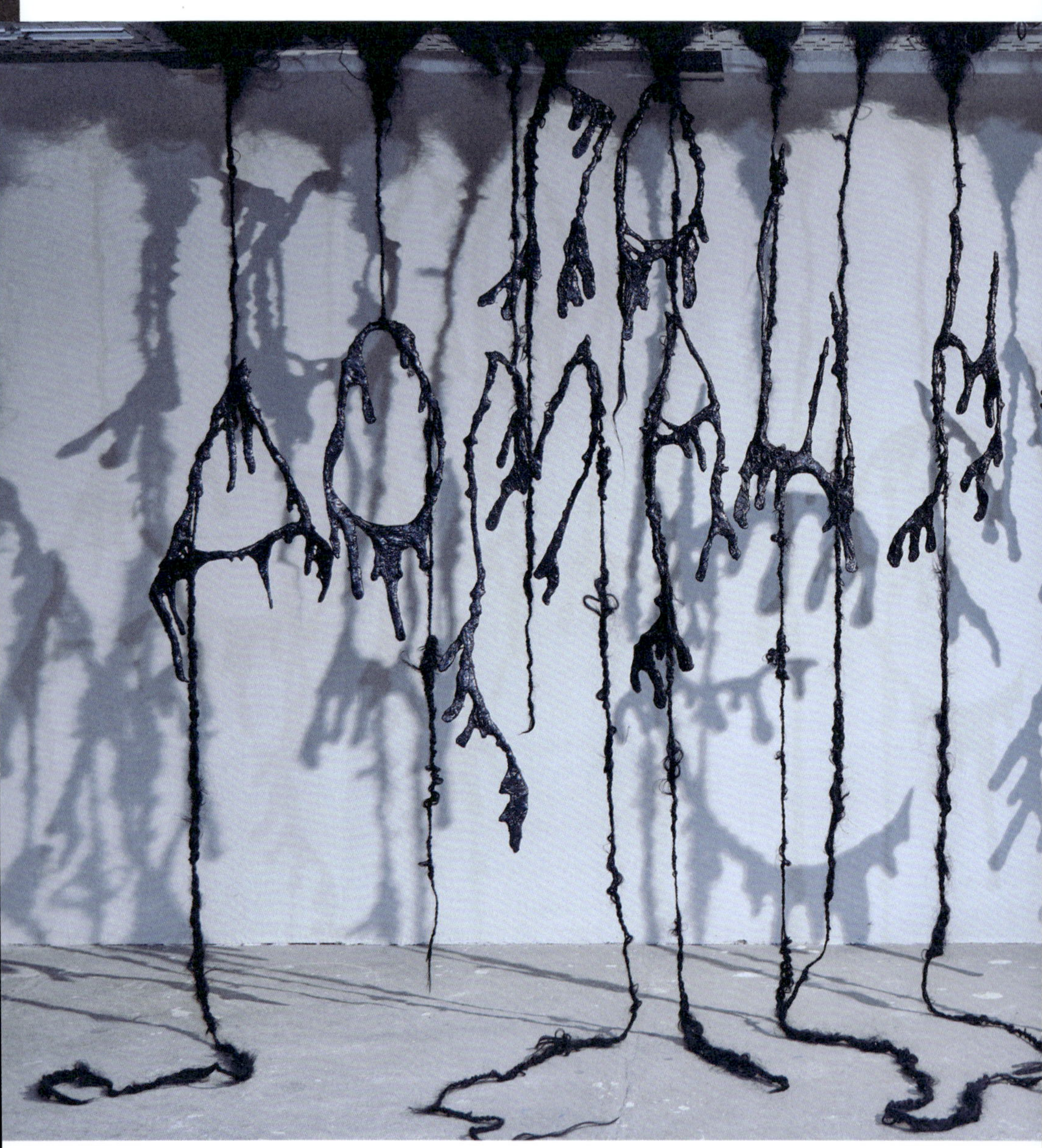

The witch's black hair beckons, wafting with magic, while the Cyrillic letters forming the word *По-домашнєму* (engl. homely) descend on the hair strands. In her new work, Alina Kleytman creates a shimmering realm—an enigmatic and inescapable world of black magic, where enchantment rituals are performed somewhere on the other side

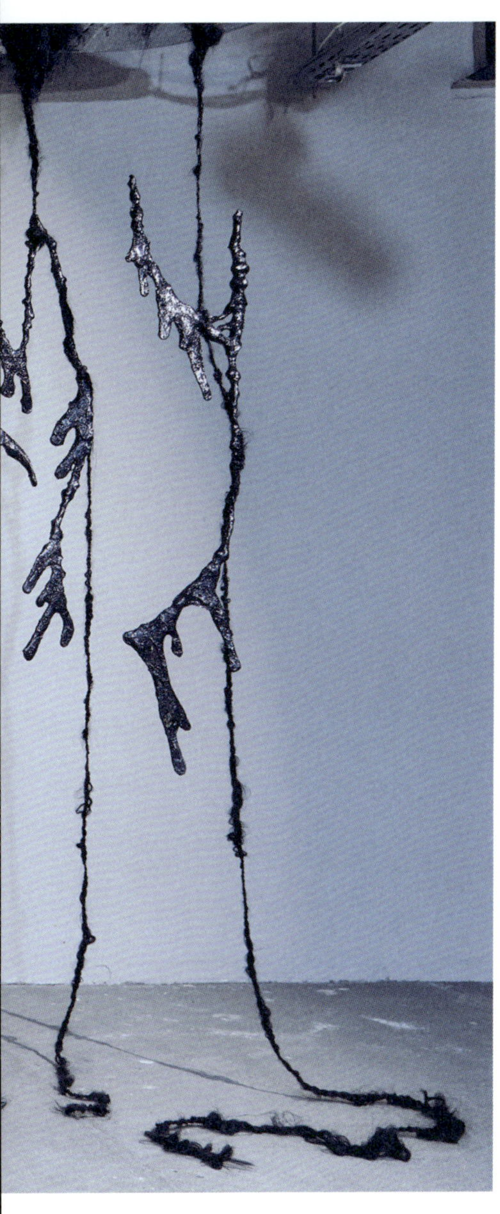

of the letters or in the thickness of the shadows. The work is part of a larger project called *Endless Shine of Human Violence*, in which the artist reflects on the complexity of the human psyche as well as the essence of violence and war. Despite each generation's vows of "never again," war and violence keep returning to our lives.

Homely encapsulates the ambivalence of the concept of safety, around which the exhibition is built. In the context of contemporary war, when every home is at risk, the idea of home still serves as an important stronghold, a place of strength and support, despite all the horrors befalling it. The notion of home is not up for debate; on the contrary, it claims the right to inviolable security.

The phrase itself, *po-domashnemu*, has become a meme and was taken from the viral video of a woman who became an "indigenous" Crimean in 2014. Home and occupation, domestication of the occupied, migration, staying or leaving—these are the complex constructs that Alina Kleytman examines. She foregrounds the ambivalent relationships between overarching political events and the human value of individual situations.

The work is most impressive for its tactile quality. It is made of medical plastic and body bags, which are then heat-shrunk so that they cling tightly to the sculpture's metal frame. Material originally designed for protection during injury, trauma, and death—often serving as a temporary or permanent coffin—is transformed into an artistic statement. Through the magical fairy tale and deliberate tactility, this work reveals the inherent human need to walk the razor's edge, to stand at the brink of life itself, risking one's safety to create it for others.

Three Shelters of the Aza Nizi Maza Studio

Borys Filonenko

I'M IN MY HAPPY PLACE

The force field *I'm in My Happy Place* is dedicated to the temporary and the elusive, to memory and imagination. These forms of inner experience give us strength and support, grounding us in the recognition of what feels familiar and close: memories of loved ones who have passed away, a lost home, children's games, or a personal sense of safety. Such moments provide continuity and meaning, especially in times of instability.
This force field is built around rituals, memory, and imagination—essential human capacities that allow us to orient ourselves toward the future while staying grounded. Central to this constellation is the idea of home: a place, or even a feeling, that offers shelter and defines the boundary between an inner world of safety and the outer environment. In situations of war, these boundaries are violently disrupted. Yet neural patterns of familiarity persist, allowing us to recognize home not only as a physical space but as a learned structure of behavior and memory. It is this habitual familiarity that appears to preserve the idea of home as something that should remain inviolable.
The impulse to claim or transform a space into one's own—to imagine it as home—becomes a strategy of survival. Even temporarily, the creation of a sense of home offers protection and restores a fragile but vital sense of safety.

Most of the art studios I know in Kharkiv are either located in basements or on the ground floor. This catacomb-like system reflects the self-image of many artists who work there—that is, underground. It also clearly illustrates the place of art in the city's social stratification. Art centers, galleries, music, and theater stages are often located underground.
And with the shift from one major disaster (COVID-19) to another (Russia's full-scale invasion of Ukraine), some cultural venues became shelters. While outdoor spaces were used during the pandemic, the subterranean floors are now being used during the war.

On 23 February 2022, on the eve of the Russian attempt to occupy Kharkiv, Mykola Kolomiets—an artist, founder, and director of the Aza Nizi Maza studio—invited his friends and acquaintances to his studios in case war broke out. The Aza Nizi Maza premises are situated underground, featuring a small sunken window that faces the backyard. On the morning when the city was hit by the first missile strikes, he posted a message in a group chat saying that his offer still stood. Aza Nizi Maza, a well-known art studio in Ukraine that works mainly with children and teenagers, thus became one of the shelters in the city center.

Today, Kolomiets recalls those weeks as "crazy activities." His studios brought together all kinds of people, from close friends to residents of the neighborhood. A nearby restaurant that had been damaged by shelling donated some food to them, including surf clams. A parrot flew around the studio, and dogs and cats lived there. A very old cat found its last refuge here and was buried in the yard. Bikers moved in with a microwave and other household appliances. A Korean student who missed his bus stayed there. A 92-year-old grandfather celebrated his birthday, sharing his memories from the German occupation. Young people played *Counter-Strike*. An elderly woman insisted there was no war. A general came and tried to calm everyone down. The mechanisms for developing a sense of safety were also different: some cooked rice in a 10-liter pot, others went on nighttime searches for iodine due to the threat of a nuclear attack. Mykola Kolomiets, who was deemed responsible for the newly created shelter, eventually went to the metro station, looking for an opportunity to work.

The city mayor estimated that 150,000–160,000 people went underground during the first weeks of the full-scale invasion:[1] hiding from shelling or living in train carriages, tents, and sleeping bags at the stations. Pavlo Dorogoi's documentary film *89 Days* (2023) about life in the Kharkiv metro also features pets, as well as young men playing *Counter-Strike* or watching a video game walkthrough.

There are numerous reports on Aza Nizi Maza's work at the Historical Museum metro station. Eventually, Kolomiets spent forty days there: first, he organized drawing classes for 5 to 6-year-old children, and later teenagers joined him. At some point, the station's decoration became a collective work, with each column given to a curator chosen from the new studio participants. Everyone could contribute to the creation of images with their own ideas and techniques, like a musical ensemble with many instruments. The artistic collaboration and publicity gave them agency, even if they had to occasionally fend off the cameras of intrusive journalists. The participants of Aza Nizi Maza experienced an invasion of their already vulnerable personal space at the stations. They were photographed while sleeping or doing their everyday routines. After a while, the photographers began to work differently, treating them with respect because of their work.

The participants of Aza Nizi Maza, who continue working in the studio to this day, did not initially plan on becoming artists. They met Mykola Kolomiets in the spring of 2022, in a place without communications, with a bizarre form of free time that they could use in a variety of ways. The military invasion and daily terrorism targeting the civilian population of Ukraine forced changes in routine activities, formed new habits and new forms of tracking time: from the air raid alarm signal to the all-clear, from the long-lasting curfews to going outside in the intervals between attacks. Every day, elderly women would come to see the artworks at the subterranean Aza Nizi Maza studio. "We can't go out now, so instead of walking, we come to see what they've painted during the day," they explained to Kolomiets. The ability to manage your time and make some effort also helps maintain one's sense of security. That spring, decorating the station turned out to be a kind of clockwork for those who came down to the metro. That changed Aza Nizi Maza, too. Kolomiets says that, in a way, "the metro still goes on, since the current team of the studio was formed right there."

Mykola Kolomiets founded the studio in 2012, continuing the work of his teacher, the artist and lecturer Yevhen Bykov, who also formed a community around himself. A few years later, the name Aza Nizi Maza emerged. Apart from being an encrypted word for anima or the soul, it is also a secret spell.

In Federico Fellini's film *8½* (1963), children wait for a late-night hour when portraits start moving their eyes. If one utters these words at that moment, one can see where the paintings direct their gaze—and that is where the treasure is to be found.

Looking at the studio's method before the full-scale invasion, it can be described as creating a space of freedom between two extremes. On the one hand, there was a rejection of studying technique and the academic approach, where drawing skills were prioritized over ideas. And on the other hand, there's a cautious attitude toward unlimited freedom, which might not help create anything new, or at least something that's uniquely yours. The studio offered multiple guidelines to help students find their own path to a work of art, with each student's concept gradually emerging through observation and discussion. "Aza Nizi Maza is a weird community that's hard to define, especially if you're talking to people who are used to thinking inside the box," says Kolomiets. Today, it is a community brought together by shared experiences. Just like in the metro, the studio's artworks become a form of creative exchange between the participants. It is a space of special safety in times of war. It is a space of fragility and strength.

Safety in Kharkiv is always an illusion. Here, a common phrase from children's outdoor games, "I'm in the house"—similar to the English "forty forty home"—makes you think about the current situation in the world. Usually, these words mean the highest degree of safety within the game, but even the phrase itself originates from the Russian-speaking context and also serves as a flickering reminder—what game are we playing? There is a grain of truth in another well-established phrase that has emerged in recent years: "We have to reinvent language to describe what is going on with us."

Despite the conventionality of security, Kolomiets says that messages such as "Everything will be okay with you" are extremely important and reflect one of the meanings of coexistence in the Aza Nizi Maza studio today. He refers to *Melancholia* (2011), a movie by Lars von Trier, where Claire, played by Charlotte Gainsbourg, tries to be cool and keep everything under control while the world is plunging into chaos. But when the apocalypse finally comes, she also freaks out. In the final scene, Claire, her son, and her sister find themselves in a primitive hut made of sticks—a magical shelter. It is the last moment of family unity before the disaster. A possible place for the phrase "I'm in the house."

Referring to this episode raises questions that have yet to be answered. How stable is this hut? When the portraits begin to move their eyes, what treasures will they see? What will the spell "Aza Nizi Maza" reveal to us? Some view this frail hut as a military target. Others observe it all from a safe distance and have time to reflect. And some are tired of watching altogether. As the story continues, we find that some of its scenes can be better seen from underground floors or basements.

1. Vadym Petrasiuk, "Hotel Underground: the people who sleep in the metro every night for fear of attacks," *Ukrainska Pravda*, 28 September 2025, https://www.pravda.com.ua/eng/articles/2025/09/28/7530493 [accessed 1 February 2026].

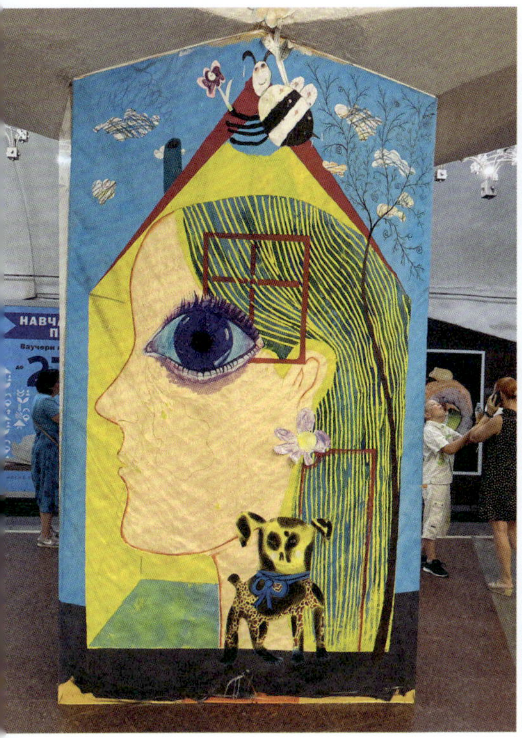

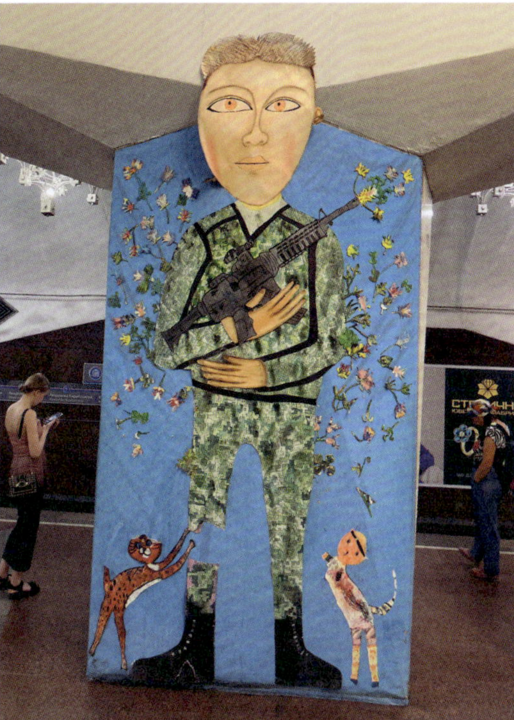

hildren's drawings from the Aza Nizi Maza art studio in the Kharkiv subway. Photo: Maxim Tyminko.

<u>\za Nizi Maza, The freedom of children in a frontline city (3'16")</u>

'his is a selection of enlarged children's drawings from the Aza Nizi Maza studio in Kharkiv. During the war, he studio relocated to the metro, where its founder, artist Mykola Kolomiiets, created a safe creative space or children. He actively helped adapt the drawings for projection in order to show local audiences the lives of hildren and their feelings during the war.

Documentation of the program for "Aza Nizi Maza, The freedom of children in a frontline city," 2024. Photo: Philipp Ziegler.

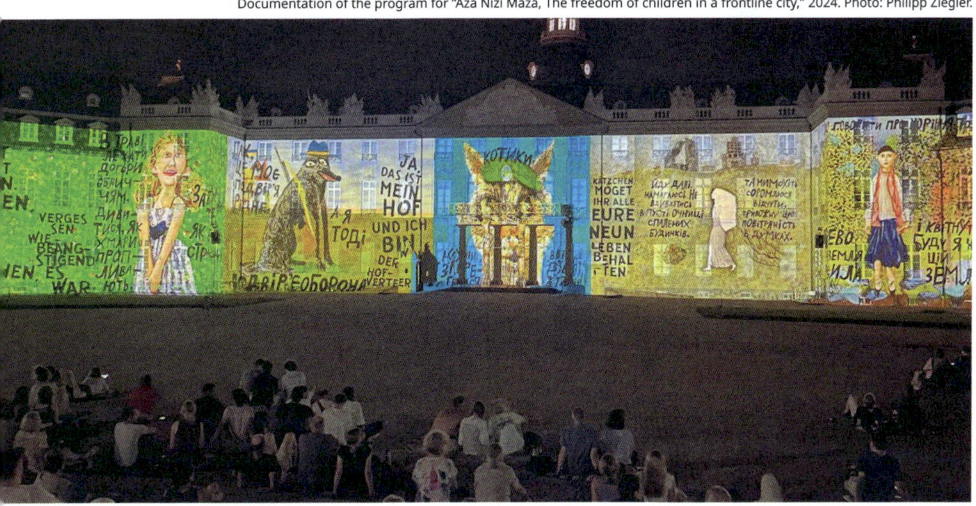

<u>CHLOSSLICHTSPIELE Karlsruhe</u>

<u>Schlossplatz, Karlsruhe (DE)</u>

<u>Large-scale outdoor video projection</u>

<u>Date</u>
01–15.09.2024

This event combined two video programs into a single immersive experience within the context of the city.

bridges of solidarity

Sense of Safety (19'25")

A selection of video works from the antiwarcoalition.art digital platform, adapted for large-scale outdoor projection, was presented on Anti-War Day in Germany, reminding audiences of ongoing conflicts and political oppression worldwide.

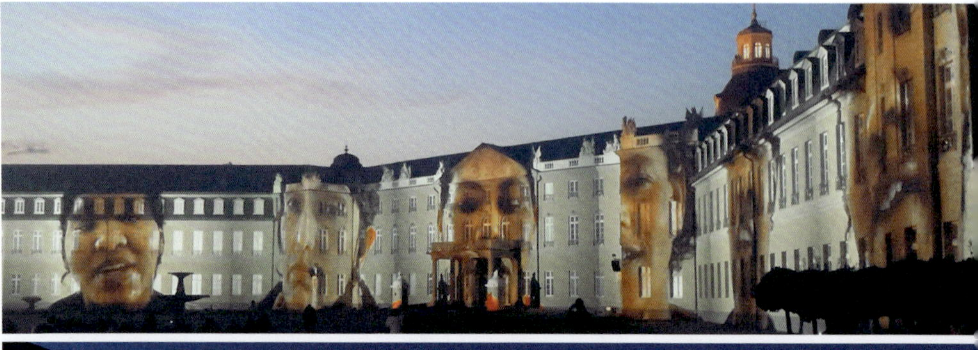

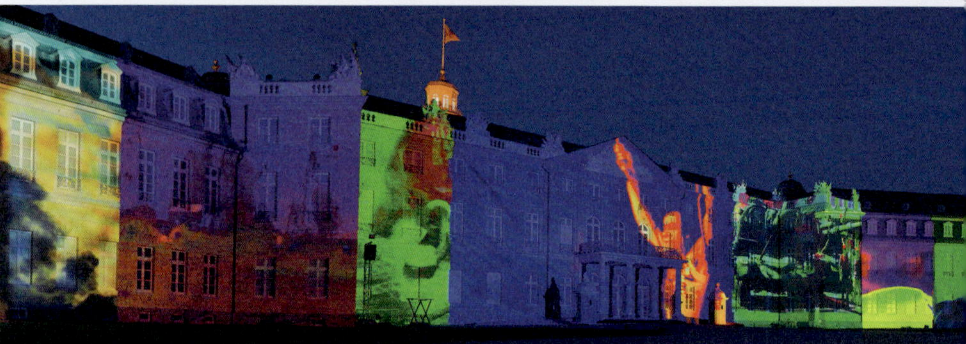

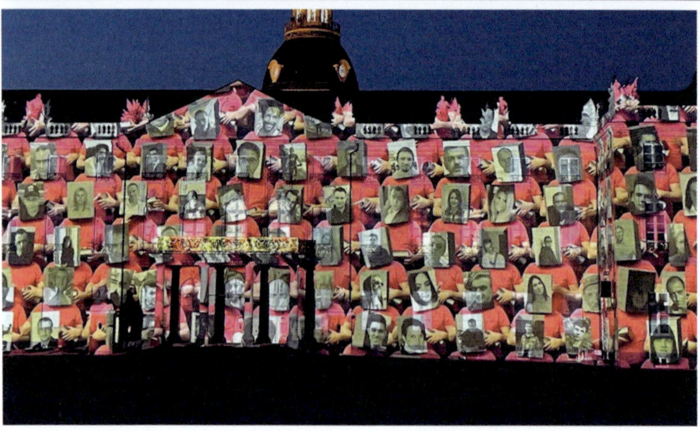

Documentation of the "Sense of Safety" program featuring:
Top image: *Personal Accounts* by Gabrielle Goliath, 2024. Photo: Helmut Schweizer.
Middle image: *In Solcher Nacht* by Helmut Schweizer, 2024. Photo: Philipp Ziegler.
Bottom image: *A Percussion Piece for Two Thousand and Nine Players* by Maxim Tyminko, 2024. Photo: Seiji Shimabukuro.

At the beginning of the screening, people settled on the lawn in front of the castle, with some standing close to the façade. When a red title screen appeared against the dark sky, the crowd grew focused and conversations fell silent.
The audience's attention only deepened with each new work, and the screening culminated in the repeated showing of the children's drawings.
It was a rare and unusual experience for an event that has already become a tradition in the city.

Alina Bukina, artist.

SCHLOSSLICHTSPIELE Karlsruhe

Large-scale outdoor video projection

Schlossplatz, Karlsruhe (DE)

Large-scale outdoor video projection

Date
01–15.09.2024

Artists
Gabrielle Goliath (ZA)
Zhanna Kadyrova (UA)
Mykyta Lyskov (UA)
Daria Sazanovich (BY)
Helmut Schweizer (DE)
Maxim Tyminko (NL)
Clemens V. Wedemeyer (DE)
fantastic little splash (UA)

Video compositing
Siarhei Navitski (PL)

Supported by
SCHLOSSLICHTSPIELE Karlsruhe (DE)
Aza Nizi Maza (UA)
Goethe-Institut Ukraine (DE/UA)
ZKM | Center for Art and Media Karlsruhe (DE)

'he video screening took place at the Leipzig Festival of Lights and the Revolutionale Festival, continuing *ense of Safety's* critical discussion on the ambivalence of safety. Building on the exhibition, the screening rought together voices and artistic perspectives from different geographical contexts, including Belarus, iermany, and Sweden. The program for *Safety as Collective Practice* presented works that examined how afety is constructed, negotiated, and contested, foregrounding its fragile and collective dimensions.

afety as Collective Practice

arge-scale outdoor video rojection

Revolutionale – Festival or Change and Leipzig estival of Lights, Leipzig DE)

Date
)9.10.2024

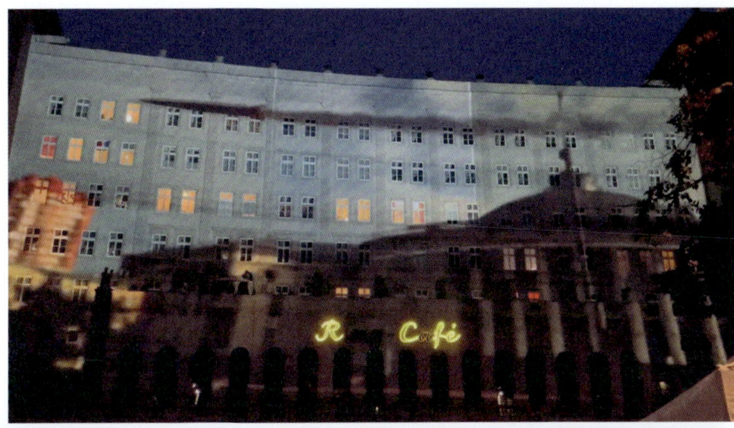

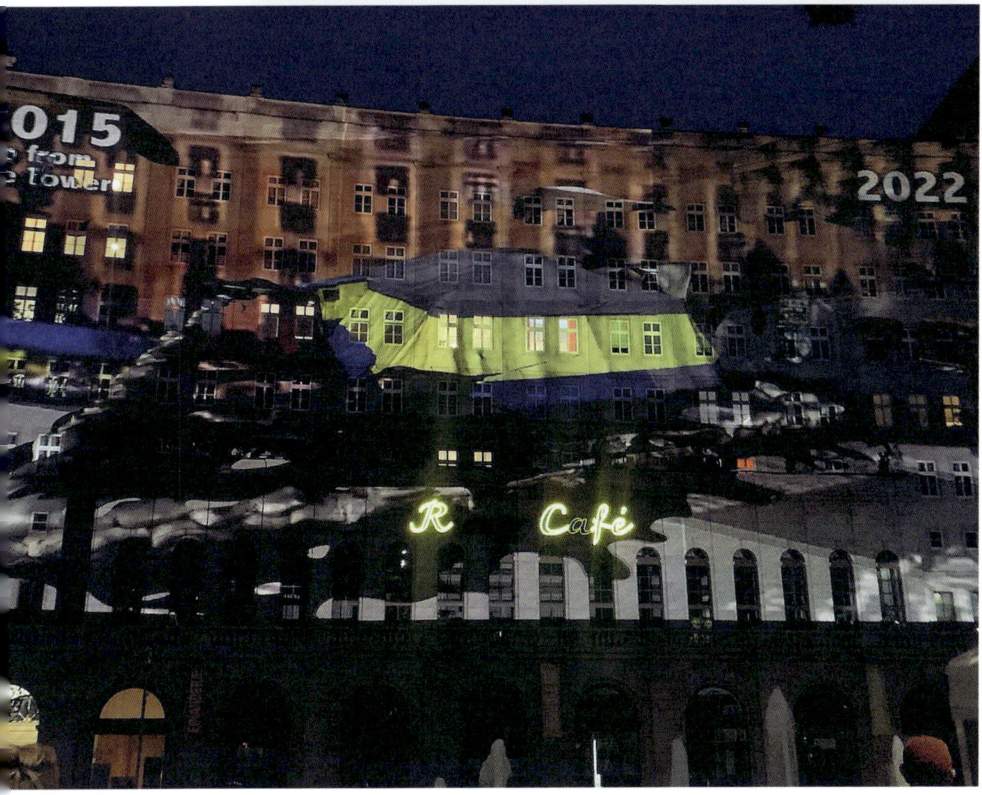

Documentation featuring works by Zhanna Kadyrova (top image) and Hito Steyerl (bottom image), 2024. Photo: Anna Chistoserdova.

rtists
la Aliyeva (AZ)
ergamot (BY)
ina El Assadi (UA)
ezzan Gümgüm (TR)
adzimir Hramovich
Y/DE)
Zhanna Kadyrova (UA)
Marina Naprushkina (DE)
Oleksandr Osipov (UA)
Nadya Sayapina (BY)
Hito Steyerl (DE)
Johan Widén, Ylva Gislén, Elin Maria Johansson (SE)

Danilo Correale

born 1982 in Naples, Italy; based in New York, USA

2024
AUDIOVISUAL INSTALLATION, 18'23" (ENG); 24'6" (UA)
COURTESY OF THE ARTIST
A UKRAINIAN VERSION OF THE WORK WAS PRODUCED
ESPECIALLY FOR *SENSE OF SAFETY*
VOICEOVER: KYRYLO LUKASH
SOUND ENGINEER: OLEKSANDR YUKHNO

Reverie, on the Liberation from Work

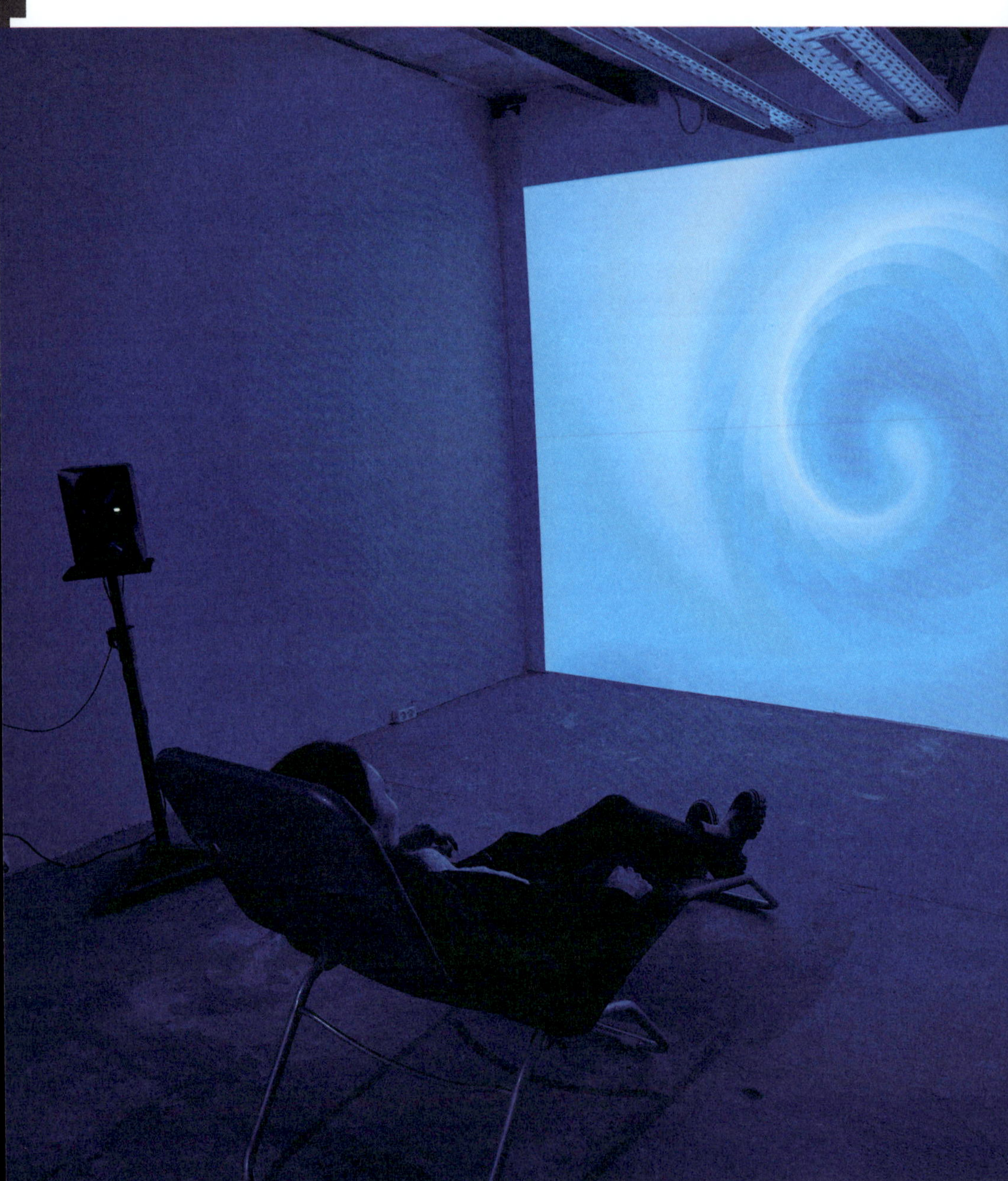

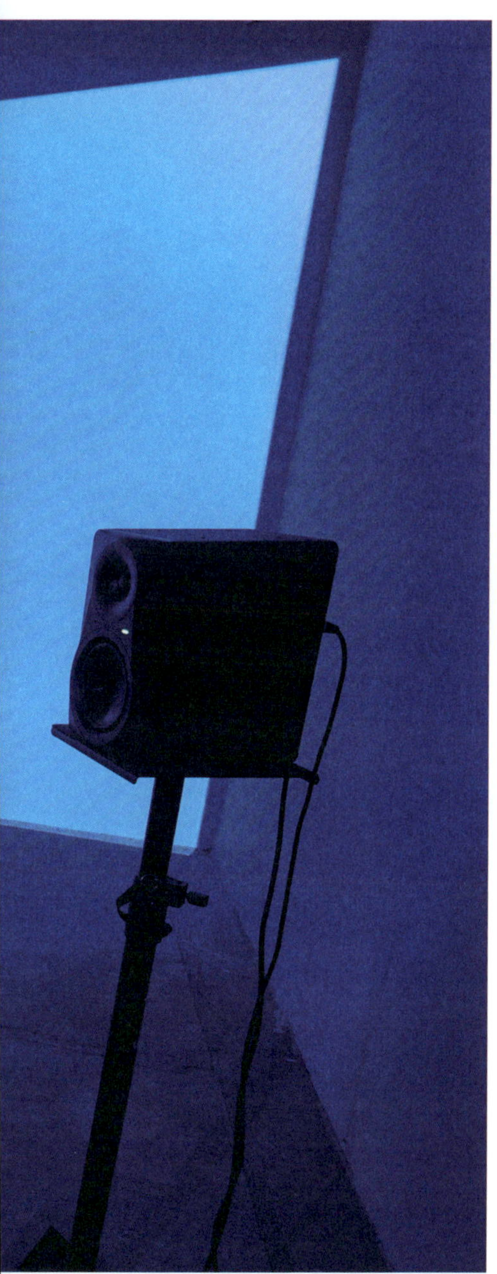

In his work, Danilo Correale explores the everyday life of a modern person: work, leisure, and day-to-day routine. The artist is interested in the experience of sleep and the way it is disrupted by the traumatic effects of capitalist urban society. He draws attention to people's bodily and psychological reactions—such as fatigue, lethargy, and boredom—and interprets them as diseases provoked by the pressures of modern life. Correale uses a variety of media to explore these reactions and reveal hidden aspects of everyday existence. His work emphasizes the need for a critical look at contemporary social structures and calls for ways to restore the balance between work and leisure. The artist emphasizes the importance of rest as an integral part of health and well-being.

As part of the *Sense of Safety* project, the author presents an audiovisual installation in which the viewer is invited to relax and reboot through meditation, freeing oneself from economic and social pressure. The installation creates conditions for immersion in deep relaxation, helping to feel safe and restore emotional balance, which becomes especially urgent given the constant stress and anxiety that accompany modern life. The work's focus on the dream of a brighter future is especially valuable. In times of war, Ukrainians often live one day at a time, but the ability to believe in better prospects is a path to recovery.

It is important to note that the author deliberately engaged Kharkiv specialists to voice the Ukrainian version of the meditation, seeking to support the city's theater actors who have had limited opportunities to perform in the aftermath of Russia's aggression.

Karen Lancel

born 1963 in Katwijk aan Zee, Netherlands; based in Amsterdam

Hermen Maat

born 1963 in Amsterdam, Netherlands; based in Amsterdam

Agora Phobia (Digitalis)

2000–2009, 2024
INSTALLATION, PERFORMANCE
COURTESY OF THE ARTISTS

THIS EDITION OF THE WORK WAS PRODUCED ESPECIALLY FOR THE EXHIBITION *SENSE OF SAFETY*.
PRODUCTION WAS SUPPORTED BY THE EMBASSY OF THE KINGDOM OF THE NETHERLANDS IN UKRAINE.
SPECIAL THANKS TO THE AIR DESIGN STUDIO — ERIK VAN DONGEN.
SINCE 2000, THE WORK HAS BEEN TRAVELING THROUGH PUBLIC SPACES IN CITIES SUCH AS AMSTERDAM, PARIS, NEW YORK, BERLIN, AND HAS RECENTLY BEEN INCLUDED IN THE DIGITAL CANON OF THE NETHERLANDS 1960–2000, A SELECTION OF 20 DIGITAL WORKS.

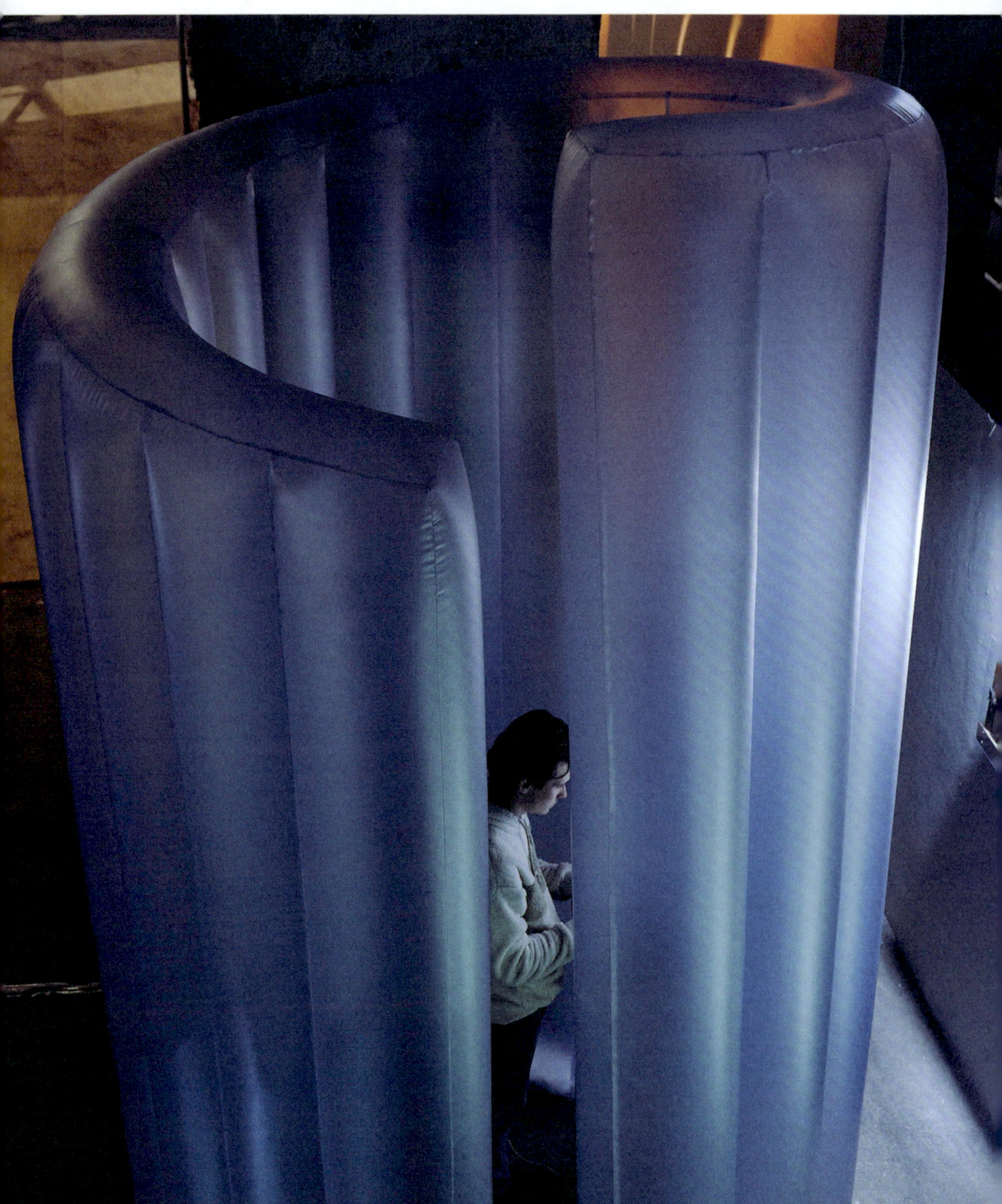

Karen Lancel and Hermen Maat are renowned artists and researchers based in Amsterdam. Their core practices involve creating intimate and empathetic connections through innovative AI technologies and public performances, encouraging people to reflect and connect in new, disrupted sensory ways.

What is a safe place for you?

How would you describe an unsafe place?

When and where do you feel isolated?

How do you control your space?

Agora Phobia (Digitalis) is an interactive installation that investigates feelings and experiences of isolation, safety, and unsafety. Originally conceived in the early 2000s, during the rise of social media and the growing dominance of the Internet, it addressed virtual communication between people. Paradoxically, this form of communication enhances social connections but also results in physical alienation and personal isolation. Digital domination thus impacts questions of personal control and safety.

Agora Phobia (Digitalis) is a mobile monument for "public isolation." The project connects social experiences in both physical and virtual space, creating a hybrid agora. It invites you into a semi-transparent, inflatable "isolation pillar," where you can feel safe in an intimate space, but simultaneously vulnerable given the lack of social or physical control over the outside. Participants can anonymously create and share a data-archive of mental images and strategies for being (un)safe and isolated.

Today, over twenty years after the conception of the work, its display in Kharkiv opens up an entirely different reading. Its meaning almost seems inverted: the possibility of secure cross-border communication comes as a relief for the audience, since the war has forced so many people into isolation.

Initially conceived as a critical reflection about the public and private sphere in a mediated society, the work is now being exhibited in an a priori unsafe context. *Agora Phobia (Digitalis)* proposes hybrid communication—online from an inflatable, tactile, almost embodied spatial environment—as a safe space, critically reflecting on such connections as a last resort for social safety. The work proposes a safe haven for personal reflection within the protective walls of the YermilovCentre and the shell of the inflatable isolation pillar. This installation underscores the changing nature of safety and interaction, inviting visitors to find comfort in communicating in a protected space during a situation of instability.

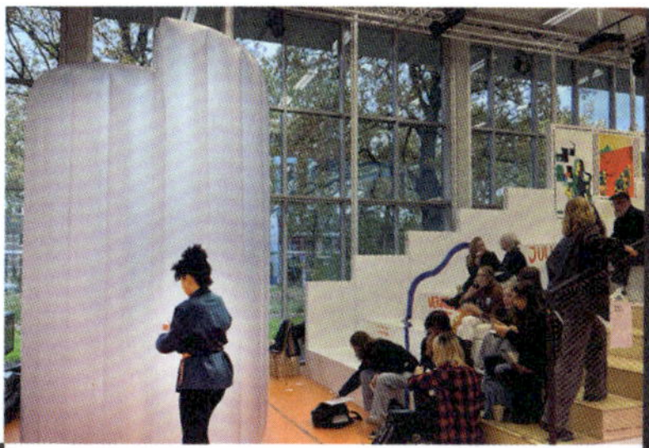

Installation and performance at ArtEZ Academy, Zwolle (NL), 2024. Photo: LancelMaat. Courtesy of the artists.

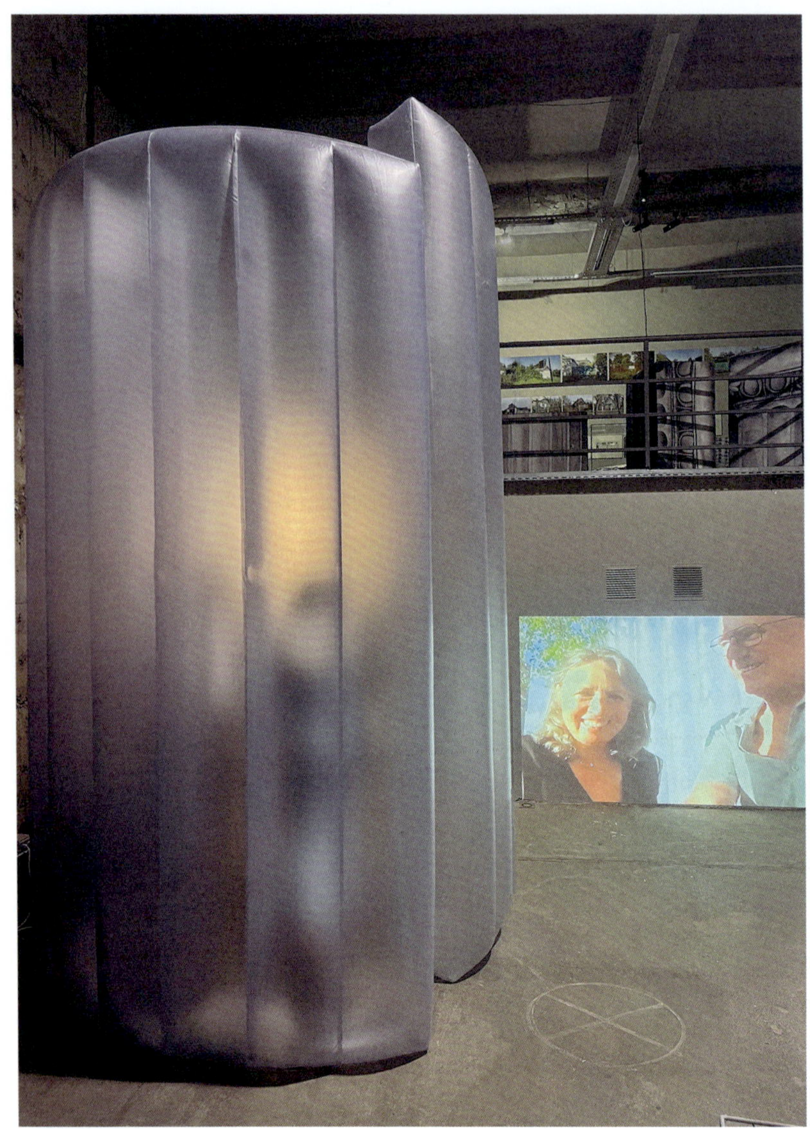

Sense of Safety, exhibition opening at YermilovCentre in Kharkiv with livestream featuring Karen Lancel and Hermen Maat from the artists' studio in Amsterdam, 2024. Photo: Maxim Tyminko.
Courtesy of the artists.

THROUGHOUT THE PROJECT, THE WORK WAS DISPLAYED AT YERMILOVCENTRE AND ALSO INSTALLED IN OTHER LOCATIONS.

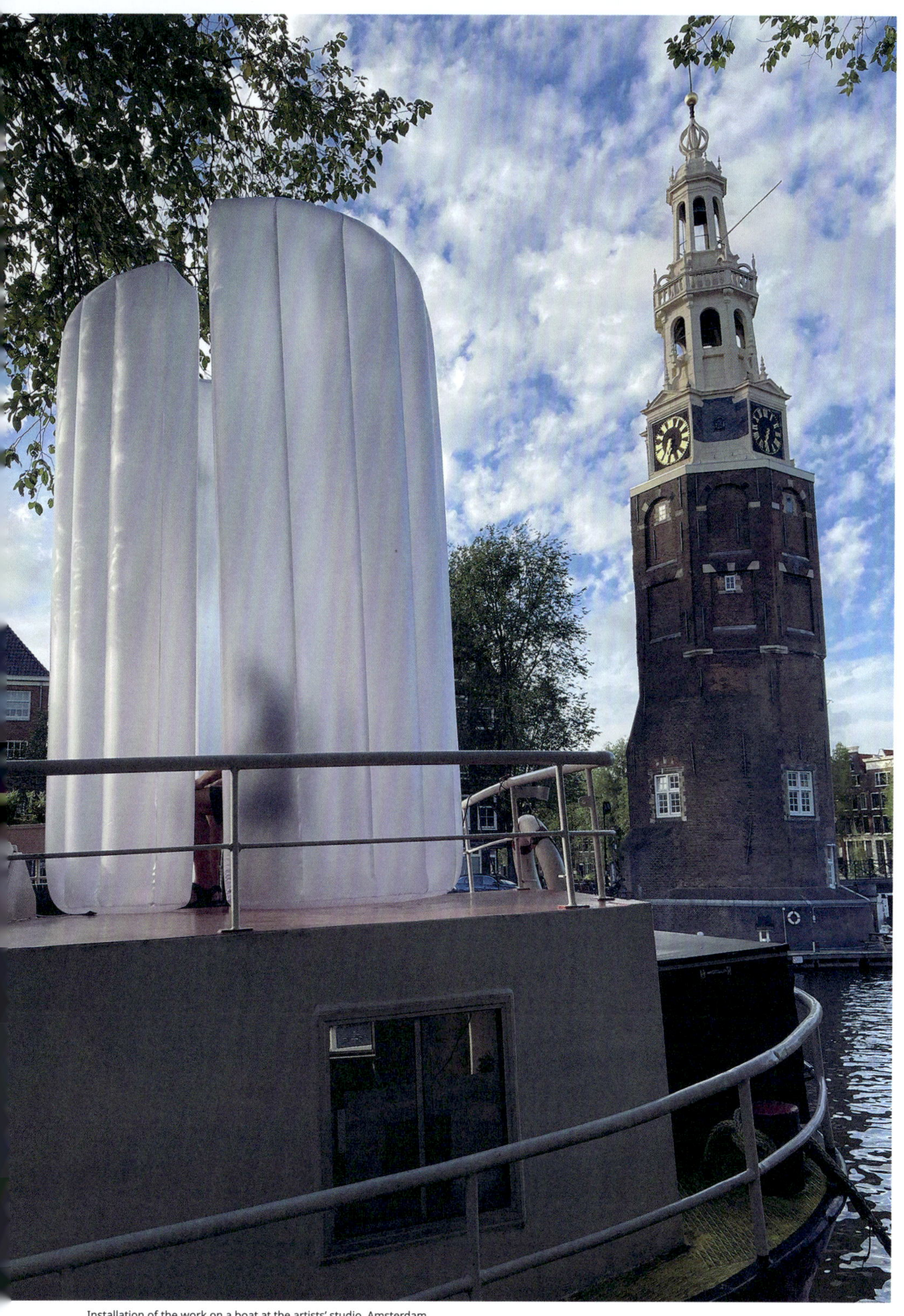

Installation of the work on a boat at the artists' studio, Amsterdam, 2024. Photo: LancelMaat. Courtesy of the artists.

Olena Afanasieva & Max Afanasyev

both born 1971 in Kherson, Ukraine

2023
ARTBOOK
COURTESY OF THE GRYNYOV ART COLLECTION

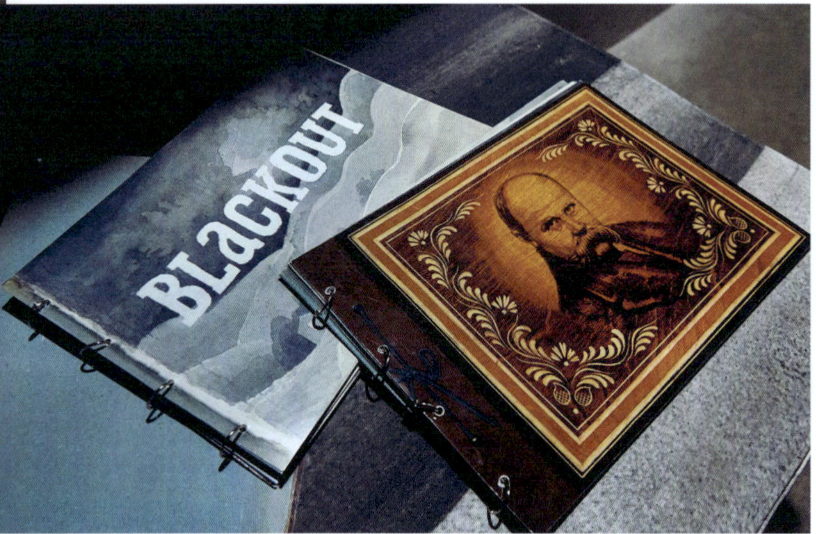

The husband and wife team Olena Afanasieva and Max Afanasyev are among the founders of the legendary Ukrainian contemporary art group Totem and regularly collaborate as a duo. Many of their projects focus on their home region of Kherson: its history, society, politics, and everyday life. During the city's occupation, the Afanasievs managed to travel to western Ukraine and helped evacuate other residents. They now temporarily reside in Uzhhorod and continue to work with the Kherson context.

The *Blackout* artbook was created in 2023 when Ukraine was left without electricity after the Russian attacks. This work was a gesture of mutual support and unity in difficult circumstances. To collect the stories, Olena Afanasieva called and corresponded with her friends, asking the question that became so important during the war: "How are you?" The artbook consists of an author's introduction and fourteen stories by cultural figures from different parts of the country about how they experienced the blackout. All the stories are accompanied by redrawn and edited photographs found in a photo album purchased at a flea market.

Each time Afanasyev redrew the photographs in ink, he turned the artistic process into a daily routine that provided a sense of control and stability in the unpredictable present. The practice of artbooking itself is usually a very intimate process. However, in this case, the artists use the artbook as a space for communication and work. They create a collective rather than individualistic practice, thus showing that safety can be achieved through collective efforts.

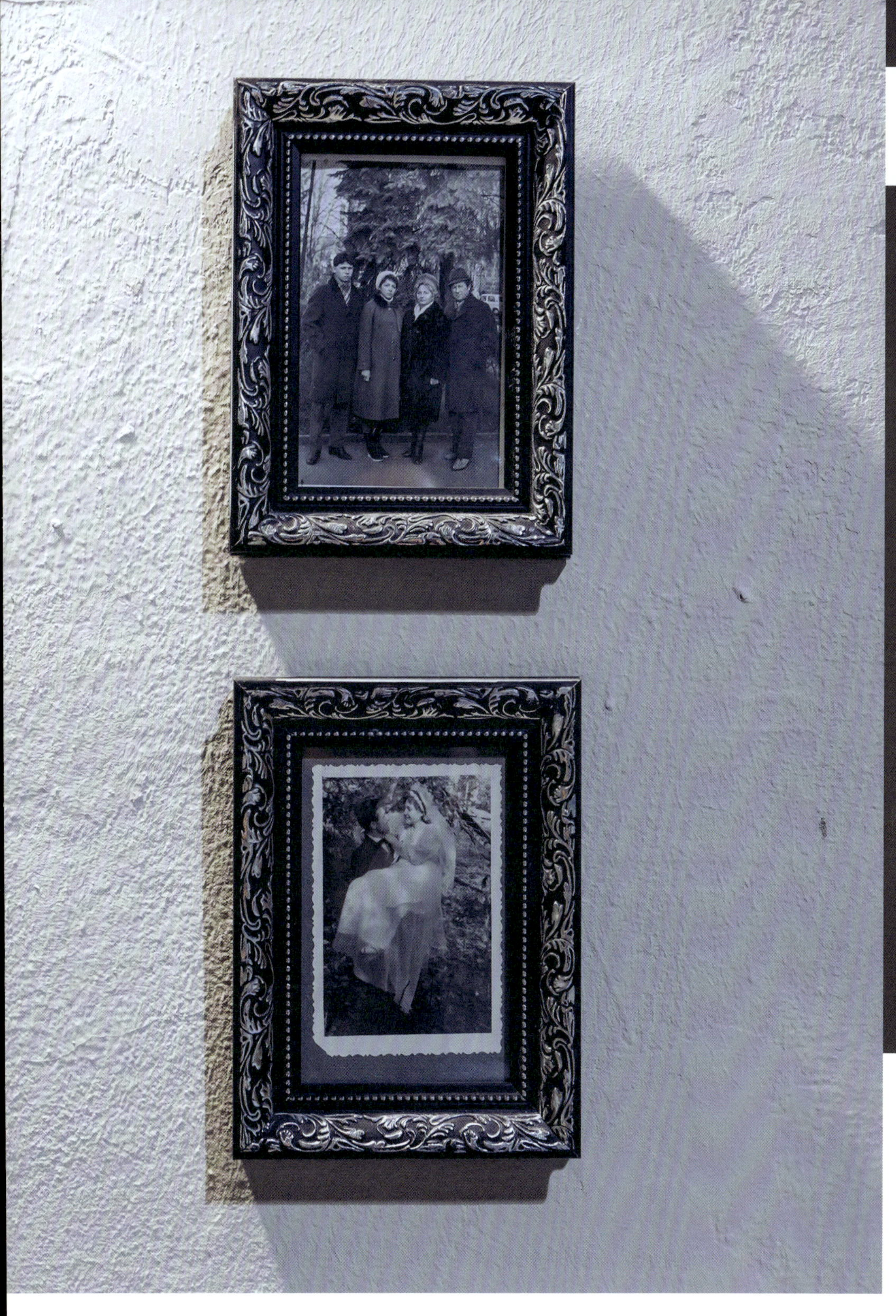

Collective Diary

Antonina Stebur

ROUTINE AS A GROUNDING PRACTICE

When life feels chaotic and unpredictable, simple daily activities like reading, cooking, or cleaning become crucial for reducing stress and anxiety. In these moments, the mind immerses itself in familiar tasks in order to regain control. Everyday rituals that were once unremarkable take on new significance as symbols of order and psychological comfort in an uncertain world. In times of war, artistic practices often serve a similar function. Creativity allows artists to process and reconsider the present, helping them maintain inner balance and discover new meanings under challenging circumstances. Activities like drawing, writing, music, and singing are no longer just forms of self-expression but also therapeutic tools for fostering mental health and combating stress. When artists share these practices with the public, they help create an atmosphere of safety and reassurance, enabling others to find stability during challenging times.

Susan Sontag, a near obsessive diarist from an early age who shaped her sense of self through this practice, wrote: "It is superficial to understand the journal as just a receptacle for one's private, secret thoughts."[1] The personal diary became a popular daily practice during the Enlightenment, alongside the growing separation of private and public life, and the formulation of the rational subject. It has never been an apolitical tool. On the contrary, the diary often records experiences of oppression and trauma for which no stable language yet exists.

The diary captures routine—that which is fleeting and constantly at risk of disappearing, and yet largely invisible. Both as a genre and in its content, the diary occupies a marginal position: a hybrid, often considered a bastard form in relation to high literature, situated in the gaps and pores between major literary genres and official historical narratives. It is precisely this shimmering position—not at the centre, but in the interstices—that gives the diary its political potential, especially in the case of collective diaries.

The practice of the *Collective Diary* proposed by Kateryna Yermolayeva during the exhibition *Sense of Safety* approaches routine during wartime as a grounding practice. In a situation of constant danger—air raids, bombings, sirens—individual experience becomes radically fragmented. What becomes crucial is not the heroic figure, but the process itself: the act of recording. Writing, here, becomes a strategy for survival.

Reading the entries of the *Collective Diary* is equally important. It becomes a way of reassembling reality, of creating a shared field—if not as a solid foundation to stand on, then at least as something familiar to lean on. The diary

"The struggle continues," a page from the *Collective D*
by Kateryna Yermolayeva, 2024. Courtesy of the artis

БОРОТЬБА ТРИВАЄ

Люди, пийте смачну кавуєвку із сінабоном-лимон ~~Гайда~~ Гайда!

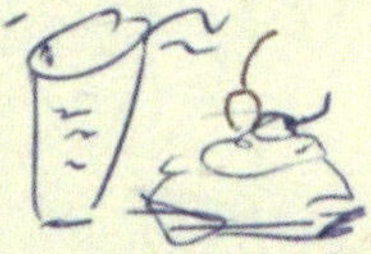

Люди, читайте книги!

...аю, що у кожного своя боротьба.
...и впораєтесь, упевнена!
...житті немає виходу тільки з одного місця...
...е інше — можна вирішити, подолати.
...рте у себе і дійте!
...юбов'ю...

Аліна В. 26.09.2024

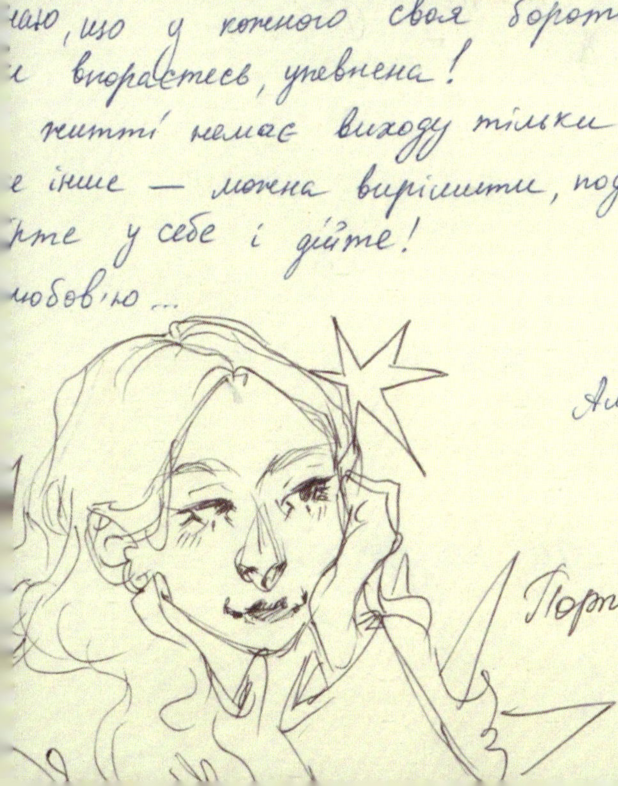

Портрет з натури моєї любої і дорогої Капюші
Rin Mench

Тут папер проста АТАС!!!..

Клас, дякую

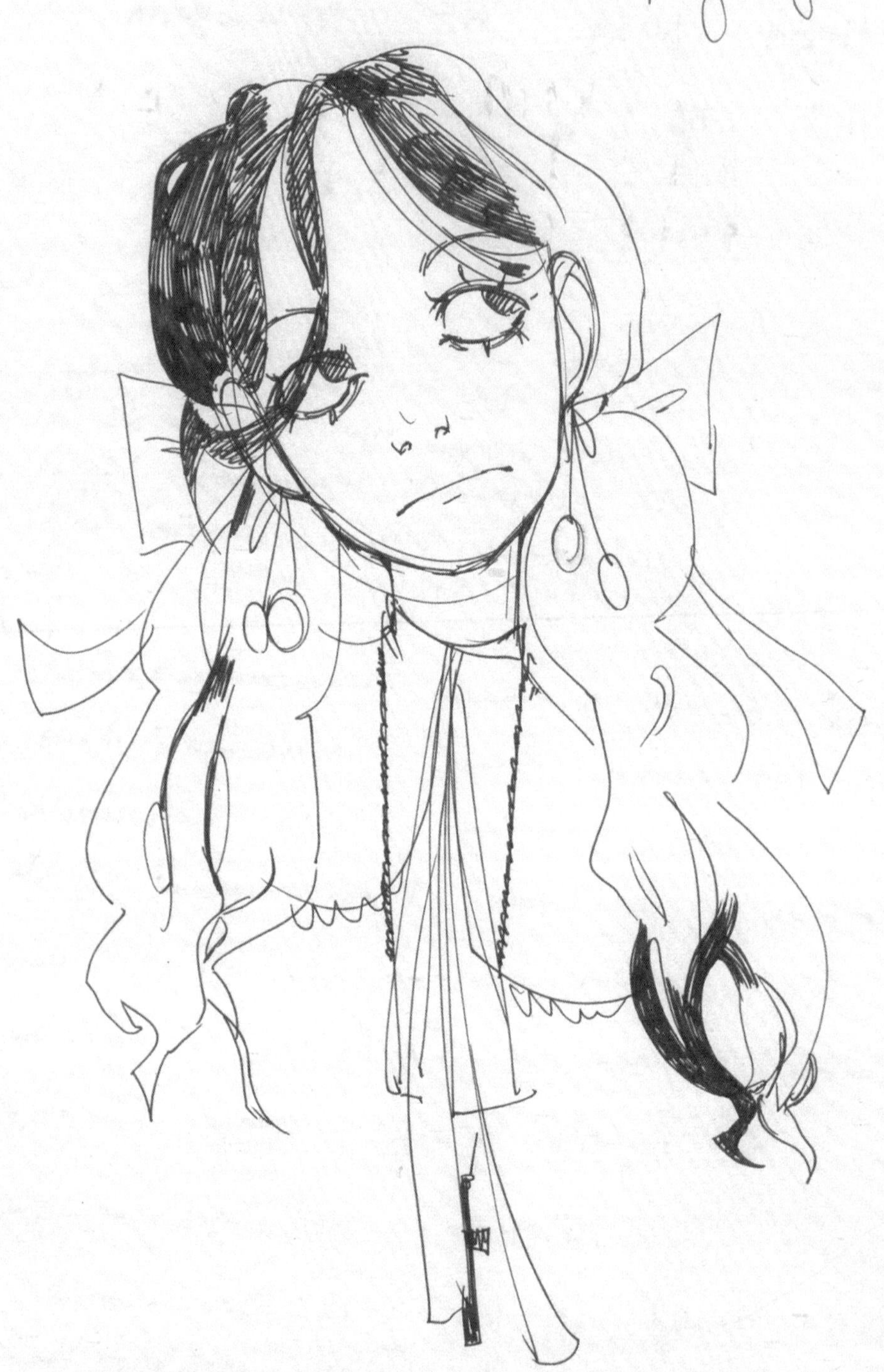

can function as a shoulder, or a set of shoulders, offering temporary support.

Over the course of two and a half months at the YermilovCentre, the *Collective Diary* remained open to anyone willing not only to read, but also to contribute their own notes. The diary was dedicated to the stories of people ready to share their memories and experiences of life after the beginning of Russia's full-scale invasion of Ukraine. The excerpts presented here form a constellation of voices—differing in age, background, and position: young adults whose coming of age coincided with the invasion, soldiers fighting on the front, doctors, and staff members of the YermilovCentre itself.

Together, these heterogeneous voices articulate the routine of war—its traumatic losses, fears, hopes, and frustrations, textures that often resist articulation or representation. They are not merely testimonies of war, but accounts of how intimacy and everyday routine themselves become political, how they turn traumatic, and how they demand constant, daily reassembly to endure.

This diary is dedicated to the stories of people who are willing to share their memories or experiences about what happened in their lives after the start of Russia's full-scale invasion of Ukraine.

I hope that your memories, anonymous or not, will also become a part of it.

Kateryna Yermolayeva

1.

My name is Ania Zvyagintseva,[2] and here is how I remember my first thoughts when I found out that the war had started. My first thought: what do I have with me from home? (At that moment, I was in Maastricht). My second thought: where are my parents hiding during the bombings? Here is what I went through in my mind: a black-and-white photo of me as a little girl with my mother; candy wrappers that my father used to roll up, which later inspired my artwork *My Father's Sculptures*; some of my grandfather's photo film archive; my grandfather's sketches and notes, "My soul stands in the fields like a tree without leaves"; a herbarium that I collected once during the summer at my dacha; my collection of scraps of paper with scribbles that people wrote while trying out pens in stationery stores; a vyshyvanka ...

2.

I'm 19 years old now. When the full-scale war began, I was 16. Kharkiv has been with me all this time, just as I have been with it.
I remember that strange feeling that it wouldn't last long. That it was all surreal and would soon be over. I still believe that it's all surreal. I still can't believe that so many of my friends have died. I didn't even get to know them well before

age from the *Collective Diary*
ateryna Yermolayeva, 2024.
rtesy of the artist.

all this started. I don't know what to write. It was scary, uncertain, and … I remember fighter jets flying over our house while we sat in the basement. Sad and terrible.

3. ______________

Hello, dear random reader! My name is Oleksandra, and my anxiety about the war began before 2022, but the fear that still haunts me every day came on the night of 24 February 2022. The first night, from 24 to 25 February, was the most terrifying. For a year and a half, I had dreams about the war every day. Here, people describe something specific, a certain memory, but for me, it is now a whole streak of fear. Of course, there were good moments during this time, too, lots of them. You know that yourself …

Bye-bye

4. ______________

Hi, I'm Annushka. I left Kha[3] at the beginning of the full-scale invasion, and every time I come back, I feel that living in another city just doesn't make any sense for me. I love Kha, I love the people here, I love everything that surrounds me here. But it's very scary … The feeling of safety has long been lost and forgotten … I want to believe that soon we will remember again what that feeling of safety is like!

5. ______________

Sometimes I wonder which of my choices were wrong. Everyone does that. What is the reason I never want to leave Kharkiv for long? Could this be trauma and fear disguised as unconditional love for the city and its people? What if everything I feel is fake?

But it's real.

6. ______________

I'm Vika. When the full-scale war began, I was 17, actually I had just turned 17 a month before it started. At the time, I was a student at KhKhU[4] and lived in a dorm in Piatykhatky. …[5]

I wasn't scared, even though I saw APCs being shot down as I was leaving Piatykhatky. But I didn't think anything could happen to me. A week after the war started, the house where I was hiding with my relatives was destroyed in an air strike. Everyone survived, but we had to leave.

…

I came back to Kharkiv a year later. Another year later, my dad was drafted, and now he's gone missing somewhere in Donetsk Oblast. I guess I wrote this just to say that I love my dad and I miss him a lot. Please come back alive. It's just really hard without you. Mom, Nastia, and I are waiting for you.

7. ______________

01.09.2024

I heard ten strikes today, and I was really scared, but I came here, listened to the meditation on post-industrial society,[6] and it made me feel better. And the fact that you are underground is also a kind of moral support; it's like a shelter.

8. ______________

I like that there are many people here.

9. ______________

My name is Nastia, and it hurts. The war took away the courage to share my feelings. I love everyone, and it hurts when people are gone. I have known many people in my 21 years of life, and I remember 99% of their birthdays.

"Vika's story," a page from the *Collective D…* by Kateryna Yermolayeva, 2024. Courtesy of the artist.

Віка. Коли почалася повномаштабна війна мені було
буквально виповнилося за місяць до початку. Я тоді
я студенткою ХХУ, жила в гуртожитку на
ятихатках. Мої батьки були вдома, на Куп'янщині.
ніяк не мали змоги доїхати, мости вдома
бомбили за день. Я залишилась у родичів, в Харко

Страшно не було, хоча виїзджаючи з П'ятихатки
підбиті БТР-и, я не думала що зі мною може
статися. Через тиждень після початку війни,
ударом було зруйновано дім, де ми з родичами
ались. Усі живі, але довелось кудись їхати.

Батьки виїхали ще через два тижні,
, ще тоді цілим, Ізюм (а може через Краматорськ
обус, що їхав за ними був розстріляний.
ми зустрілись.

Я повернулась до Харкова через рік.
Через рік мого батька мобілізували,
зараз він зниклий безвісти десь на
ечині. Напевно, я це
ла тільки щоб сказати,
люблю свого батька
дуже скучаю. Повернись
им. Просто без тебе
складно. Я, мама і Настя
емо.

♡

10.

22.09.2024

I am fine, as I used to be. Isn't it interesting that in my past life, I only had the starry sky, and now there are flashes and explosions. Is that how it should be? Why should our people see war? There is only a white wall between us and the outside world. Right now, I listen to Ukrainian songs, watch American TV series, and browse through Kharkiv news. Art and books keep me grounded, I don't know, soon curfew will start again, and I will be sitting in the dark again, or rather, in my head. A moment later, I dive deep into my thoughts. I have to try hard not to drown in textures. Above all, I should not let myself become indifferent. I have to stay kind even when anger flows through my veins. That feeling when there is a smile on your face, but pure rage in your eyes. When I look in the mirror, I should see myself, but there is only a shadow, some kind of devastated predator. It's hard to live in this broken world. Now there are only ruins where the houses used to be … seconds, minutes, hours, days, and we continue to water our wilted flowers to meet in our Kha …

11.

03.09.2024

I look at the trampoline and realize that less than a week ago, a person who is no longer alive was jumping here. Eternal memory to Nika![7]

For me, as an artist, the worst thing was losing my imagination completely during the first long months after the war began. I could only imagine darkness. Frightened by death, we fall in love with life even more. We don't choose the times we live in, but we can choose how to live. I choose love and life, and it will be mutual.

Olena

12.

I was in Kharkiv when the war began, waking up at 5 am to the sound of explosions. I had no illusions and made no attempt to calm myself, because it was obvious what those explosions were. I had heard them before, in Donetsk, in 2014. I packed my backpack and stood by the window, and an endless stream of cars was passing by my house. I really wanted to get into one of them and drive away from what was approaching, apparently from the northeast. So I stood there for a few more minutes, started calling my friends and family, and telling them that the war had begun. At 7 am, I decided to go to work at the hospital as usual. On that first day we discharged as many patients as we could, while all around us there was a heavy and incredibly anxious atmosphere of despair. The next day, I decided to pack up all my belongings and move them to the hospital where I had been living and working until May. To keep this short I will leave you with my most vivid impressions

- The smell of blood and gunpowder lingered in the operating room after the wounded were brought in.
- Indifference to the explosions that sounded so often and so loudly that there was no strength left to be scared.
- The amazing starry sky and the red glow on the horizon. The sense of safety and calmness when it got dark, and everyone got together in the lounge for dinner.

13.

It doesn't matter what my name is. When the full-scale war began, I was 20 years old. … Now I'm advancing in the military sphere, unfortunately. But that's how it should be. Civilians don't understand this. They don't ınderstand these, let's say, subtleties. Although that's not right to say like that. I don't know what I want. Peace? But you understand that this won't happen, right? Because these are people, aggressive, selfish creatures, and it won't be like in the general utopian understanding. I'm tired. Honestly. I just want to be left alone. Calmness. Silence. As if you've dived into water …

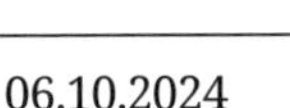

4.

06.10.2024

My name is Taisiya. I have been working at YC8 for nine months already. This place has become a sense of safety for me. Not only because of its location, but also because of its team.

1. Susan Sontag, *Reborn: Journals and Notebooks, 1947–1963*, ed. David Rieff (New York: Farrar, Straus and Giroux, 2008).
2. Anna Zvyagintseva is a Ukrainian artist and a participant in the project *Sense of Safety*.
3. Kha functions as an affectionate diminutive for Kharkiv, indicating proximity, familiarity, and everyday forms of relational attachment to the city.
4. KhKhU is an abbreviation for Kharkivs'ke Khudozhnye Uchylyshche (the Kharkiv State School of Art).
5. Piatykhatky is a former *khutir*, now a neighbourhood in Kharkiv's Kyivskyi District.
6. Danilo Correale, *Reverie, on the Liberation from Work*, audiovisual installation, 24′06″, at the exhibition Sense of Safety, YermilovCentre, Kharkiv.
7. Ukrainian artist Veronika "Nika" Kozhushko was killed in a Russian airstrike on Kharkiv on 30 August 2024, a day after the opening of the exhibition *Sense of Safety*. She was 18 years old. The trampoline here refers to the work *Jump Up!* by Ahmet Öğüt, an artwork activated during the opening night, when Nika was jumping on it.
8. Means YermilovCentre.

Sense of Safety, installation view at YermilovCentre.
Photo: Viktoriia Yakymenko. →

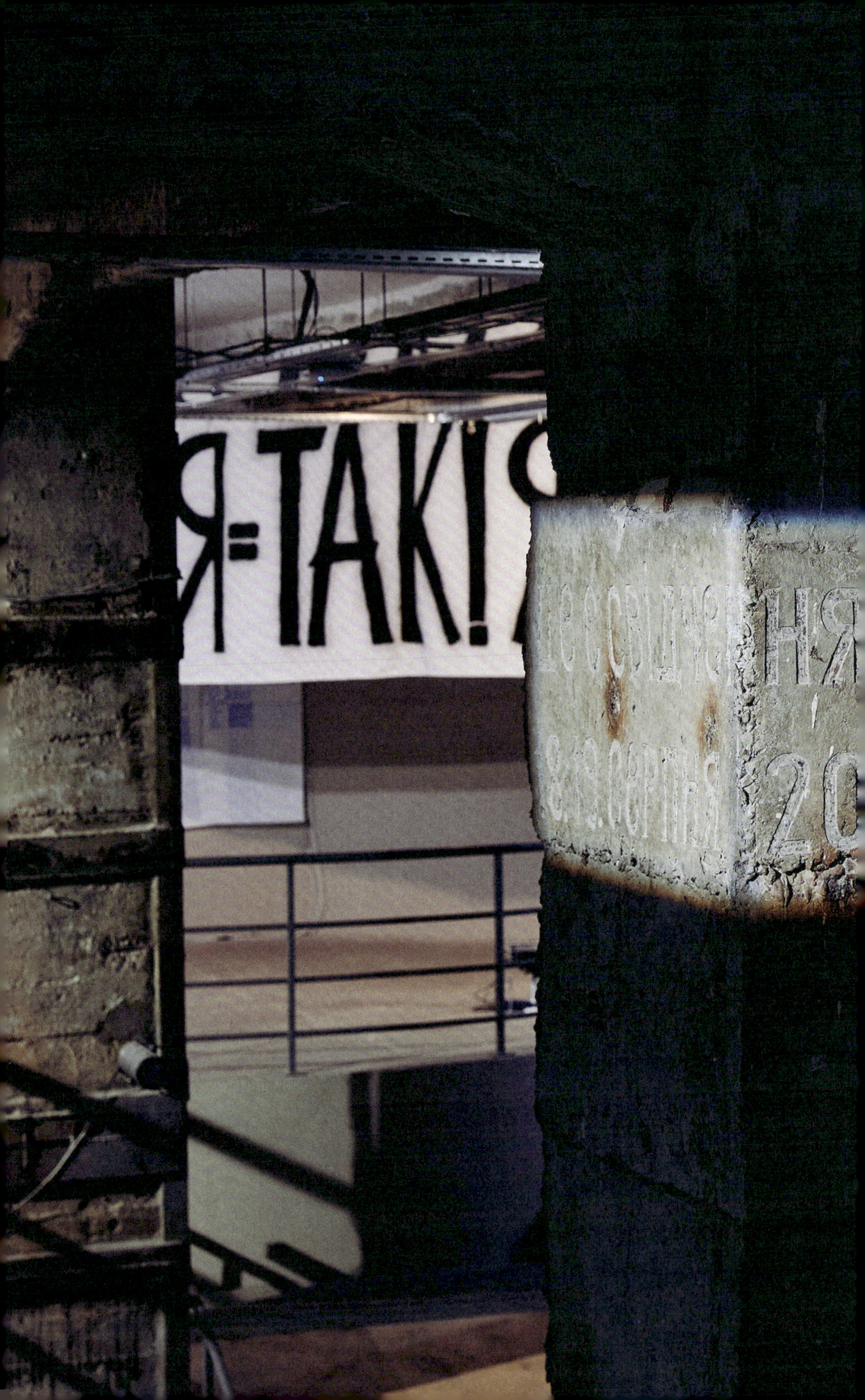
Я=ТАК!

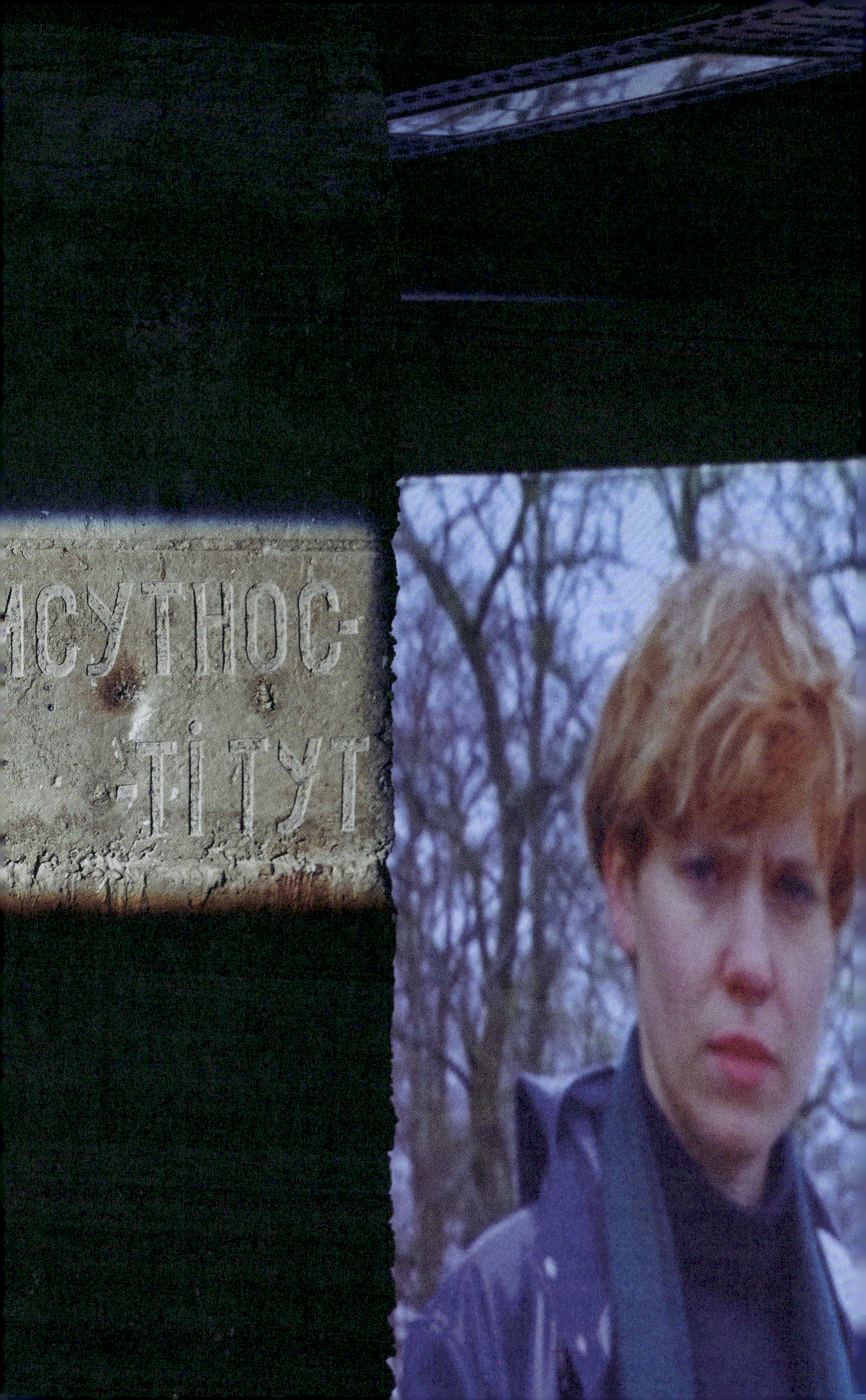
ІСУТНОС-
-ТІ ТУТ

_mediaklub

founded in 2020

Rehearsal of the Victory Day Gig

2022–ONGOING
AUDIO PERFORMANCE

PARTICIPANTS: ANNA IVCHENKO, DARIA MAYER, LIERA POLIANSKOVA, MAX ROBOTOV, DMYTRO TENTIUK

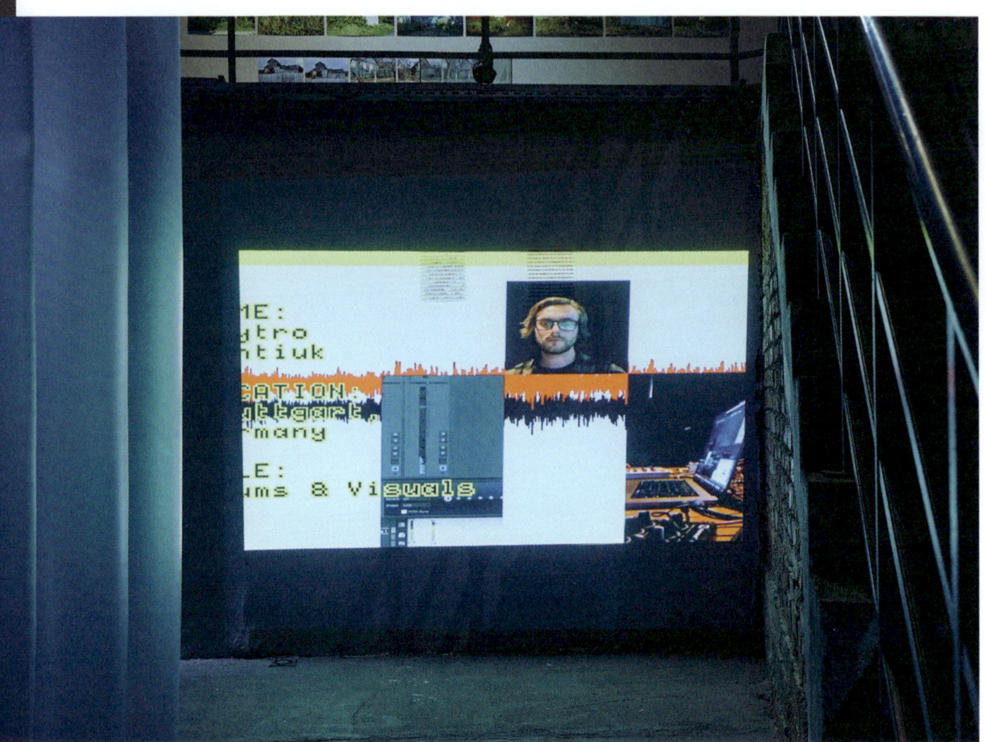

The experimental music band _mediaklub was founded in 2020 on the basis of Photinus, an educational platform for the development of new media art initiated by artists Liera Polianskova, Georgiy Potopalskiy, Max Robotov, and Ivan Svitlychnyi. Over time, the platform has become Ukraine's most influential media community.

Like Photinus, _mediaklub is a community of like-minded people united by shared practices in electronic music and media art. Synthesizing electronic and analog instruments in their practice, the members of _mediaklub explore interaction with each other through unusual musical forms. The principle of their work is based on openness, both in the choice of medium (from sound to visuals) and in the composition of the participants. The lineup is fluid, with different members of the Photinus community joining from concert to concert. Each iteration develops a new combination of sounds so that no performance is ever the same.

Rehearsal of the Victory Day Gig emerged after Russia's full-scale invasion of Ukraine. On the one hand, there was the need to preserve the community, and on the other hand to help Max Robotov—who has been serving in the Armed Forces of Ukraine

the use of a barrel has been

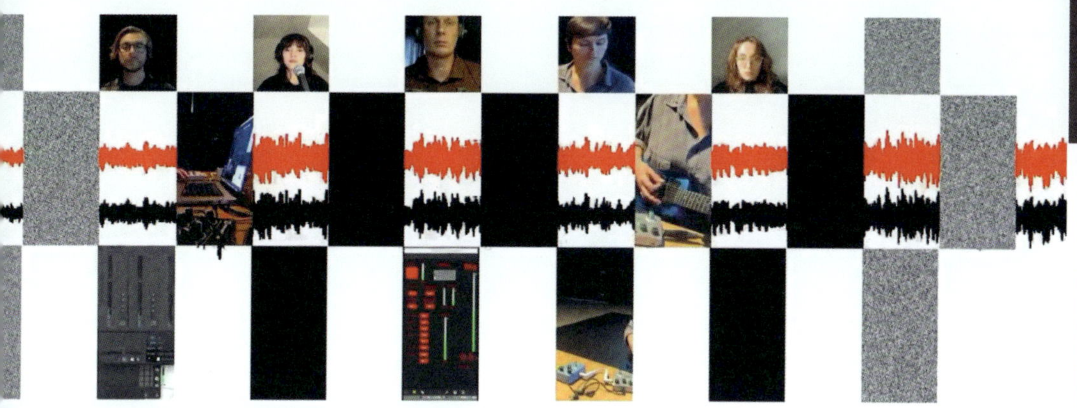

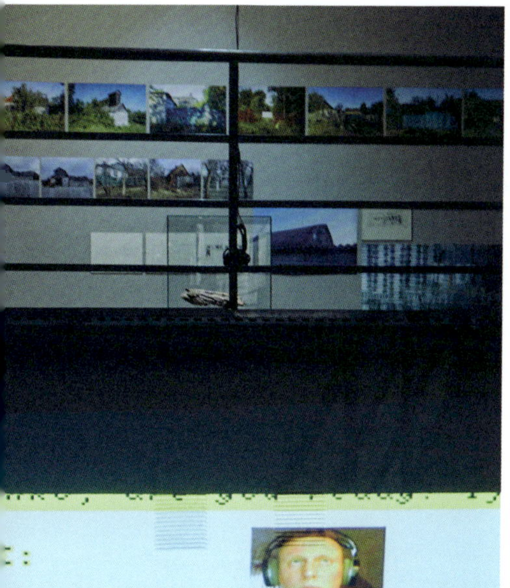

since the beginning of the war—stay involved in the artistic process and feel part of the community. The communication and interaction of the participants create an imagined safe space that allows the community to continue living and creating.

Rehearsal of the Victory Day Gig is a musical improvisation that takes the form of an open rehearsal. It is designed so that participants from different geographical locations can connect and merge in real-time. Max Robotov plays the role of a "conductor" here, directing when each instrument, voice, and participant should interact. Every performance involves an element of risk and the possibility of failure. Max Robotov's work is impossible to secure, but the artist himself is one of those who secure our lives today.

Hybrid performances are an essential part of _mediaklub's artistic practice, as they allow participants to maintain a sense of community across geographic distances and borders. This hybrid concert was conceived as a simultaneous presence in Stuttgart and Kharkiv. However, the Kharkiv musicians were unable to participate live due to the war. The concert was thus streamed into the YermilovCentre, which corresponded to the work's premise of embracing the possibility of failure. Two participants performed live in Stuttgart, while three others joined online. All elements merged into a single live sound in real time. During the Stuttgart performance the audience in Kharkiv and at the YermilovCentre observed the livestream, which created a shared space of presence. Later, the audiovisual stream from the concert was exhibited, extending this collective space despite distance and constraints.

Hybrid concert taking place at Musik der Jahrhunderte in Stuttgart, 2024. Photo: Tatiana Kochubinska.

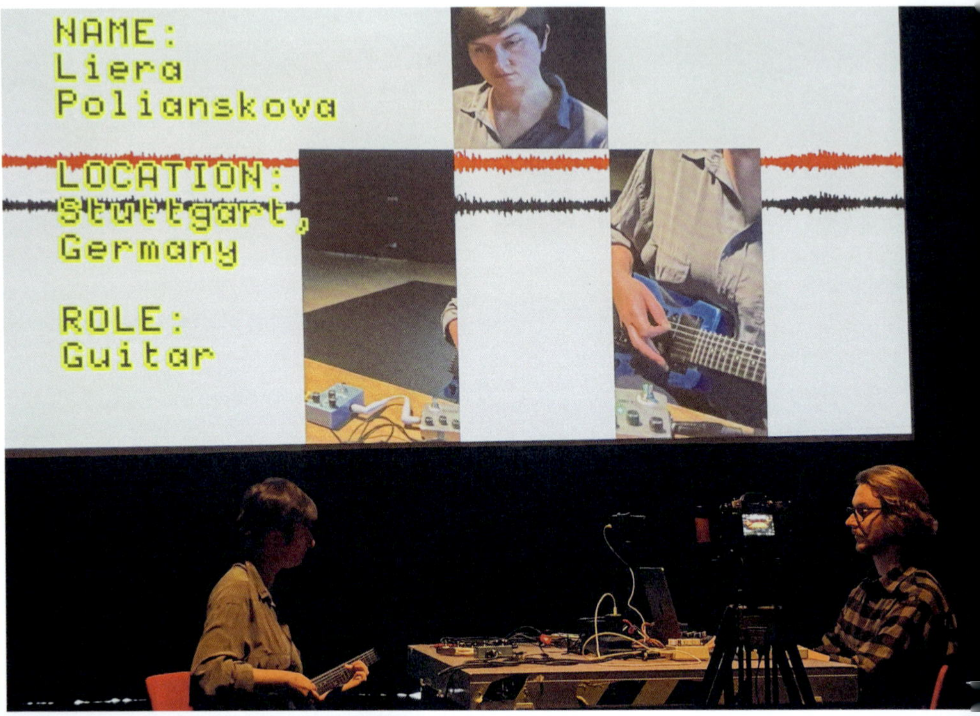

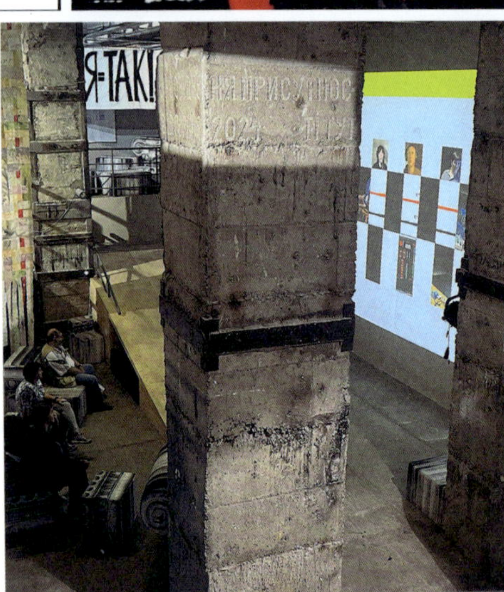

Rehearsal of the Victory Day Gig # 9

Audiovisual performance

Musik der Jahrhunderte, Stuttgart (DE)
YermilovCentre, Kharkiv (UA)
Online stream

Date
24.09.2024

Hybrid concert taking place at Musik der Jahrhunderte in Stuttgart transmitted live to the YermilovCentre in Kharkiv, 2024. Photo: Lera Borokh.

Participants
_mediaklub: Anna Ivchenko, Daria Mayer, Liera Polianskova, Max Robotov, Dmytro Tentiuk

Supported by
Musik der Jahrhunderte (DE)
Platform B (DE)

he hip-hop collective Fo Sho, founded in 2019 by sisters Bethlehem (Betty), Miriam, and Siona Endale, gave concert for the opening of the international exhibition project *Sense of Safety*, which was realized in collab-ration with the YermilovCentre in Kharkiv. The group's music combines contemporary genres—from trap nd hip-hop to R'n'B and rock—and is grounded in personal experience, bodily presence, and performative nergy. As daughters of Ethiopian Jewish migrants, the members of the group grew up in Kharkiv, where their lentities developed at the intersection of different cultures and experiences of persistent "otherness." After ussia's full-scale invasion began, they were forced to leave Kharkiv and relocate to the outskirts of Stuttgart, 'here music became a form of expression, resistance, and solidarity for them. The concert was streamed /e from the ZKM Media Theater to the YermilovCentre in Kharkiv, enabling a shared presence of audiences both cities and creating a space of connection between the artistic communities of Karlsruhe and Kharkiv nder conditions of war.

Sho concert at ZKM, 2024. Photo: Karolina Sobel © ZKM | Center for Art and Media Karlsruhe.

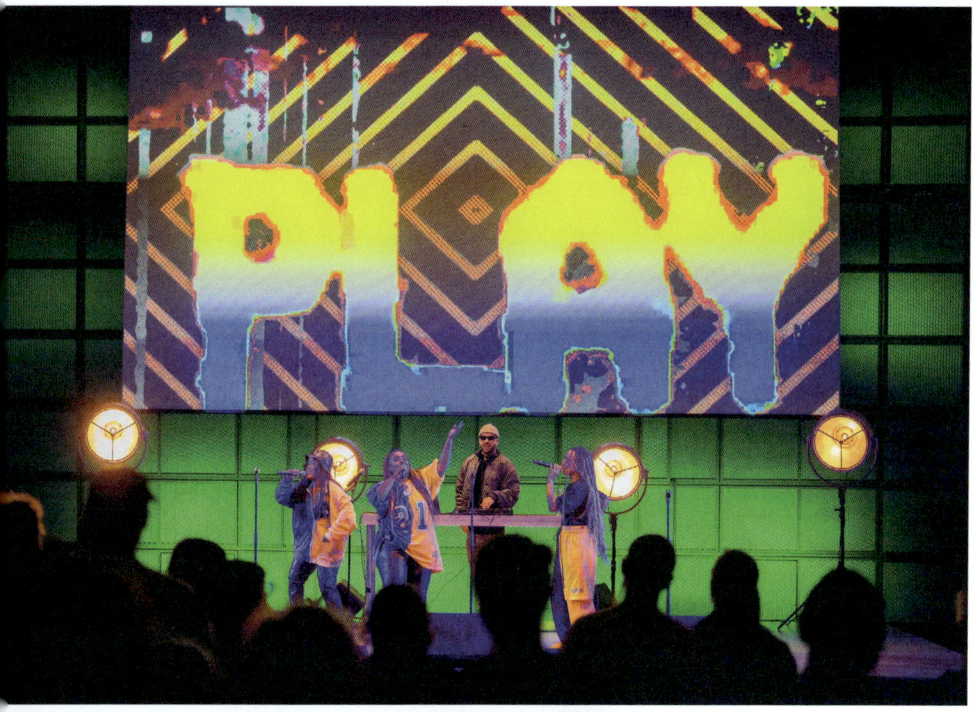

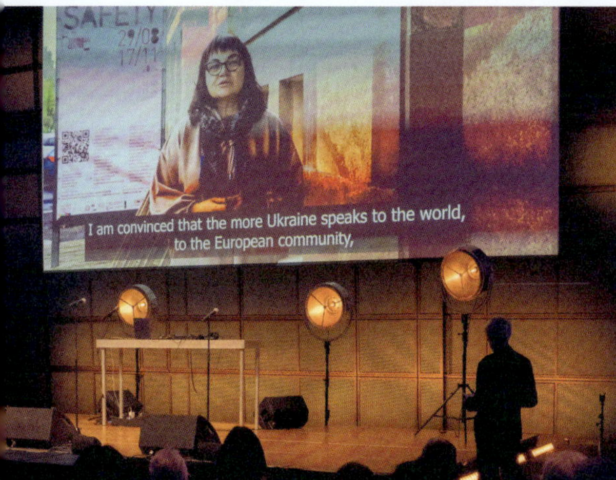

se of Safety, opening of the expanded exhibition at ZKM featuring the stream from Kharkiv of Nataliia Ivanova, YermilovCentre's director, 2024. to: Karolina Sobel © ZKM | Center for Art and Media Karlsruhe.

Sense of Safety @ ZKM, opening and concert featuring Fo Sho

ZKM | Center for Art and Media Karlsruhe

Date
18.10.2024

Speakers
Alistair Hudson, Scientific-artistic CEO, ZKM | Karlsruhe (UK)
Nataliia Ivanova, Director of Yermi-lovCentre, Kharkiv (online) (UA)
Tatiana Kochubinska, curator (UA)

Featuring
Fo Sho

This bridge functioned as a virtual continuation of the exhibition at the YermilovCentre. All video works were site-specifically adapted for the ZKM space. Using specially developed programming, the works were interspersed with a livestream of the YermilovCentre and its audience, transmitting the simultaneous presence of the experience and creating a shared, hybrid artistic space. The YermilovCentre in Kharkiv was virtually brought into the physical space of another institution, establishing a platform for interaction.

Livestream from YermilovCentre.

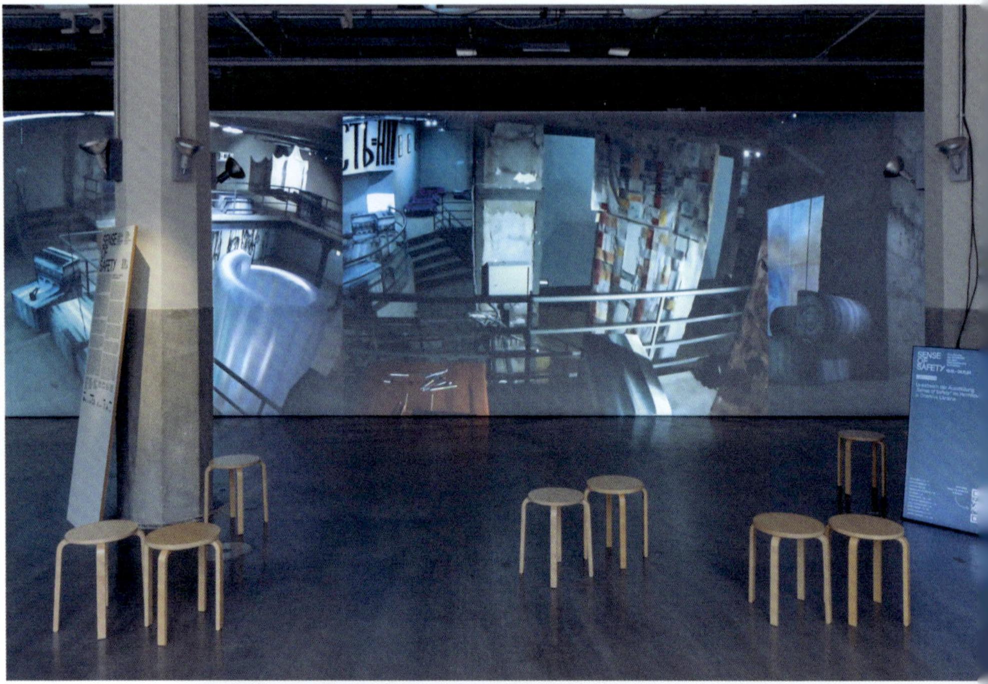

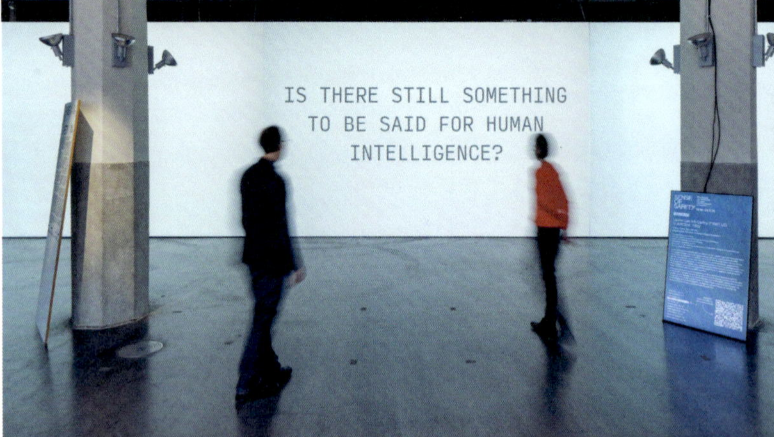

Work by Lauren Lee McCarth

Sense of Safety, expanded exhibition

ZKM | Center for Art and Media Karlsruhe

Date
19.10–25.11.2024

Artists
Francis Alÿs (MX)
Sergey Bratkov (UA/DE)
Danilo Correale (IT/USA)
Uli Golub (UA/USA)
Lauren Lee McCarthy (USA)
Katya Lesiv (UA/FI)
Rhona Mühlebach (CH)
Mark Požlep (SI/BE)
Stas Volyazlovsky (UA)
Kateryna Yermolayeva (UA)
_mediaklub (UA)

Video installation and adaptation of works
Maxim Tyminko (AWC)

Technical setup
Daniel Heiss (ZKM)
Claudius Böhm (ZKM)
Marc Schütze (ZKM)

Video selection
antiwarcoalition.art

Supported by
ZKM | Center for Art and Media Karlsruhe

Sense of Safety, expanded exhibition at ZKM, installation view, 2024.
Photo: Karolina Sobel © ZKM | Center for Art and Media Karlsruhe.

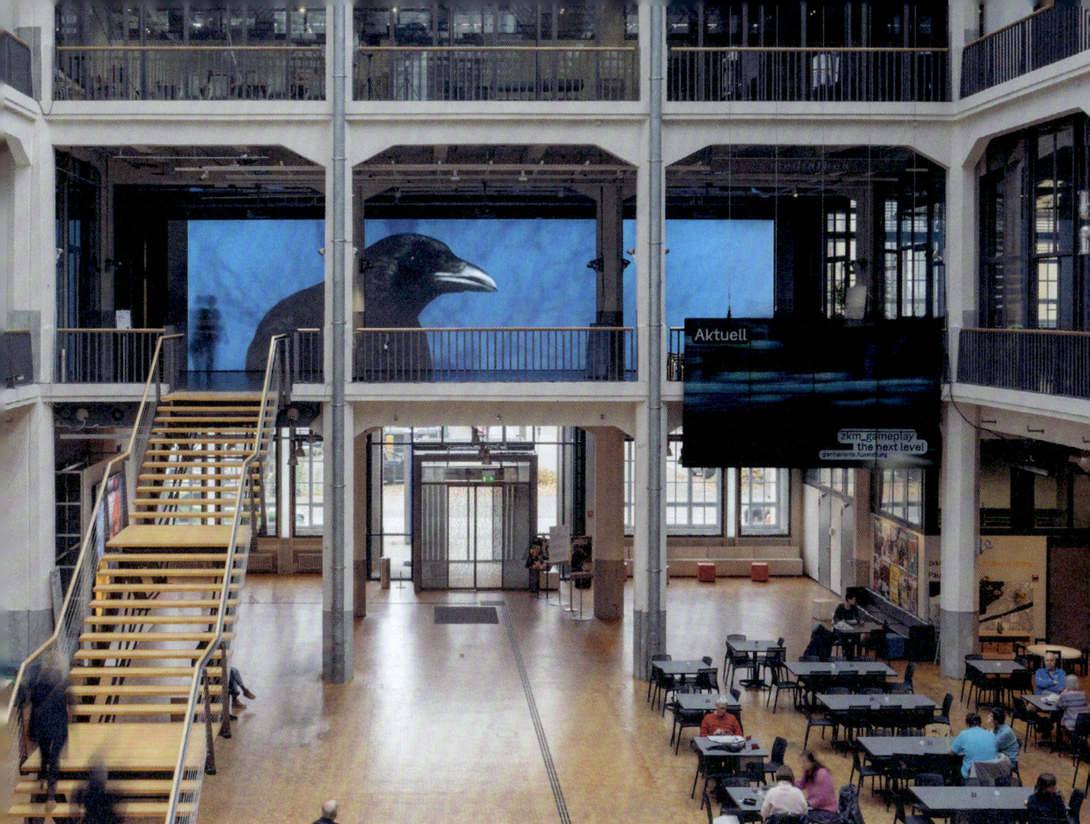

Work by Rhona Mühlebach.

Since Russia's full-scale invasion of Ukraine in 2022, there has been a close and enduring partnership between antiwarcoalition.art and the ZKM | Center for Art and Media Karlsruhe. This partnership has already led to numerous collaborations, including Bridges of Solidarity. Among them, Sense of Safety was undoubtedly the most significant collaboration to date.

On 1 September 2024—International Anti-War Day—antiwarcoalition.art contributed to the Schlosslichtspiele in Karlsruhe, one of Europe's largest open-air media festivals devoted to projection mapping. Each year, the Schlosslichtspiele brings together hundreds of thousands of visitors to experience the works projected onto the 170-meter-long façade of Karlsruhe Palace. With its contribution—which included artist videos as well as animated children's drawings from Aza Nizi Maza's studio in Kharkiv—antiwarcoalition.art sent a powerful message against forgetting.

An expanded version of Sense of Safety was subsequently presented at ZKM. The exhibition featured video works from Kharkiv projected on an approximately 12-meter-wide projection, combined with live transmissions from the exhibition space at YermilovCentre. With its rich program, Bridges of Solidarity demonstrated how crucial it is—in times of existential risk, war, and the most brutal violations of international law—to foster international solidarity among cultural practitioners, institutional actors, and local audiences. In that sense, the digitally mediated sense of togetherness built a strong bridge of solidarity and functioned as a true sign of hope and humanity.

Daria Mille and Philipp Ziegler, curators, ZKM

Work by Mark Požlep. →

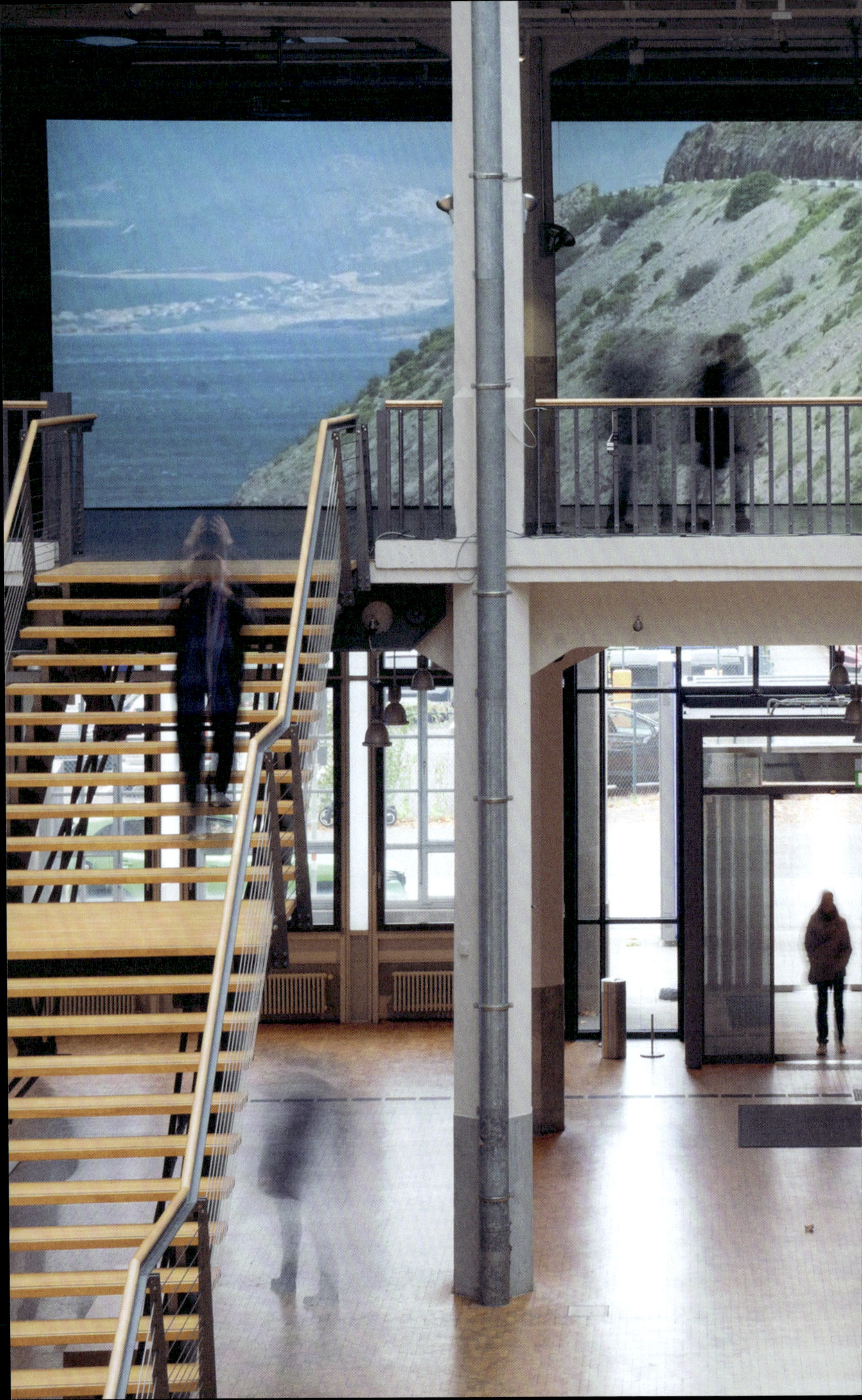

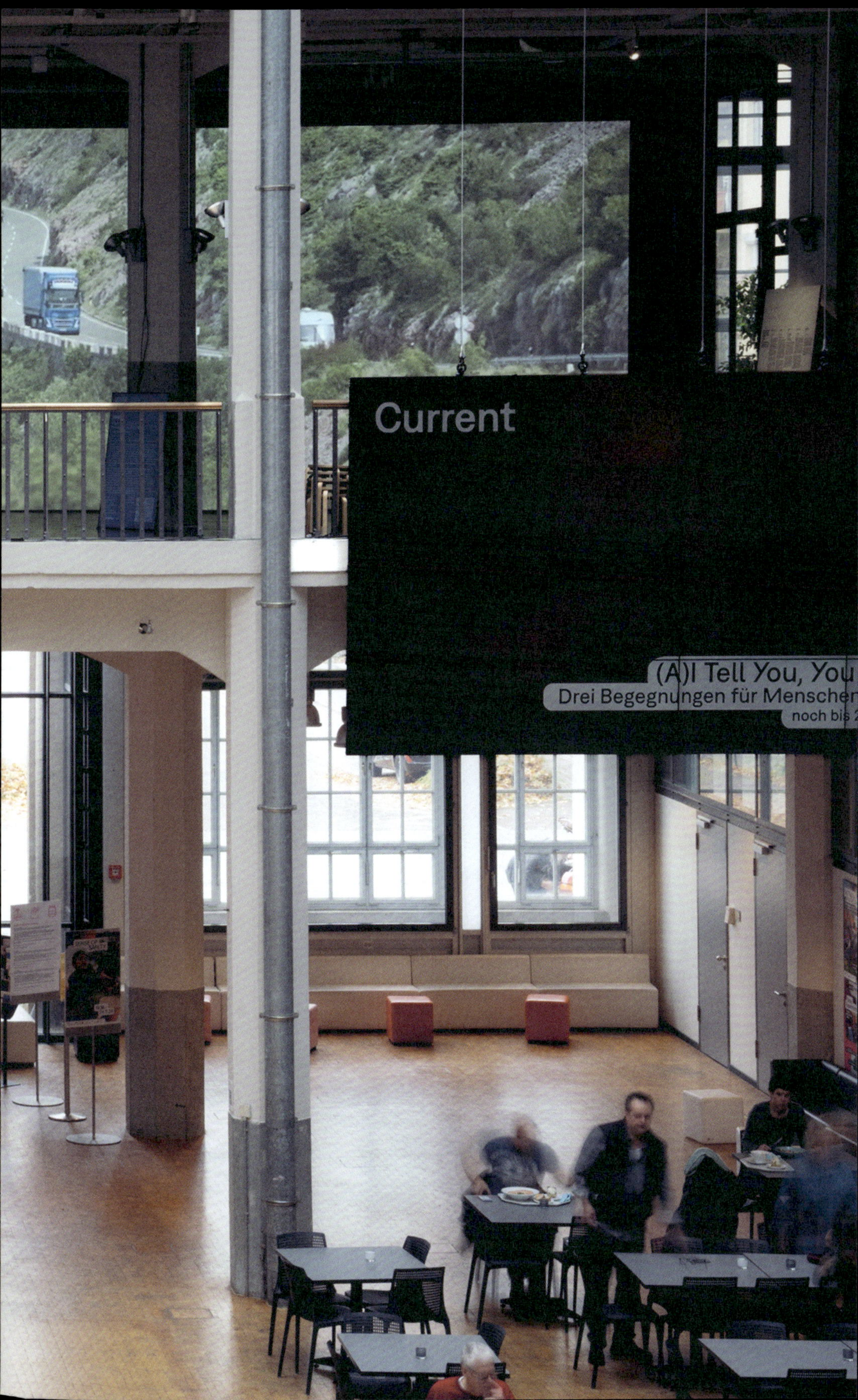
Current
(A)I Tell You, You
Drei Begegnungen für
noch bis

Contributors

Barshynova Oksana is an art historian, curator, and researcher. She serves as Deputy Director for Exhibitions at the National Art Museum of Ukraine (NAMU, where she co-developed the museum's new strategy for exhibiting and collecting modern and contemporary art. She has curated numerous exhibitions in Ukraine and internationally, authored several publications on modern and contemporary Ukrainian art, and regularly organizes conferences and panel discussions. Her recent publications include *From "The Ukraine" to Ukraine. A Contemporary History, 1991–2021*, edited by Matthew Rojansky, Georgiy Kasianov, and Mykhailo Minakov (Stuttgart: ibidem-Verlag, 2021); *In the Eye of the Storm: Modernism in Ukraine, 1900–1930s*, edited by Katia Denysova, Konstantin Akinsha, and Olena Kashuba-Volvach (London: Thames & Hudson, 2022); and *Entangled Art Histories in Ukraine*, edited by Stefaniia Demchuk and Illia Levchenko (New York: Routledge, 2024). From 2022 to 2023, she was a fellow of the PAUSE program at Musée d'Orsay and Centre Pompidou in Paris, where she studied the representation of Ukrainian art in museum collections.

Boris Buden is a writer and cultural theorist based in Berlin. Born in the former Yugoslavia, he studied philosophy in Zagreb and received his PhD in cultural theory from Humboldt University in Berlin. Since the early 1980s, Buden has published essays and books on critical and cultural theory, psychoanalysis, politics, and contemporary art in Croatian, German, and English. He is a permanent fellow at the European Institute for Progressive Cultural Policies in Vienna and teaches at various universities in Europe. His recent books include *Transition to Nowhere: Art in History After 1989* (Berlin: Archive Books, 2020) and *Past: An Introduction to the Problem* (Novi Sad: Iskra Books, 2024).

Borys Filonenko is an art critic, curator, lecturer, and editor-in-chief of ist publishing. He co-curated Ukraine's national pavilion at the 59th Venice Biennale (2022) and the 18th Venice Architecture Biennale (2023), as well as the 2nd Biennale of Young Art in Kharkiv (2019). He was co-curator of the exhibitions *Szilvashi Circles* (Ukrainian House, Kyiv, 2024) and *Our Years, Our Words, Our Losses, Our Searches, Our Us* (Jam Factory, Lviv, 2023), and was previously a curator of the Come In gallery (Kharkiv, 2015–2019), the Aza Nizi Maza gallery and its lecture program (Kharkiv, 2016–2020). He regularly writes texts on contemporary art in Ukraine, including the collection *Culture Under Pressure* (Kyiv: ist publishing, 2024), as well as comics. He lives and works in Lviv, Kyiv, and Kharkiv.

Nataliia Ivanova is the Director of the YermilovCentre for Contemporary Art and a co-founder of the public organization YermilovCentre. Art Laboratory. She is also a lecturer at the Department of Theory of Culture and Philosophy of Science, Faculty of Philosophy, V. N. Karazin Kharkiv National University, where she teaches the course in art management. From 2017 to 2020, she was a member of the Expert Council on Contemporary Art at the Ministry of Culture of Ukraine. In 2018, she served as Chair of the

election Committee for the curator of the national pavilion at the 58th Venice Biennale under the Ministry of Culture of Ukraine. In 2021, she founded the Art Kuzemyn art residency in the village of Kuzemyn, Sumy region, Ukraine. In 2025, she became a laureate of the Women in Arts Award in the category Women in Cultural Management. She holds the honorary title of Merited Worker of Culture of Ukraine.

Alona Karavai is a cultural manager, curator, and essayist originating from Donetsk Oblast. She is co-founder of the Asortymentna Kimnata gallery and the Frankivsk School of Contemporary Art fra fra fra. She worked at the IZOLYATSIA Center for Contemporary Art when it was based in Donetsk, lived and worked in Berlin, and co-curated several site-specific art projects in Ivano-Frankivsk. In 2023, she won the Kairos Prize, a European award for cultural figures, and in 2022 she organized emergency art residencies within Ukraine and coordinated the evacuation of non-state collections of art. Since 2023, her work has focused on the connections between Ukrainian artists in Ukraine and abroad, in particular within the framework of the *Scattered Communities* project and the Place to Return exhibition series. She also explores the topics of periphery(ies), absence, and local art communities. She was involved in the organization of *Bridges of Solidarity* as part of the *Sense of Safety* project.

Tatiana Kochubinska is an independent curator, art historian, writer, and lecturer focusing on contemporary art, memory, and the legacies of the 1990s in post-Soviet society. She has co-curated major international projects, including *Kaleidoscope of (Hi)stories: Ukrainian Art 1912–2023* (Dresden, 2023), *Maybe We Can Have Fun Together* (Białystok, 2024), *Landscapes of an Ongoing Past* (Essen, 2024), *Sense of Safety* (Kharkiv, 2024), and *Pairs Skating: Boris Mikhailov and Wolfgang Tillmans* (Kharkiv, 2025).
She has co-edited and compiled publications including *Kaleidoscope of (Hi)stories. Art from Ukraine* (Zwolle: Waanders Publishers, 2023), *Fedir Tetianych. Frypulia* (Kyiv: PinchukArtCentre, 2022), *Parcommune. Place. Community. Phenomenon* (Kyiv: PinchukArtCentre, 2019), and *Euphoria and Fatigue: Ukrainian Art and Society after 2014* (Obieg journal, 2020). Since 2022, she has been part of the curatorial team at antiwarcoalition.art, where she contributes to projects exploring responsibility, collective memory, and the psychological impact of historical events through contemporary art.

Maryna Konieva is an art historian, cultural manager, contemporary art curator, and author of academic and journalistic articles on contemporary art in Ukraine. She is the Deputy Director at the Kharkiv Municipal Gallery. Between 2008 and 2014, she was the curator of the Non-Stop Media festivals, the initiator of the Night of Museums campaign in Kharkiv, and the curator of its citywide program until 2016. She is currently a lecturer in the Department of Art History at the Kharkiv State Academy of Culture and Chair of the Board of the Grynyov Art Collection NGO. She also co-curated the *Sense of Safety* project. She lives and works in Kharkiv.

Bojana Piškur is a senior curator at Moderna galerija in Ljubljana. Her research and curatorial work focus on the Yugoslav and post-Yugoslav context, the Non-Aligned Movement, and the evolving concept of the "East(s)," particularly in relation to art, culture, and politics. Since 2019, Piškur has curated and co-curated the Southern Constellations exhibition series, exploring the legacies of political and cultural resistance, at institutions such as Moderna galerija, Asia Culture Center in Gwangju, Museum of Contemporary Art of Montenegro, the Qattan Foundation in Ramallah, and The Mosaic Rooms in London. She recently participated in the Kyiv Biennale in Warsaw with her research project *East of East*.

Lena Prents is a German art historian and curator of Belarusian origin. She studied German philology in Minsk, as well as art history and German literature at the Free University of Berlin. Over the course of her career, she has worked as an art historian, curator, cultural manager, and author in the international cultural sector. At the time of this interview, she headed the municipal Galerie Prater in Berlin; she now directs the Goethe-Institut in Slovenia. Her professional focus lies at the intersection of art and exhibition practices with socio-political discourses, as well as on art and culture in Eastern Europe during state socialism and today.

Tetyana Pylypchuk is the Director of the Kharkiv Literary Museum, a researcher of Ukrainian literature of the 1920s and 1930s, member of the Supervisory Board of ICOM Ukraine, consultant to the Penn Museum and Penn Cultural Heritage Center (USA), and laureate of the Vasyl Stus Prize (2024). Her recent initiatives include: organizing the City on(the)line dialogue platform (2024–present), participating in the development of the educational program Heritage: Space for Work (2024–present), running the Slovo Art Residency in Kharkiv (2021–present), managing the projects In the *Name of the City* (2023–2024), *Skovorodance* (2023), *Fifth Kharkiv* (2022–2024), and others.

Maxim Rosenfeld is an artist-architect, historian of architecture, PhD in architecture, associate professor in the Graphic Arts Department of the Kharkiv Academy of Design and Arts, and a storyteller.

Oleksandr Sorokin is a corresponding member of the National Academy of Sciences of Ukraine, Doctor of Physics and Mathematics, professor, Deputy Director of Science and leading researcher at the Institute of Scintillation Materials of the National Academy of Sciences of Ukraine (ISMA). He is the author of nearly 300 scientific papers, a winner of the President of Ukraine and Verkhovna Rada of Ukraine awards for young scientists, and a lecturer of a number of courses at V. N. Karazin Kharkiv National University, Kyiv Academic University, and ISMA graduate school. He is actively involved in several popular science activities that encourage young people to engage in science through lectures, outreach events, and guided tours to the institute.

Antonina Stebur is a curator and researcher who explores contemporary art as a tool for infrastructural and political imagination.

She is Editor-in-Chief of *AWC Journal* and founder of Mycelium [Грыбніца], a decolonial research lab. Stebur is curator of the transmediale 2027 exhibition. As part of antiwarcoalition.art, she has contributed to documenta 15, Manifesta 14, and ZKM, among others.

Asia Tsisar is a Ukrainian curator, writer, and researcher specializing in Central and Eastern Europe. She holds degrees in Cultural Studies (Kharkiv State Academy of Culture, Ukraine) and East European Studies (University of Warsaw, Poland). Her work operates at the intersection of art, cultural studies, and political history. Tsisar employs methods of artistic research and creative storytelling, working with archives, memory, and the analysis of narratives. From 2020 to 2022, she served as the chief curator of Secondary Archive—the largest digital archive dedicated to women artists from Central and Eastern Europe. Her projects have been presented at Manifesta 14 (Kosovo), the 14th Gwangju Biennale (South Korea), EVA International – Ireland's Biennial, the Mystetskyi Arsenal (Ukraine), and CZKD (Serbia). In 2025, she founded the solidarity-based podcast Radio Unheard. She currently lives in Ukraine and curates the visual art program at the Jam Factory Art Center in Lviv.

Serhiy Zhadan is a Ukrainian writer, musician, translator, and social activist. He has been one of the most influential figures in the Kharkiv scene since the early 1990s. He made his literary debut at 17 and has since published numerous volumes of poetry and prose. His novel *Voroshilovgrad* (2010) was awarded both the Jan Michalski Prize and the Brücke Berlin Prize. In 2022, Zhadan was named Man of the Year by *Gazeta Wyborcza* (Poland) and awarded the prestigious Peace Prize of the German Book Trade for his "outstanding artistic work and his humanitarian stance with which he turns to the people suffering from war and helps them at the risk of his own life." Zhadan lives in Kharkiv and has been a soldier in the Ukrainian army since 2024.

Colophon

SENSE OF SAFETY International Art Project
29 August –
17 November
2024

Concept of the project
The International Coalition
of Cultural Workers
in Solidarity with Ukraine,
YermilovCentre &
Maryna Konieva

The International Coalition of Cultural Workers in Solidarity with Ukraine
Anna Chistoserdova
Valentina Kiselyova
Tatiana Kochubinska
Aleksander Komarov
Antonina Stebur
Maxim Tyminko

YermilovCentre
Nataliia Ivanova
Yelyzaveta Koval

Exhibition

Artists
Olena Afanasieva &
Max Afanasyev
Francis Alÿs
Andreas Angelidakis
Babi Badalov
Sergey Bratkov
Danilo Correale
Uli Golub
Thomas Hirschhorn
Nadira Husain
Taras Kamennoy
Alina Kleytman
Vitalii Kokhan
Dmytro Kolomoitsev
Yulia Kostereva &
Yuriy Kruchak
Vladyslav Krasnoshchok
Karen Lancel & Hermen Maat
Lauren Lee McCarthy
Katya Lesiv
Iryna Loskot
Kateryna Lysovenko
Pavlo Makov
Boris Mikhailov
Rhona Mühlebach
Ahmet Öğüt
Mark Požlep
Karina Synytsia
Stas Volyazlovsky
Kateryna Yermolayeva
Anna Zvyagintseva
*foundationClass
_mediaklub

Curators
Tatiana Kochubinska
Aleksander Komarov
Maryna Konieva
Antonina Stebur
Maxim Tyminko

Architecture
Ivan Svitlychnyi
Maxim Tyminko

Executive architect
Viktor Dvornikov

Texts
Tatiana Kochubinska
Maryna Konieva
Antonina Stebur

Editing / translation
lisa deikun
Viktoriia Kantemyr
Svitlana Skliar

Online platform
Danil Siabro
Maxim Tyminko
Andrus Winzig

Bridges of Solidarity*

Institutions
YermilovCentre (UA)
SCHLOSSLICHTSPIELE
Karlsruhe (DE)
Aza Nizi Maza (UA)
Goethe-Institut
Ukraine (DE/UA)
ZKM | Center for Art and
Media Karlsruhe (DE)
Freie Radios Berlin
Brandenburg (DE)
ABA AIR Salon (DE)
Haus der Statistik (DE)
UKRAiNATV (PL/UA)
Asortymentna Kimnata (UA)
Galeria Arsenał (PL)
nGbk (DE)
Ziegel. Atelier Gemeinschaft
ukrainischer Künstler:innen (AT)
Artists' studio on Lierenfelder
Strasse, Düsseldorf (DE)
Musik der Jahrhunderte (DE)
Platform B (DE)
Framer Framed (NL)
Video studio of the
V. N. Karazin Kharkiv
National University (UA)
StreamArtStudio, Kraków (PL)
Let Me Show You Something
Beautiful (GE)
Revolutionale – Festival
for Change (DE)
Leipzig Festival of Lights (DE)
Charkiw-Park, Berlin (DE)
Tbilisi Photography & Multi-
media Museum (GE)
The VOID (NL)
Ambasada Kultury (DE/LT)
ZAMEK Culture Centre (PL)
Poznań Palm House (PL)
Poznań Fortress Days (PL)
Domie, Poznań (PL)
City of Poznań (PL)
Nema Playback Theater (UA)
De Balie (NL)
European Cultural
Foundation (ECF) (NL)
International Docu-
mentary Festival
Amsterdam (IDFA) (NL)
Uq-Bar-A-Ba project space (DE)
PRADMOVA festival (PL)
PLACCC International Festival
of Site-Specific Art and
Art in Public Space (HU)
Nordic Council of Ministers
Office in Lithuania (LT)
The Danish Cultural
Institute (LV)
Skövde Kulturhus (SE)
ICA-Sofia (BG)
Voloshyn Gallery (UA)
Siemiradzki Gallery (UA)
Jam Factory Art Center (UA)
The Roma Community Centre (PL)

Participants
Ahou Alagha
Lala Aliyeva
Francis Alÿs
Volha Arkhipava
Tasha Arlova
Medina Bazargali
Kateryna Berezovska
Sergey Bratkov
Tamara Olga Briks
Agnieszka Bułacik
Olga Bubich
Tommaso Campagna
Natasha Chychasova
Anna Chistoserdova
Danilo Correale
Mina Đorđević
(r)Hlib Dovzhuk
Rom Dziadkiewicz
Alina El Assadi
Olia Fedorova
Eleonora Frolov
Taras Gembik
Zhanna Gladko
Jura Golik
Gabrielle Goliath
Uli Golub
Maria Gorshkova
Rezzan Gümgüm
Danylo Halkin
Ihar Hancharuk
Viktoryia Hrabennikava
Uladzimir Hramovich
Thomas Hirschhorn
Alistair Hudson
Anna Ivchenko
Dobrinya Ivanov
Kostiantyn Ivanov
Nataliia Ivanova
Yurii Ivantsyk
Magda Jaroszewicz
Zhanna Kadyrova
Alevtina Kakhidze
Oksana Kami
Alona Karavai
Anton Karyuk
Dana Kavelina
Irina Kh.
Khatuna Khabuliani
Nastia Khlestova
Valentina Kiselyova
Tatiana Kochubinska
Aleksander Komarov
Maryna Konieva
Yulia Kostereva
Yulia Kostereva &
Yuriy Kruchak
Yelyzaveta Koval
Agnieszka Kucharska
Sasha Kurmaz
Kata Kwiatkowska
Sophia Lapiashvili
tony lashden
Lauren Lee McCarthy
Julia Legezynska
Olena Lemberska
Katya Lesiv
Mikita Lewkowicz
Rosanna Lovell
Mykyta Lyskov
Elturan Mammadov
Wojciech Mania
Marie Manushka
Timothy Maxymenko
Daria Mayer
Serhiy Melnychenko
Ada Metryka
Doro Michalak
Ana Mikadze
Rhona Mühlebach
Marina Naprushkina
Siarhei Navitski
Thomas Neumann
Julia Niedziejko
Ahmet Öğüt
Oleksandr Osipov
Stanislav Ostrous
Bozhena Pelenska
Lesia Pcholka
Dan Perjovschi
Valentyna Petrova
Sergiy Petlyuk
Anna Pohoryelova
Liera Polianskova
Olya Polyak
Serhiy Popov
Mark Požlep
Kateryna Radushynska
Vlada Ralko
Juri Rechinsky
Daniil Revkovsky &
Andriy Rachinskiy
Sofiia Reznichenko
Mykola Ridnyi
Max Robotov
Vlada Rusina
Ainur Sakisheva
Nadya Sayapina
Daria Sazanovich
Helmut Schweizer
Sergey Shabohin
Liene Šilde
Olia Sosnovskaya & A.Z.H.
Amilia Stanevich
Dmytro Starusev
Antonina Stebur
Lizaveta Stecko
Hito Steyerl
Zuza Szczepanska
Monika Szewczyk
Dmytro Tentiuk
Giulia Timi
Anton Tkachenko
Napsugár Trömböczki
Maxim Tyminko
Natalia Vatsadze
Alisa Volkova
Stas Volyazlovsky
Johan Widén, Ylva Gislén
& Elin Maria Johansson
Clemens V. Wedemeyer
Daniela Weiss
Katarzyna Wojtczak
Vitaliy Yankovy
Olena Yermishkina
Kateryna Yermolayeva
Vera Zalutskaya
Vita Zelenska
Ola Zielinska
_mediaklub
Art Project "Revolution"
Bergamot
Bouillon Group
eeefff
fantastic little splash
Fo Sho
Otucha collectiv

Project team
General management

Ambasada Kultury
Anna Chistoserdova
Valentina Kiselyova

YermilovCentre
Nataliia Ivanova
Yelyzaveta Koval

Logistics management
Asortymentna kimnata
Alona Karavai
Sofia Kozubash
Yulia Nepyk

Visual concept
Maxim Tyminko

Technical team
Front Pictures
Yuri Kostenko
Vadym Kozakivskyi

Photinus
Evgeny Arlov
Oleh Kodrul
Pavlo Sirko

Communication PR
Tetyana Landesman

SMM
Liza Mas
Yuliia Baglyk

Design
Andrei Stseburaka
Maxim Tyminko

Photographers
Oleksandr Osipov
Andrei Stseburaka
Viktoriia Yakymenko

We are thankful to

Individuals
Oksana Barshynova
Olena Bykovets
Sebastian Cichocki
Yevhen Demyanenko
Michiel Driebergen
Esselien Van Eerten
Lore Gablier
Jakub Gawkowski
Taras Gembik
Oleksandr Golubov
Maryna Grachova
Martin Hoernes
Maria Isserlis
Tetiana Kaganovska
Oleksandr Kaplia
Oksana Karpovets
Maksym Khodak
Eugenia Kochubinska
Anatoly Kochubinskyi
Anna Kolomiitseva
Susanne Kriemann
Taisia Kryvko
Kostiantyn Lahunovskyi
Irina Leonenko
Kyrylo Lukash
Iuliia Lytvynets
Kotryna Markevičiutė
Daria Mille
Olexii Minko
Marina Naprushkina
Siarhei Navitski
Oleksandr Osipov
Dmytro Paziura
Lena Prents
Tetyana Pylypchuk
Mykhailo Protsenko
Sasha Razor
Yan Sakovich
Serhii Seleznov
Artem Shevchenko
Georgiy Shevchenko
Nicolay Spesivtsev
Anastasiia Spirenkova
Iaroslava Strikha
Kateryna Tsyhykalo
Asia Tsisar
Tjitske Wildervanck
Volodymyr Yefimenko
Oleksandr Yukhno
Dzina Zhuk
Philipp Ziegler

Institutions
Air Design Studio –
Erik van Dongen (NL)
BELARUSIAN YOUTH HUB (PL)
European Cultural
Foundation (NL)
NAMU (UA)
Solidarny Dom Kultury
"Słonecznik" (PL)

**Bridges of Solidarity* could only happen thanks to the collective efforts of many people involved in the project, whose empathy made this work possible. We made every effort to acknowledge everyone who contributed. We apologize if anyone has been unintentionally omitted.

Supported by

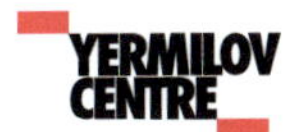

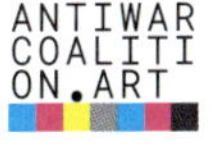

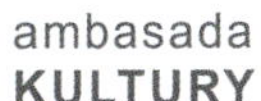

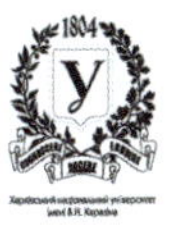

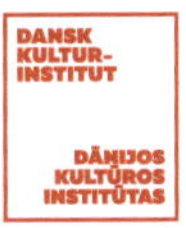

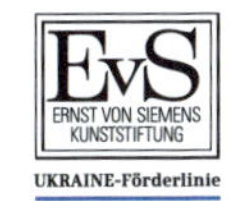

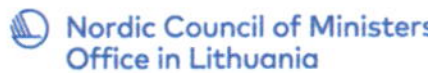

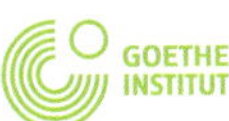

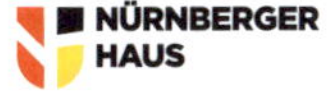

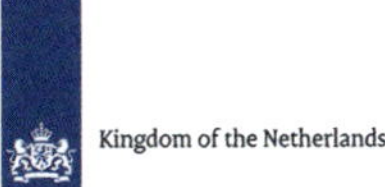

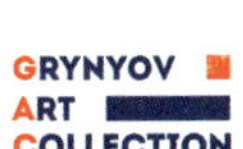

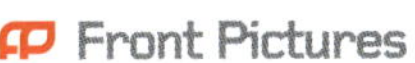

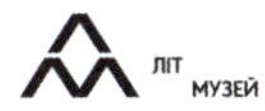

SENSE OF SAFETY
Art in a Time of War

This book is published on the occasion of the international art project *Sense of Safety* at the YermilovCentre, Kharkiv, Ukraine and across Europe from 29 August to 17 November 2024.

Concept
Foundation
antiwarcoaliton.art
www.antiwarcoalition.art

Editor-in-chief
Tatiana Kochubinska

Editors
Maryna Konieva
Antonina Stebur

Picture editor
Maxim Tyminko

Design
Aliona Solomadina

Authors

Essays
Oksana Barshynova
Boris Buden
Borys Filonenko
Alona Karavai
Tatiana Kochubinska
Maryna Konieva
Bojana Piškur
Lena Prents & Nataliia Ivanova
Tetyana Pylypchuk
Maxim Rosenfeld
Oleksandr Sorokin
Antonina Stebur
Asia Tsisar
Serhiy Zhadan

Catalog texts
Tatiana Kochubinska
Maryna Konieva
Antonina Stebur

Translation

Essays
Ukrainian-English,
English-Ukrainian:
Yulia Didokha
Tania Rodionova

Catalog texts
Viktoriia Kantemyr
Tatiana Kochubinska

Copy editing
Stanton Taylor, Good and Cheap Art Translators

Photo credits

Installation and artworks
Oleksandr Osipov
(pp. 13, 38, 48, 52, 87, 93, 128 (right), 151)

Karolina Sobel
(pp. 165–169)

Andrei Stseburaka
(pp. 37, 43, 72–73)

Viktoriia Yakymenko
(pp. 36, 40–42, 44–47, 49, 53, 62–63, 77–78, 88–92, 102, 104–106, 108–109, 128 (left), 129–137, 144–146, 150, 160–163)

Other contributors
Levan Adikashvili
Iuliia Bondarenko
Lera Borokh
Sergey Bratkov
Anna Chistoserdova
Yelyzaveta Koval
Mateusz "Kronos" Stosik
Pavlo Makov
Vlad Nikorchuk
Mykhailo Protsenko
Marharyta Rubanenko
Helmut Schweizer
Seiji Shimabukuro
Taras Telishchak
Maxim Tyminko
Philipp Ziegler

Image editing
Aliona Solomadina

Production management
Charlotte Riggert,
DISTANZ Verlag

Printing and binding
optimal media GmbH,
Röbel/Müritz

ISBN 978-3-95476-792-2 (EN)

Printed in Germany

Published by
DISTANZ Verlag
www.distanz.de

DISTANZ

Co-published by
ilostmylibrary
www.ilostmylibrary.org

I lost my library

The publication is kindly supported by

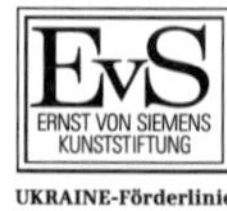

UKRAINE-Förderlinie

ZKM Center for Art and Media Karlsruhe

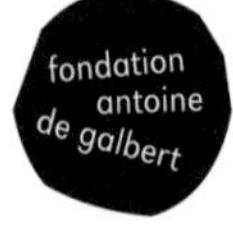

ambasada KULTURY